Hooligans or Rebels?

KING AL ~~~~ **COLLEG**

2

2

12

For Sal

STEPHEN HUMPHRIES

Hooligans or Rebels?

*An Oral History of Working-Class Childhood
and Youth 1889—1939*

BLACKWELL
Oxford UK & Cambridge USA

First published 1981
Paperback edition 1983
Reprinted 1984
Reissued in paperback 1995

Blackwell Publishers Ltd
108 Cowley Road, Oxford OX4 1JF, England

Blackwell Publishers Inc.
238 Main Street
Cambridge, Massachusetts 02142, USA

British Library Cataloguing in Publication Data

Humphries, Stephen
  Hooligans or rebels?
  1. Labor and Laboring classes – Great Britain
  2. Great Britain – Social life and customs –
  19th century
  3. Great Britain – Social life and customs –
  20th century
  I. Title
  941.082'0880623   DA566.4

ISBN 0–631–19984–5 (Pbk)

Typesetting by Pioneer, East Sussex
Printed in Great Britain by
T. J. Press (Padstow) Ltd, Padstow,
Cornwall

This book is printed on acid-free paper

Contents

Acknowledgements

I would like to thank all the people who have helped directly or indirectly in the preparation of this book. Most of all I am indebted to Sally Mullen, without whose care and support the book would not have been written. Sally's mother, Madge Mullen, helped enormously, especially with her excellent typing of the interviews and manuscripts. I owe a great debt to my mum and dad, Marjorie and Jim Humphries, who have always encouraged me to value education and learning, partly because both were forced by economic necessity to sacrifice their own secondary education at the age of fourteen. Thanks also to the other members of my family and friends who helped in various ways, especially Mike and Sue Humphries, Joan Mitchell, Phil Gardner, Geoffrey and Evelyn Spittal, Charles Hannam, Marie Hill, Iris Hutchings and Ruth Richardson.

Many of the recollections that appear in the book were collected as part of the Bristol People's Oral History Project, and I am very grateful to all those who took part in it. Special thanks are due to Pam Scull, Irena Czapska, Jane Dunstan, Tracy Morefield, Kathy Lye, Linda Vickers and Anne Oakley for their skilful taperecording and transcribing of many interviews with old people. The project was made possible by the financial and administrative support of the Manpower Services Commission, the Resources for Learning and Development Unit and the Avon County Central Library, and I would like to thank the staff of all these organizations, in particular Ivor Bolt, Philip Waterhouse and Geoff Langley, for the advice and assistance they generously gave to us. I am also indebted to all the people we interviewed for their friendly co-operation, and to the wardens of the old people's dwellings in Bristol and the West Country who helped us to arrange most of the interviews.

Other interview extracts that appear in the book have been drawn from Paul Thompson and Thea Vigne's 'Family Life and Work Experience Before 1918' collection at the University of Essex, and from the Manchester Studies collection of tapes and transcripts at Manchester Polytechnic. I am very grateful to Paul Thompson for his hospitality, advice and permission to use material held in the Essex archive, and to Bill Williams, Audrey Linkman, Jill Liddington and the staff of the Manchester Studies Unit for their friendly and valuable assistance.

I should like to thank the staff of the many libraries and record offices — too numerous to be mentioned here — where I have worked or with which I have corresponded during my research. In particular, I am indebted to the staff of the Avon County Reference Library for their generous and efficient help over a number of years. I have also received much kind assistance from Ian Dewhirst of Keighley Reference Library, Margaret de Motte of Manchester Central Library and Miss E. Wilmott of Bradford Central Library. The editors of many provincial newspapers all over Britain have kindly inserted appeals for reminiscences of working-class childhood, and I am extremely grateful to them and to all those who responded to these requests for information. Some of the material collected in this way has been incorporated into the book and is acknowledged in the notes.

Finally, I am indebted to my tutors and friends at the University of Sussex, Stephen Yeo and Alun Howkins, who supervised the thesis upon which this book is based and who have given me much valuable advice and support. And last but not least I should like to thank John Davey of Blackwell for enthusiastically backing the idea of a book on young working class rebels and Elizabeth Bland for her excellent copy-editing of the manuscript. Any errors of fact and interpretation that remain are, of course, my own responsibility.

For permission to reproduce line drawings and photographs the author and publisher gratefully acknowledge the following: B.T. Batsford Ltd for page 201, from Richard Whitmore, *Victorian Crime and Punishment* (London, 1978); BBC Hulton Picture Library for pages 99, 100, 157, 163, 194, 202; Mr F.W.E. Bidmead, St Barnabas School, Bristol for page 30 (photograph Simon Isaacs); Trustees of the British Museum for page 180; Edinburgh City Libraries for page 162; Fox Photos Ltd for page 148; Greater London Council Photograph Library for pages 47 and 227; Hodder & Stoughton Ltd for page 15, from Cyril Burt, *The Young Delinquent* (London, 1931); IPC Magazines Ltd for page 127; Muller's

Orphanage, Bristol for page 210; Routledge & Kegan Paul Ltd for page 181, from W.F. Lestrange, *Wasted Lives* (London, 1936); Spalding Gentlemen's Society, Spalding, Lincs for page 67; Welfare History Picture Library, Milngavie for page 195; Mr Reece Winstone, Bristol for page 159. The photograph on page 228 is taken from Sydney A. Moseley, *The Truth about Borstal* (London, 1926).

CHAPTER 1

Deprivation and Depravity

A Review of the Theory

Working-class children and youth have probably attracted more theorizing and moralizing in the past century than almost any other social group. Coupled with this concern, there has been a dramatic increase in state intervention governing many aspects of working-class family life, education, work and leisure activities. In this book I argue that the development and proliferation of institutions in these key areas are part of a complex process of class conflict, involving the resistance of working-class youth to powerful attempts to inculcate conformist modes of behaviour (products of the dominant middle-class culture) through various bourgeois agencies of control, manipulation and exploitation. The behaviour that I contend can be regarded as resistance is the persistent rule-breaking and opposition to authority characteristic of working-class youth culture that has traditionally been viewed as indiscipline or delinquency. The most conspicuous activities with which this study is concerned are disaffection from school work, classroom disobedience, school strikes, larking about, social crime, street-gang violence, rebellious sexual behaviour, absenteeism and acts of industrial sabotage, activities that oral and documentary evidence suggest have recurred with some continuity during the past century.

The book has two principal and related aims. First, it will examine critically the theoretical and empirical traditions that have informed the study of working-class youth and its delinquent cultural forms. It will seek to demonstrate that constant reference to theories of mass culture and deprivation have tended to trivialize and devalue these cultural forms. This will necessarily involve exposing and dismantling the theoretical prejudice and depersonalizing imagery that surrounds the study of this particular group, and the explanations offered by the moral entrepreneurs, psychologists,

1

criminologists and sociologists who have dominated this field will
be subjected to critical analysis. Second, in the process of reviewing
received theories about working-class youth, the book will offer an
alternative, class-based interpretation of its behaviour, which will
situate resistance within various class formations and relationships,
showing the continuity and similarity between working-class youth
and parent cultures.

To begin with, it is necessary to outline briefly my theoretical
position. I will adopt a theoretical perspective similar to that of the
emerging revisionist school of Marxist sociologists and historians
who during the past decade have challenged the method and
metaphor upon which the orthodox literature on youth has been
based. The method, it is alleged, has failed to relate the development
of educational, welfare and penal institutions provided for youth to
wider social and political structures. In fact, the method adopted
by most writers has borne a close resemblance to Whig historiography, for the history of childhood and youth has often been
represented as a history of progress and enlightened reform, moving
irrevocably towards more humane standards of care, protection
and learning. The metaphor has portrayed provision for working-
class youth as a flower of democracy, inspired by liberal and
collectivist ideals, the aim of which has been to extend the rights
and opportunities enjoyed by the middle-class to the deprived and
brutalized sections of the community.[1] However, revisionist
historians are beginning to penetrate the altruistic rhetoric of the
social welfare and schoolteaching professions. They seek to
demonstrate that this rhetoric has disguised an essentially
bureaucratic response to the imperatives of class control, which
has necessitated the expansion of statutory and voluntary
organizations in order to regulate and reproduce capitalist society.
The most influential revisionist historians, such as Michael Katz in
America and Richard Johnson in Britain, have made use of
Gramsci's concept of hegemony and the notion of a dialectic between
a hegemonic dominant culture and a subordinate working-class
culture.[2] They argue that a hegemonic cultural order operates by
incorporating the subordinate class in the key institutions that
support the social authority of the dominant order. And, they
argue, the development of a complex web of institutions in the past
century, seeking, through a combination of coercion and consent, to
shape youthful behaviour, can most usefully be seen within such a
framework of hegemonic incorporation. The revisionists see these
institutions as functional instruments designed to mould the minds
and morality of working-class youth in ways intended to re-

invigorate capitalism and to encourage a more harmonious and more stable relationship between the classes in the next generation.[3]

So far, their analysis is largely convincing. However, revisionist historians have tended to concentrate attention on the intentions and policies of legislators and have ignored the grass-roots response of working-class children and youth to the organizations provided for them. As a result, their resistance is an area that remains under-recorded and under-researched. Clearly, any account of an under-privileged and largely anonymous group like working-class youth requires a methodological approach different from that ordinarily employed by historians. Since the control of manuscript and printed evidence by adults (normally middle-class adults) is absolute, most documentary sources present a biased and distorted view of the resistance of working-class youth. This book will attempt to redress the balance by rewriting the history of working-class childhood and youth largely in the words of working-class people who themselves experienced it between 1889 and 1939; official accounts of disruptive and delinquent behaviour will be assessed in the light of their reminiscences. However, although it will be argued that the spoken testimony of working-class people is of fundamental importance in reconstructing an accurate history of their resistance to authority, the vast accumulation of theory and evidence that has emerged from the perspective of middle-class investigators and fills libraries and records offices cannot simply be dismissed as ideological prejudice or distortion. For if this evidence were taken at face value, then the history of working-class youth that emerged would be mainly a catalogue of ignorance and immorality testifying to the struggle of the state to rescue youth from the destructive effects of its culture and environment. In order to challenge previous interpretations, the precise nature of the ideological and conceptual distortion of such records must be specified.

There have been two major traditions in the conceptualization of working-class youth, which have shaped both theoretical and common-sense assumptions about its culture. These can broadly be termed theories of mass culture and theories of deprivation. Although the substance of the book focuses upon the period 1889 to 1939, I will extend my analysis of these traditions to the present day, because they continue to exercise a profound influence on our ways of viewing working-class youth culture.

The first tradition, the mass-society theory, has exerted a considerable influence since its development in the mid-nineteenth century. It does not constitute a unified body of theory but rather consists of a number of loosely defined views, sharing certain key concerns and rooted in an ambivalent and antagonistic response to industrialization and urbanization. The fear, common to many sociologists and social reformers in the past century, is that the combined forces of mass production, mass consumption, mass communication and mass democracy tend to undermine traditional values and to dissolve the individual's moral strength and the community's social purpose in an undifferentiated and desocialized mass.[4] Of course, this fear, which is present in the writings of cultural critics such as Matthew Arnold, T.S. Eliot and F.R. Leavis and political theorists such as John Stuart Mill, Alexis de Tocqueville and Ortega y Gasset, to name but a few, has normally been directed at modern culture as a whole. However, many observers, drawing on this tradition, have identified working-class youth, by virtue of its supposed ignorance and immaturity, as the group most vulnerable to the debilitating effects of a mass society. Starting from this position, they have tended to approach working-class youth using concepts closely related to the sociological theory of anomie, which stresses atomization and the consequent disintegration of moral control. In the literature on working-class youth this aimless condition finds expression in four broad forms of behaviour — instability, conformity, escapist fantasy and violence — which are consistently referred to as being characteristic of its culture. Naturally, different observers have stressed different characteristics of working-class youth, just as they have attributed various causes to these types of behaviour. Thus, while radical or Marxist critics have emphasized manipulation and repression as causes, conservative critics have tended to stress the innate inferiority of working-class youth and its incapacity to attain a higher level of consciousness. Although these concepts appear to have a solid and indisputable empirical base, the behaviour that they purport to describe might be explained equally well in terms of other motives and meanings, requiring different concepts: it is contended here that some aspects of this behaviour can more accurately be regarded as resistance, for traditional labels have been most vigorously applied to those sections of working-class youth that have in some way resisted, through withdrawal from, rejection of, or opposition to the institutions within which they are incorporated.

Each of these concepts requires a detailed and extended study, which cannot be attempted here. However, in order to illustrate some of the fundamental continuities in the mass-culture theory during the past century, it may be useful to examine in a little more detail some of the terminology and imagery associated with the concepts that have commonly been used to analyse working-class youth. Instability, of course, is central to a great deal of psychological and sociological theory. However, reformers and writers concerned with working-class youth have tended to simplify such theory (for example, Durkheim's original typology of anomie) and to reduce it to a series of labels and epithets. Thus, although ubiquitous references are made by writers to the instability of working-class youth, this term is often used interchangeably with other popular labels, such as 'uncertainty', 'purposelessness', 'insecurity', 'aimlessness', 'excitability', 'confusion' and 'restlessness'. Helen Dendy, for example, describing working-class culture in London in the 1890s, observed:

the excitement of a town life tells very greatly upon children. . . . the dark rings under their eyes tell of the nervous strain which is breaking down their health, and their very restlessness is the restlessness of fatigue and nervous exhaustion.[5]

Reginald Bray portrayed an even more disturbing stereotype of the city child restlessly searching for momentary stimulation and excitement on the streets as an escape from a meaningless existence:

Hour by hour, day by day, year in, year out, beats in upon him with remorseless persistence the lesson of his own utter insignificance in the multitudinous energy of a great city's life. . . . The aimless wandering of a child down the street is symbolic of his whole existence. He is dodging now this vehicle and now that; he is halting now to gather dusty treasures from a coster's barrow providentially upset, now to watch a herd of bullocks swept into the slaughterhouse . . . here walking, here running, here idling, now laughing, now crying, now shouting, he drifts in gentle aimlessness down the roadway. But in all this busy and exciting pilgrimage there is for him, unlike the ordinary passenger, no particular destination to be reached, no special street to be crossed, no definite task to be worked through, and no final goal of all desire to be attained.[6]

Following from these assumptions that city life has produced psychological imbalance and instability, those sections of working-class youth that have not internalized the values imposed by school, work and youth organizations have tended to be regarded as masses of rootless individuals. According to Fyvel,

Teddy boy society . . . like a magnet, draws in the most psychologically insecure among working-class adolescents. . . . Teddy boy society is a concentration of the insecure, of unstable adolescents, those with weak family ties . . . who are drawn to this nightly café life as to a drug, to hold back their anxieties.[7]

This type of analysis is also prominent in the post-war glut of reports and literature on working-class youth, which views them as the victims of rapid social change that has undermined traditional institutions and authority and has dislocated behavioural norms and expectations. Thus in the 1950s the main preoccupation of youth organizations was the problem of the 'unclubbables', and in the 1960s the 'unattached'.[8] Both of these problem types assume a model of working-class youth that is desocialized and inadequately integrated into society. Clearly, however, much of the behaviour of working-class youth subcultures that is conventionally stigmatized as antisocial can alternatively be conceptualized as resistance and viewed to some extent as an indictment of oppressive institutions.

Conformity, with its associations of low intelligence and poor taste reduced to the level of the lowest common denominator, has been another concept popular with critics, who have detected in the mass culture of working-class youth a particular gullibility and a tendency to imitate the antisocial behaviour retailed, for example, by comics, cinema and television. Thus in the late nineteenth century the dramatic growth of juvenile literature, especially the penny dreadfuls, aroused moral panic among sections of the middle class, which linked these pernicious influences directly with resistance to authority and crimes committed by working-class youth.[9] As Edward Salmon put it, 'a child accustomed to read of nothing but burglaries, and bushranging, and murder, cannot fail to develop many ferocious traits.' He warned that this corruption and debasement of working-class youth was a 'matter of such vital moment in the social economy of the masses as to justify high-handed action on the part of the state'.[10] To many reformers state intervention in the form of compulsory continuation classes and extended schooling seemed the most effective means of combating the mass conformity and mediocrity of working-class culture, a view symptomatic of an elitism that is particularly evident in the thinking of Masterman, who wrote of the East End of London: 'Into this mass, the School Boards have attempted to introduce as leaven the Evening Schools, flashing lanterns in their faces.'[11] Fears of mass conformity have been constantly echoed and elaborated throughout the century and have been repeated with particular urgency in the past three decades with the advent of commercial radio and television; for, in the words of cultural critic Richard Hoggart, 'there is something warming in the feeling that you are with everyone else . . . taking part in some mass activity . . . being able to feel one of the main herd.' Although Hoggart has contributed much towards our understanding of working-class culture, his view of the post-war generations as 'unbending the springs' of community solidarity and action is unnecessarily pessimistic. For example, he has written that less intelligent members of working-class youth are 'even more exposed than others to the debilitating mass trends of the day', as is evidenced by the appearance of subcultures such as 'Juke Box Boys . . . the directionless and tamed helots of a machine-minding class'.[12]

Closely related to the concept of conformity are those of manipulation and the manufacture of a fantasy world of film, music and sporting stars in which working-class youth submerges itself,[13] both of which are based on what can usefully be termed a 'hypodermic needle' theory of the effects of mass communications and entertainment industries. Mass culture is seen as a drug, injected through various communications media, which blunts individual awareness and produces a predictable mass response. Like the soma of Huxley's dystopia *Brave New World*, it provides a fantasy escape from an aimless and monotonous existence. George Orwell, in a much quoted passage, has described the experience of watching a cinema film as 'one which gradually overwhelms you — feeling the waves of its silliness lap around you till you seem to be drawn, intoxicated, in a viscous sea — after all, it's the kind of drug we need.'[14] Fears of the moral dangers of mass-entertainment industries inducing fantasy escapism have, during the present century, found frequent expression in moral reform movements aimed principally at protecting children and youth, such as the Social Purity League of the 1900s and, more recently, Mary Whitehouse's Viewers' and Listeners' Association.[15] This tradition clearly influenced Christopher Booker's *The Neophiliacs*, in which the three related concepts of insecurity, conformity and escapist fantasy merge to produce a disturbing image of contemporary youth culture:

The modern entertainment industry is almost entirely concerned with producing day dreams and day dream heroes. . . . there is no dream so powerful as one generated and subscribed to by a whole mass of people simultaneously — one of those mass projections of innumerable individual neuroses which we may call a group-fantasy . . . such as the teenage subculture based on dress and music. But the individuals making up the mass are not of course united in any real sense. . . . Behind their conformist exteriors they remain individually as insecure as ever . . . for mass advertising . . . is continually aggravating their fantasy selves and appealing to them through their insecurities to merge themselves in the mass ever more completely.[16]

The final preoccupation of mass culture critics has been the apparently aimless and gratuitous violence of working-class youth. Viewed through the mass-society lens, violence has consistently been explained in terms of the erosion of traditional authority and community control and by the development of depersonalized mass institutions and living conditions. Thus delinquency has commonly been seen as a consequence of the lack of defensible space on anonymous housing estates, as an expression of frustration experienced in depersonalized conditions at work and as the imitation of violent behaviour transmitted by communications media.[17] The most chronic symptom commonly ascribed to this urban malaise has been social disorganization, involving the breakdown of civilized behaviour and the formation of violent gangs in inner-city slum neighborhoods.[18] This theory of urban degeneration has for the past century constituted one of the most important traditions in sociological thought and cultural criticism.[19] Thus in the 1890s William Morrison argued that the contemporary increase in crime committed by juveniles was due partly to the development of a mass society:

the restraining eye of the village community is no longer upon them. In many cases they find themselves in a large city without friends, without family ties, and belonging to no social circle in which their conduct is either scrutinized or observed.[20]

Sociologist Bryan Wilson summarizes this line of argument in his alarming indictment of working-class youth subcultures in the post-World War II period.

The growing youth problem reflects deep-seated changes in the structure of industrial society. . . . It reflects the trend towards centralization, bigger firms, bigger schools, and bigger towns. . . . As long as this process affected only the middle classes, personal behaviour did not deteriorate. The middle classes had for a long time demanded inhibition and self-discipline in their children. But once the working classes were inducted into large institutions and once their community life became impersonal, vital elements in social control were lost. Control amongst the working classes was much more a feature of community and much less a matter of the internalization of a distinctive set of values. When working-class folk culture was replaced by mass culture, so the least socialized sections of society inevitably passed out of effective control. . . . Working-class youngsters . . . have discovered something about mass action. . . . They arrive, congregate in groups, fight, and when the police arrive, drive off swiftly and anonymously.[21]

As is indicated by both these quotations, the key to mass-culture explanations of delinquency or resistance is the reduction or disintegration of social control. This focus on the concept of control closely parallels, and draws upon, functionalist theories, which emphasize the importance of control and socializing functions for system maintenance. Until fairly recently, sociological and historical inquiry into juvenile delinquency was heavily influenced by assumptions derived from functionalist and mass-culture theory, particularly the functionalist maxim that systems undergoing rapid social change, such as urbanization, experience a temporary loosening of control mechanisms.[22] Thus Tobias, for example, has concluded that the huge increase in juvenile crime and the development of delinquent youth subcultures in the first half of the nineteenth century

was not to any important extent a consequence of poverty . . . but . . . lay fundamentally in the failure of the economic and social system to adjust sufficiently rapidly to the great upsurge of population . . . internal migration . . . and bewildering changes. The people of those towns were jerked out of centuries of certainty into an uncertain world. . . . The feeling of uncertainty thus engendered was all the more important because of the youth of many of the migrants. . . . The control of the young [was] weakened by these circumstances. . . . These youngsters were criminals in England because of lack of work and because of the pernicious effects of a morally unhealthy urban environment. . . . the upsurge of population growth . . . provided greater opportunities for crime and weakened many of the barriers against crime. In so far as the evidence bears any conclusions, crime, and especially juvenile crime, in the first half of the nineteenth century was the crime of a society in violent economic and social transition.[23]

The view that working-class children and youth are much more vulnerable than any other social group to the disorienting and destructive forces of urbanization, city life and rapid social change has a long tradition. It is rooted in the ideology of community that, closely coupled with the ideology of social imperialism, developed from the mid-nineteenth century onwards and has since been a potent influence on social policy.[24] One important concern shared by these ideologies has been the promotion of state intervention to prevent and counteract the moral and physical damage inflicted upon working-class youth by the experience of work in an industrial capitalist society. This concern found its most profound expression in the reports and protective legislation generated by the boy and girl labour problem that emerged at the turn of the century, based on the discovery that approximately two-thirds of working-class youth entered semi-skilled or unskilled jobs in the early teens, as a result of which many became unemployed or unemployable in later life.[25] The problem was created by the structural increase in 'blind alley' jobs produced by mechanization, specialization and the rapid growth of the retail and distributive trades, and by the corresponding decline in craft trades, apprenticeships and skilled opportunities for working-class youth.[26] Characteristically, the de-skilling of work, the depersonalization of relationships between employers and employees and unemployment were seen as dysfunctions of a rapidly changing industrial society, which could to a large extent be rectified by extended schooling and compulsory continuation classes for young workers.[27] These, it was assumed, would enable moral control to be maintained during the critical period of adolescence, which many reformers believed was an impressionable stage of life, of immense importance in the making or breaking of reliable workers and responsible citizens. Thus fundamental contradictions of a capitalist economy were viewed in mass-society terms as problems of industrialization, necessitating state intervention to educate and regulate the lives of working-class youth, thereby protecting them from an amoral and aimless life in the city and promoting long-term national efficiency and stability.[28] Following from this perspective, the antisocial behaviour of 'blind alley' youth tended to be regarded as amorality and aimless violence rather than as class-mediated resistance. For example, Reginald Bray, one of the most influential writers on the boy labour problem, believed that inadequate control of youth at work was generating a restless spirit of rebellion among young people in general, of which hooliganism was only one particularly extreme expression. He wrote:

it must not be assumed that all boys become hooligans or criminals, but all do suffer from the want of control and the need of a more disciplined life. Hooliganism is merely an extreme type of disease which in a milder form fastens upon the boys who are allowed unrestrained liberty. The disease is the disease of restlessness — the restlessness of the town, the dislike of regularity. . . . This disease . . . leads into unemployment when the age of manhood is reached.[29]

It was this image of a precocious and delinquent working-class youth culture, corrupted by the temptations of the city, that motivated several generations of middle-class child savers in a crusade to revitalize family and community life. The growth of the child welfare movement was closely related to the process of urbanization and the associated middle-class fear of a rootless mass culture,[30] which, it is contended, has with some consistency found symbolic form in the image of a brutalized working-class youth, a portent of moral decline and cultural disintegration.

The most pervasive and disturbing images used to depict the violent behaviour of working-class youth during the nineteenth and early twentieth centuries derived from middle-class anxiety about pollution from the city's refuse dumps, drains and sewers. In fact, the lurid metaphors of the 'gutter', 'excrement' and 'pestilence' with which commentators commonly portrayed the activities of street gangs were themselves extensions of the depersonalizing language used to describe the moral and physical condition of the casual poor or the 'residuum'.[31] Another powerful metaphor that captured fears of the degeneracy of youth was the image of the jungle, with its associations of primitive sexuality, tribal savagery, bestiality and plain bovine stupidity. This jungle metaphor (which, for example, portrays young 'slum monkeys' and 'brutal savages' who 'ape' undesirable practices and are vulnerable to 'herd trends')[32] has become a predominant source of pejorative labels in the twentieth century, primarily as a consequence of the influence of social Darwinism and the obsessive concern of critics with the permissive sexuality of youth. In moments of widespread anxiety about the disorderly behaviour of young people in the post-World War II period these two sets of images have been manipulated by the mass media to produce alarming stereotypes of rebellious youth, which have become the symbolic folk devils of their generation.[33] Thus, for example, during the mid-1960s the media's condemnation of mods and rocker gangs as 'animals', 'dregs', 'vermin', 'rat-packs' and so on helped to create a moral panic that reinforced and legitimized repressive measures of social control by the police and the courts.[34] Clearly, these images, together with the broader assumptions made by mass-culture theories of working-class youth, have an implicit political dimension, which must be explored in more detail.

The theoretical orientation and the evidence produced by the mass-society conception has two principal defects that blur our vision of the cultural forms of working-class youth. The first is that much mass-culture theorizing has an in-built elitist or class bias —

a bias that is particularly evident in the value-laden labels frequently used to stigmatize working-class youth and often tells us more about the values and expectations of the observer than it does about the behaviour of youth. What it reveals most of all is a fundamental concern with class. Left-wing critics have expressed anxiety that class-consciousness is being diluted or even obliterated by the commercialized, classless content of communication systems. Their stock response to what they perceive to be the increasingly apolitical and amoral culture of working-class youth has been to characterize it as the passive victim of a manipulative capitalist culture industry.[35] Charles Parker, for example, has concluded that 'pop is, in fact, now cherished by a ruling class as a peerless form of social control.'[36] Liberal and conservative critics, on the other hand, have feared that mass leisure and entertainment industries, by reflecting and reinforcing the mediocre taste and brutal passions of working-class youth, are eroding traditional values and institutions that are necessary for social order.[37] Patricia Morgan, for example, in a recent study, has warned of a 'new barbarism . . . the spread of . . . a delinquent syndrome, a conglomeration of behaviour, speech, appearance and attitudes, a frightening ugliness and hostility which pervades human interaction, a flaunting contempt for other human beings, a delight in crudity, cruelty and violence', which she attributes to be 'in some places . . . the main cause of urban decay.'[38] Thus the elitist analyses of both left- and right-wing observers have failed to do justice to the creative responses of working-class youth and have often denied its cultural forms any validity whatsoever.

The second major criticism of mass-culture theory is that it disguises political problems of class inequality and exploitation by its use of the depoliticized concepts of the individual as opposed to the masses and the masses as opposed to the elites. The difference between masses and elites has usually been defined in cultural terms; that between classes, normally in economic terms. Thus although this theory does to some extent focus on work rather than leisure, the main thrust of mass-culture analysis has been directed at the developing mass media, and attention has been concentrated on leisure and education as opposed to work activities and experiences.[39] Further, this view of class relationships as the domination and deprivation of an atomized mass reduces, or even precludes, any possibility of class conflict or class-mediated resistance. Mass-culture theory, particularly in its functionalist variations, does, of course, conceptualize conflict between social groupings based on shared interests and identities. Society is not regarded simply as comprising a mass of atomized individuals. However, in the case of youth this theory tends to see shared age position and shared membership of a particular generation as far more potent factors in the development of a common consciousness than class position. This adds a further complication, for many of the cultural forms that might be seen as providing evidence of class-based resistance have instead commonly been viewed in terms of generational conflict.[40] In formulating their youth-culture theories sociologists have, to some extent, merely been giving academic expression to the popular, centuries-old notion of generational conflict between youth and adults, which features prominently in much of the evidence relating to youth. However, the youth-culture and generational theories of sociologists such as Talcott Parsons and Mannheim, originally formulated in the inter-war period, have come to exert a powerful influence today, mainly because they have fitted neatly with the various interpretations of post-war change, principally the theories of affluence, consumerism and *embourgeoisement*, that have claimed that the working class is disappearing.[41] Stated simply, it was assumed by such sociologists that status, assessed by reference to age and a combination of educational, employment and consumption achievements was replacing class as the basis of social stratification. One major new social type which was emerging, it was claimed, was the teenager, who formed part of an increasingly classless young generation.

This conceptualization has had two principal effects relevant to this study. First, it has masked the persistence of class inequality in twentieth-century Britain and has mystified our understanding of the cultural forms of working-class youth, which, although conventionally viewed as hedonism and aimless violence, can in some circumstances be seen alternatively as an expression of class feeling or nascent class-consciousness.[42] Second, its emphasis on generational consciousness and generational conflict as far more important than class-consciousness and class conflict has exercised a major influence on the emerging historiography of youth, for most recent historians of youth culture have borrowed the conceptual framework of generational conflict between teenagers and adults and put it to use as the most powerful lens through which to view the resistance of working-class youth to authority.[43] Given this starting point, those who have investigated the resistance of youth have tended to ignore its potential for a class interpretation and have seen little connection between generational conflict and class conflict.[44] However, as we shall see later, the testimony of elderly working-class people suggests that their experience of class relations and class inequality was the most important factor in motivating their resistance to control.

The other major tradition in the conceptualization of working-class youth is deprivation theory. The first type that has commonly been applied to working-class youth has concerned itself with a hereditary lack of potential for intellectual and emotional development. The concept of intelligence as an innate and scientifically measurable entity was closely associated with the ideology of social Darwinism and the eugenics movement, which emerged in the late nineteenth century and proposed that each nation contained a fixed proportion of bright and dull people (Galton referred to the latter as 'the vast abundance of mediocrity').[45] The main social problem to which theories of intelligence and personality were addressed was that of the biological and psychological condition of working-class children and youth, who, it was assumed, were hereditarily and genetically inferior to their middle-class counterparts and whose culture symbolized for many observers the physical and mental deterioration of the British race.[46] George Sims, for example, insisted:

the vital factor in the future of the British Empire is the child. . . . Thousands of the tortured children who suffer and survive will only do so with stunted bodies and enfeebled minds to become the physical, moral and mental wreckage which burdens the state and fills the lunatic asylums, the workhouses and the jails. Against the guilt of race suicide our men of science are everywhere preaching their sermons today. It is against the guilt of race murder that the cry of the children should ring through the land.[47]

This image of a feebleminded and degenerate generation to come impelled numerous statutory and voluntary attempts to improve the moral fibre and physical strength of the nation. It is from this civilizing mission of social imperialism that much of the evidence on working-class youth culture from the 1880s to the 1930s derives.[48] The evidence and explanations produced by this movement must be treated with extreme caution, for they tend to collapse the complexities of youthful behaviour into a set of disturbing images. Most important, it was the sections of working-class youth that most flagrantly flouted middle-class norms of orderly and obedient behaviour and violently resisted authority that aroused the most anxious and most vicious condemnation. Thus Arnold Freeman, who boasted that his investigation into the boy labour problem was a pioneering work because he had 'considered the problem from the standpoint of the boy as well as from that of industry', wrote of a 'young wastrel' in 1914: 'his character was as good as might be expected with such blood in his veins. . . . a glance at his face is sufficient to convince the least observant person that there is a kind of moral rottenness in him.'[49] Even more sensitive observers,

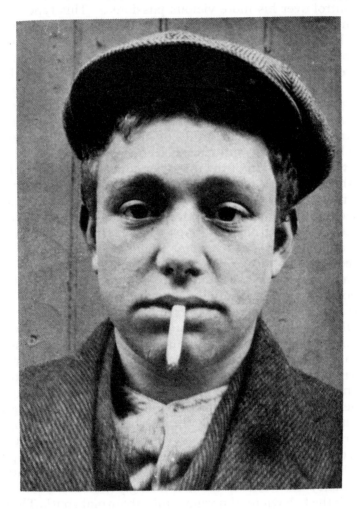

This picture of a 15-year-old delinquent, photographed in the 1920s, was used as the frontispiece for Cyril Burt's The Young Delinquent, *one of the most influential books on juvenile delinquency in the inter-war period. Although Burt thought that the youth's face expressed the psychological disturbance of the adolescent years, it could equally well be seen as expressive of justifiable anger, rebellion and stubborn independence.*

such as Charles Russell, were often reduced to the use of abusive epithets when confronted with violent resistance or antisocial behaviour. In 1905 Russell characterized the individual member of the Ike gangs of Manchester as 'a loafer, an idler . . . a stupid fellow, who, from constant indulgence in vicious habits of many kinds has lost control over his more vicious passions'.[50] This type of moral condemnation of resistance to authority and delinquency, expressed through depersonalizing images derived from social Darwinism, was common at least until the 1930s. From this period onwards, however, the moralistic approach was gradually superseded by the use of more scientific methods and language, culminating in the development of psychometric psychology, which has been concerned with the analysis of personality types and the measurement of different levels of intelligence. This theorizing, which has been hugely influential on educational and social policy, led to the justification of the three-tier education system inherited from the nineteenth century by appeals to psychometric evidence. Thus the 1944 modification of the tripartite education system claimed to correspond to three clearly defined types of intellect and character, ranging from those capable of 'abstract thought' to those who could not progress beyond 'concrete thought'. Given this perspective, acts of resistance and rule-breaking committed by working-class youth have tended to be viewed as expressions of psychological and intellectual deficiency.

The rebellious behaviour regarded as juvenile delinquency and normally investigated in case studies has constituted the main encounter of psychology and criminology with working-class youth and has generated a vast literature of diagnosis and recommended corrective treatment. One influential tradition of criminological thought has seen young delinquents as the tainted offspring of the degenerate and morally retarded residuum of the working class, characterized by instinctively brutal behaviour and a physical appearance similar to apes or savages.[51] However, although the image of the subhuman 'slum monkey' has persisted to the present day, since the late nineteenth century much of the literature on delinquency has drawn an increasingly narrow dividing line between the behaviour of normal and subnormal youth. Thus Cyril Burt, for example, who from the 1930s onwards became one of the leading theorists in this field, aimed much of his work at the teaching profession, for, as he put it, 'I am convinced the psychology of the young criminal will throw great light upon the daily disciplinary problems of the classroom and upon the misconduct of the difficult child.'[52] The development of this pathological view of young people was due principally to the influence of theories of adolescence, which contended that it was a stage of life characterized by inner turmoil and uncertainty, commonly expressed in egotistic, cruel and criminal behaviour.[53] Working-class adolescents were thought to be most likely to display delinquent and rebellious characteristics during this 'storm and stress' period in the life cycle because it was widely assumed that working-class parents exercised inadequate control over brutal adolescent instincts. Theories of adolescent psychopathology remain fashionable today, and psycho-historians, applying the iron laws of adolescent development to the study of the past, often ascribe patterns of rebellious behaviour to inadequate socialization and the disturbance of the maturation process.

Clearly, acceptance or partial acceptance of such theories and evidence of psychological deficiency would seriously undermine any attempt to demonstrate the rational and discriminating resistance of working-class youth to authority. However, the historical value of these psychological theories is extremely limited, for there is much evidence to suggest that adolescence is not a universal experience but has been created artificially through a convergence of social, economic and demographic changes. During the late nineteenth century many middle-class social reformers sought to impose adolescence, as a period of enforced and extended dependence, on adults through the educational, welfare and leisure organizations that they controlled.[54] This child-saving movement had a considerable influence and impact, principally because the discovery of adolescence was interrelated with the introduction and extension of compulsory education, the decline of apprenticeship and wage labour for children and the development of protective child-welfare legislation. Although the ideology of adolescence was imposed on middle-class youth with a high degree of success, however, the resilient, independent traditions of working-class youth remained to a large extent impervious to control and penetration. During the past century horrified middle-class investigators have continually expressed concern at the coarse language, the rough games, the exuberant and extrovert behaviour, the territorial conflicts between rival gangs, the early initiation into adult pleasures such as smoking and drinking and the courting of young lovers in public places that have traditionally been characteristic of working-class youth culture.[55] Yet this failure of working-class youth to respond to the education and protective treatment thought appropriate for adolescents did not lead to the abandonment of the theory of adolescence as a crucial stage in character development. Instead the concept of adolescence was stretched to explain 'precocious' and 'antisocial' forms of behaviour by reference to the incompetence of working-class parents, who, it was frequently claimed, failed to treat their children with the correct affectionate and authoritarian control during this traumatic stage of life. Often the condemnation of dissolute working-class parents was abusive and hysterical in its tone, as is shown by the following address to the National Union of Teachers in 1901:

My first plea is for the child, the neglected child, whose present condition deserves public attention, because there are not wanting indications that the welfare of society and of the nation are seriously menaced by the lawlessness which springs from defective control, mainly owing to the unwillingness or inability of parents to carry out the duties of their position. The hooligan, or street blackguard, is not a sudden growth. He is the product of street education. . . . The thoughtful student of modern life sees nothing sadder than the crowds of boys and girls in the streets late at night, exposed to many and serious dangers, acquiring evil habits, and generally laying the foundations of a life of idleness, vice or crime. . . . The boisterous, rude behaviour, the vulgar and coarse language, and the inculcation of positively sinful deeds are facts which must be faced and fought. There is no parental influence here. . . . And there are mothers! When we think of 'mother' what endearing and noble images arise in the mind. Yet there are mothers so degraded, so utterly unworthy of their name, so lost to all sense of their duties and privileges, that savage women ignorant of all Christianity are in such respects their superiors. . . . How can the schools and their purer atmosphere overcome the habitual intimacy which springs from debased and debasing surroundings? The difficulty — a grave one — is to enforce the obligation on the parent, which the violent, the drunken, the dissolute and the idle are ever seeking to evade.[56]

Many schoolteachers and youth workers shared Stanley Hall's view that during the teenage years 'the young man is fighting the hottest battles of his life with the Devil.'[57] However, since very few working-class interviewees recollected any moral conflict, emotional disturbance or identity crisis when they were young, it seems probable that the experience of adolescence is class-specific. For while adolescent theories of personal crisis may correspond to some extent to a middle-class culture characterized by individualistic values and a prolonged dependency on parents, they have little explanatory power when applied to a working-class culture typified by group solidarity and a rapid transition from childhood to adulthood. Thus the resistance of working-class youth to adult control at school, at work and at leisure will be viewed as symptomatic of class-cultural conflict rather than of the adolescent neurosis favoured by psychologists.

Similarly, the influential tradition of psychological and criminological thought that has emphasized the importance of hereditary and biological factors in determining delinquent and antisocial behaviour must also be reviewed in class terms. The task of dismantling this tradition will not be attempted here, however, as a critical revision has already been undertaken, mainly by the academic disciplines of sociology and educational sociology, which expanded, especially from the 1950s onwards, in close connection with a reformist educational ideology. These disciplines have reversed the traditional emphasis on heredity and instead place primacy on environmental factors as the major determinant of working-class youth culture. The main achievement of this school of thought has been to expose and discredit the pathological view of delinquency and resistance principally on the grounds that it commits the cardinal sin of reductionism, reducing explanations that require sociological and historical treatment to biological and psychological elements. Thus the bulk of delinquent case studies produced by the pathological school are at best of limited historical value and at worst directly misleading, for although they provide a wealth of detail about individual attitudes, temperament, parentage and so on, they use a faulty methodology for measuring intelligence and personality and fail to situate behaviour in the broader class context of poverty, inequality and exploitation.[58]

The bulk of sociological literature produced in the 1950s and 1960s, then, insisted that analysis of delinquent and antisocial behaviour should focus on the environmental factor of social class. Thus the persistent social problem of an aggressive and semi-delinquent working-class youth culture often came to be viewed within a class, as opposed to a pathological, framework. However, social class was conceived in terms not of social and economic relationships but of a category indicating cultural deprivation.[59] The origins of this deprivation were to a large extent traced to faulty family socialization processes, such as authoritarian patterns of thought and action, the erratic and inconsistent application of discipline, restricted conceptual and linguistic codes and low expectations of achievement, all of which, it was claimed, contributed to a culture of poverty.[60] The cluster of theories that constitute the foundation of the bulk of contemporary research on working-class childhood and youth tend to place a strong emphasis on the transmission of an anti-intellectual culture of resignation, low expectation and immediate gratification to successive generations in explaining the cycle of deprivation and inequality.[61] Clearly, these theories have a lot to say about the origins, the nature and the consequences of the resistance of working-class youth to authority. A study that seeks to explain the resistance of youth cannot simply ignore the huge amount of empirical research inspired by theories of cultural deprivation; it must modify or reject these theories, for the explanations they produce and the evidence they select have important consequences. For example, some sociological research into working-class youth has concluded that, by virtue of its innumerable deficits, it is simply without morality. Thus in 1969 McDonald, in a study of delinquent behaviour in school, work and leisure time, wrote:

awareness of wrongdoing . . . means very different things to the middle-class and the working-class person. For the person with only a restricted code . . . guilt and shame are not experienced . . . as they would be for a speaker of the elaborated code. In the case of delinquent activity . . . a restricted code speaker probably would not be thinking of theft as such, or its rightness or wrongness.[62]

Although the cultural deprivation argument was heralded in the 1950s and 1960s as a breakthrough in the understanding of the continual pattern of working-class failure and low achievement at school, leading to a Government policy of positive discrimination and small-scale attempts at cultural engineering, it only requires an elementary historical knowledge to realize that the problem of a deprived culture has been a constant preoccupation of social investigators and reformers since the early nineteenth century. For despite the belief that hereditary and psychological deficits fixed and limited the potential of the majority of working-class youth, it was widely assumed that the harmful influence of an ignorant culture, geared to living for the present, was a significant factor in shaping its behaviour. Reginald Bray, for example, in his study of boy life in the city in 1904, wrote that working-class parents

condemn . . . dirty habits, noisy ways and rough practices in the house . . . but this disapproval is due much more to the personal comfort of the parents than to any delicate distinction between right and wrong. . . . In many cases the boy has daily impressed on him by the lives of his parents the lesson that nothing matters, provided detection is impossible, while vice may become virtuous when whitened by a spacious and ingenious falsehood. They have no idea of the meaning of character. Acts and not motives count for anything. Their lessons take the form of 'do' and 'don't', and never reach that higher level where the command is to 'be this and not that'.[63]

Thus a historian of working-class youth who followed Trevor Roper's advice and 'tested the models of the social scientist . . . by . . . running them through the dimension of time'[64] would find ample evidence for cultural deprivation theories, principally because they are often little more than pseudo-scientific elaborations of the moral judgements originally made by social investigators.

Cultural deprivation theory has many dimensions, and these will be subjected to critical analysis in subsequent chapters through a detailed examination of oral evidence, which in many instances suggests alternative explanations for the cultural forms of working-class youth. However, it is necessary here to focus on one crucial aspect of cultural deprivation theory, the working class 'authoritarianism' thesis, for it has particularly important consequences for the construction of a theory of resistance. Clearly, acceptance of this thesis, which attributes to working-class culture qualities of violence, brutality and intolerance, would invalidate any attempt to establish the purposeful resistance of working-class youth to bourgeois institutions.[65] In its preoccupation with violence the working-class authoritarianism thesis provides an important link between cultural deprivation and mass-culture theory. A fear of totalitarianism or anarchy, and the subsequent obliteration of the liberal principles of freedom, tolerance and justice, has exerted a powerful influence on social and political thought in the past century. The European experience of Fascism and the fear of communism have convinced many that liberal democracy is the most just and most viable political system possible and that it must be resolutely protected from threats of violence from whatever quarter.[66] Crucially, some of this theorizing is infused with an implicit or explicit class prejudice, which identifies the working class as the main enemy and threat to freedom and democracy. Thus, according to Lipset, working-class culture is distinguished by its 'profoundly anti-democratic tendencies';[67] Bernstein in his early work argued that it was characterized by a 'volatile patterning of behaviour';[68] while Eysenck claims that the working class tends to be 'tough-minded', whereas the middle class is 'tender-minded', in their social and political principles. Many historians have been influenced by these assumptions about working-class authoritarianism and have viewed state and voluntary provision for working-class children and youth as a progressive civilizing force that protects them from the harmful and destructive influences of their own culture. Pinchbeck and Hewitt, for example, argued that the progress of state protection of children 'against exploitation, cruelty and neglect and against exposure to any kind of moral or physical danger or unnecessary suffering of any kind', was the result of 'middle-class . . . social reformers who judged working-class conditions by their own middle-class standards . . . to make it possible for the working-class family to adopt a pattern . . . of life not so offensively different from their own'.[69]

The stereotype of deeply embedded authoritarianism, particularly among the rough or unskilled sections of the working class, is based on an overwhelming body of evidence accumulated by investigators during the past century. For example, one recurring theme in child-saving literature was the national disgrace of a drunken and dissolute slum culture in which child abuse was endemic.[70] Thus John Samuelson, in a typically moralistic and class-prejudiced view of cruelty to children, claimed:

slum children have been starved, tortured, assaulted, neglected, morally and physically outraged, employed as beggars and subjected to various forms of cruelty and suffering by their parents or guardians, whose duty it was to protect and cherish them, and until recently this has been done with impunity and often even without rebuke. . . . But the 'silver lining' which is now apparent through the intervention of humane and indignant men and women of the middle and upper classes, is daily broadening, and out of the evil which God in his wisdom permits, some of the noblest qualities of mankind are being evolved.[71]

And although labour historians, tending to focus on skilled, organized and politically conscious workers, have documented a noble struggle to create a democratic culture among an educated minority, few would dispute Gareth Stedman Jones's view of the unskilled as 'ignorant, inarticulate' and characterized by their 'rootless volatility'.[72] This tendency to accept allegations of the authoritarianism and viciousness of large sections of the working class has led many historians to ignore or dismiss potential evidence of class-based resistance. It has, for example, discouraged educational historians from seriously studying reports of classroom conflict in school log and punishment books, in the press and in oral interviews; for, following Lowndes, they have tended to see 'those teachers and school attendance officers who went down into the slums of our great cities' as 'the pioneers of a new age', achieving 'that great feat of national organization . . . the formation of manners . . . cleanliness, orderliness, sobriety and self-respect . . . in a child population sadly uncivilized by modern standards'.[73] Given this perspective, the violent opposition of older pupils to school authority, for example, or of street gangs to uniformed youth organizations and the police can be dismissed as brutal expressions of a culture of poverty. For although it is acknowledged that the rough sections of the working class have strongly resisted outside penetration, it is generally argued that this resistance has been rooted in an ignorant, insular and conservative culture, which has rejected all organizations, whatever their social purpose, in favour of the immediate release and gratification offered by violence and drink.[74] In subsequent chapters I will attempt to show that this type of explanation is misleading because it fails to situate violence within its detailed historical context of class-cultural conflict, thereby ignoring the social meaning of violence. It will be argued that patterns of violence at school, at work and in the working-class neighbourhood can most usefully be explained in terms of a specific response to the deficiencies of the providers rather than in terms of generalized theories of the cultural deficiencies of working-class children and youth.

Another common fault of cultural deprivation theories, which they share with the mass-society conceptualization of working-class youth, is the frequent use of value-laden, pejorative labels to deride their subjects of study. In attempting to dismantle this class prejudice, it is useful to adopt the perspective of cultural relativism derived from interpretive sociology and anthropology, which argues that by definition nobody can be deprived of his own culture and that images of deprivation are manufactured by dominant groups that possess the power to impose their own definitions of social worth upon subordinate groups.[75] Thus, stated simply, the cultural relativist would regard the language, thought and behaviour of working-class youth as components of a different, rather than a deficient, culture. This approach is particularly valuable in exposing the in-built class bias of the terminology used by social investigators and critics, for, as many relativists have pointed out, the positive or negative associations of certain cultural forms can be reversed simply by attaching different labels to them.[76] For example, working-class 'aggression' and 'volatility' can be reinterpreted as desirable forms of immediate emotional expression, just as a middle-class preference for deferred gratification and a concern for the future might be reformulated as a stifling lack of spontaneity. This approach is also valuable in giving back to working-class youth some form of self-respect and rationality, qualities that hostile outside observers have often denied it. As we shall see later, oral interviews suggest that the aggressive street gangs and territorial conflicts between rival gangs that alarmed middle-class observers have often condemned as evidence of animal brutality are to a large extent ritualized and involve customary constraints that prevent serious injury.

However, this relativist approach, when taken to its logical conclusion, can lead to romanticism or the celebration of cultural forms that should more realistically be seen, in the context of class inequality and oppression, as a defence against, or an attempt to compensate for, harsh living and working conditions. An illustration of the inadequacy of this approach is provided by the recent ethnographic studies of football hooliganism by Peter Marsh and the Contemporary Violence Research Centre in Oxford, which argue that the 'bovver-boy' element in working-class youth should be viewed as liberated rather than alienated, for 'aggro is a way of ritualizing and expressing aggression in a relatively non-injurious manner. . . . By trying to eradicate aggro we end up with something far more sinister. . . . aggression doesn't go away and the champions of pacifist ideals have never had history on their side.'[77] According to Marsh and a number of other relativists and interactionists who tend to adopt a pluralistic model of society, working-class youth's resistance to authority is rooted in the latter's intolerant refusal to accept youth culture on its own terms, and delinquency is manufactured by the imposition of derogatory labels on working-class youth, thereby escalating cultural conflict and producing moral panics.[78] This relativist view of working-class youth must be rejected for a number of reasons: it reduces class-cultural conflict to cultural conflict, and it lacks a historical or structural dimension and is consequently blind to the process by which the values of the dominant culture tend to be rewarded and those of the subordinate culture penalized. Even more seriously, it dispenses with concepts such as class-consciousness and class feeling, which are fundamental to an understanding of the process of resistance. For although the vast majority of acts of resistance committed by working-class youth have not taken an explicitly political form, its most resilient cultural traditions — for example, larking about and social crime — can to some extent be seen as nascent expressions of class-consciousness. Similarly, the related concept of class feeling is extremely important in constructing a theory of resistance, because the experience of subordination and of deep-seated social division in which working-class youth's resistance is rooted is often not articulated in class-conscious terms. Many studies, including my own research, show that hostility has frequently been aimed at localized and personalized targets, such as a schoolteacher, a policeman or an immigrant group, victimized as scapegoats for the economic decline of a neighbourhood.[79] Clearly, the use of a concept such as class feeling to account for working-class youth's lack of awareness of the real causes of, and solutions to, its grievances implies a concession to some form of deprivation theory. For the failure of the majority of working-class youth to conceptualize its resistance in a self-conscious political form in the past century cannot be explained simply in terms of repression and ideological manipulation. A comprehensive theory of resistance must focus on the role played by working-class culture and on the way in which the transmission of values and focal concerns from parent to youth culture shapes and limits the potential strategies for opposition available to youth. However, an analysis of this process need not involve acceptance of the cultural deprivation theories that have been criticized above.

Two important points must be made here. First, working-class culture can, of course, broadly be reformulated as an effect rather than a cause of structural inequality. For example, so-called typical working-class values, such as roughness and the prizing of immediate pleasure as opposed to long-term planning, can be viewed as rational adaptations to harsh and uncertain living and working conditions.[80] The complicated relationship between class location and cultural response will not be entered into here, neither will the problematical nature of working-class values and institutions, as these have been the subject of lengthy sociological and historical debate.[81] However, a second, closely related point must be examined in a little more detail; it is that some historians, including Marxist historians, having grounded working-class culture in the context of economic structures and developments, then have an unfortunate habit of feeling justified in adopting concepts derived from cultural deprivation theory as analytical tools. This tendency is present, for example, either explicitly or implicitly, in the work of Richard Price and Gareth Stedman Jones on the remaking of British working-class culture during the period 1870 to 1914.

Richard Price has urged that the history of working-class culture be rewritten, taking into account 'the difference . . . that exists in the values, thought processes and frames of reference between the "articulate" and the "inarticulate"', for 'the working class does not use the same frames of reference that the more formally educated would.'[82] Thus Price concludes that during the Boer War 'young clerks were more eager to volunteer than young labourers' because 'imperialism as a concept was too tenuous for working-class society to react to. . . . working-class objections to imperialism were based upon what was a typical working-class characteristic: a concern for the immediate and the material.'[83] From this perspective, one would presumably regard as deprivation rather than resistance the limited success of schools in inculcating imperialist sentiments during the period under study. However, oral interviews indicate a far more diverse response to imperialism among working-class youth and, in particular, a more complex conceptual understanding that this theory can contain. In chapter 2 I attempt to show how this opposition was rooted in young people's experience of the contradictions between the rhetoric of imperialism and the daily reality of class discrimination and inequality.

Gareth Stedman Jones's analysis of working-class culture in some ways parallels the work of Price. By decoding the lyrics of pre-World War I music hall songs, he concludes that the humorous songs and sketches enjoyed by the working class played an essentially conformist role, providing an antidote to suffering and a harmless release for feelings of class resentment and expressing a cheerful accommodation to poverty and hardship. He argues that implicit in the 'comic realism' of the songs is the assumption that 'class is a life sentence as final as any caste system',[84] and he considers the innocuous entertainment and fatalistic humour purveyed by music halls to be of some importance because they were 'a reflection and reinforcement of the major trends in London working class life from the 1870s to the 1900s'.[85] Although this approach provides us with interesting insights, it does tend however, to overlook the powerful elements of resistance contained within working-class humour, which in some contexts can represent an aggressive and irreverent challenge to the dominant culture. In chapter 5 I argue that working-class youth drew from this rich tradition of humour to develop one of its most important cultural forms, larking about, expressed in a wide range of activities such as parody singing, practical joking, sabotage tactics at school and work and so on, all of which helped to loosen the bonds of obedience and deference that many institutions were attempting to secure. What is relevant here is not so much the content of that chapter but the method that gave it conceptual shape. The usefulness of the concept of larking about as an important cultural tradition of working-class youth was suggested to me by the frequency with which respondents used the phrase to describe devious techniques of resistance to authoritarian control. It seems to me that to the extent that historians show a sensitivity to the language and concepts used by working-class people and a willingness to incorporate these concepts into cultural theory, oral history has enormous potential for generating a more firmly grounded understanding of working-class culture. Of course, this is not the only possible method of analysing working-class youth culture. Phil Cohen has shown that it can be misleading to concentrate exclusively on verbalizations of consciousness, and that contemporary working-class youth subcultures are best understood by decoding their symbolic style and working back to their class base.[86] However, the great advantage of grounded concepts (like, for example, larking about) is that they express directly the motives and meanings of the people whom they purport to describe. Consequently, they have greater explanatory power than the concepts used by middle-class investigators — such as instability, immorality, ignorance and so on — which impose built-in ideological preconceptions and prejudices on their subjects of study. This chapter has attempted to demonstrate how these concepts have tended to be accepted uncritically by sociologists, psychologists and historians and elevated into mass-culture and cultural deprivation theories that in the past century have devalued or denied the class-based resistance of working-class youth. The potential power of oral history is that it offers a viable method of placing this class resistance back at the centre of analysis. This book aims to rescue some of the most important traditions of resistance that emerged during the period 1889 to 1939 by documenting the testimony of old people who participated in the making of a working-class youth culture.

CHAPTER 2

Subverting
the School Syllabus

The teachers couldn't control the kids, even in them days. They was proper little monkeys, all of them, not one no more than another. They did go to school in gangs an' they did vent all their feelings out and the teacher 'ad a job to keep 'em down. There was so many in a class, if she could keep 'em quiet, she was a good teacher, no learning 'em or anything. You could never open the school door and walk in and the kids there was quiet, you could always hear some class in uproar and the headmistress 'ud 'ave to go in an' sort it out. Many's the time I've seen a teacher break down and cry. When they did cry, it did get on their nerves and work them up to such a pitch that they couldn't stand a minute longer. They couldn't take any more. 'Cos if the kids didn't want a lesson, they didn't have that lesson, because they used to cause so much commotion with one thing an' another that the teacher couldn't give that lesson. The kids was either playin' around with bits of paper or throwin' things, chatting, laughing, sniggering quietly, you know, she couldn't put it over. If it was a subject that we kids didn't like, the teacher might just's well 'ave closed the book and said, 'Well, I'll read you a story.' The only time they could control the kids was in singing lessons, 'cos the kids liked singing, so that was alright. Apart from that nobody took no blind notice.[1]

Ada Iles's harrowing description of lesson disruption at Two Mile Hill school, Bristol, in the early part of the century, like many other old people's memories of classroom conflict, challenges the popular stereotype and academic orthodoxy that portrays pupils in the pre-1939 period as disciplined, conformist and submissive to school authority. This image of obedience has, of course, in recent years been viewed by commentators as evidence of laudable standards of formal instruction, stifling regimentation or class oppression, according to their conservative, liberal or Marxist perspectives. However, despite such differences of interpretation, it is generally agreed that authoritarian control was effectively established in the classroom. The rare moments of resistance to authority conceded by this view have tended to be explained away in terms of the brutalization and cultural deficiencies of rough, working-class children. The next two chapters will seek to expose this misleading stereotype by tracing the extensive nature of pupil opposition to provided schooling and by demonstrating the purposeful and discriminating character of resistance to control and manipulation in the classroom. They will examine three key areas of conflict, focusing upon working-class children's resistance to the content, the structure and the form of the developing state education system.

Interviews are a particularly valuable source of evidence in illuminating the precise circumstances and consequences of opposition to school authority because official records often distort the motives and underestimate the frequency of children's resistance. It was not in the interests of headteachers to record pupils' disobedience accurately, for a lengthy catalogue of classroom conflict gave an impression of inefficient instruction to school inspectors and managers, upon whom teachers depended for their future employment and salary. Also the discrepancy between the elaborate strategies to defeat teachers' dictates recalled by old people and the brief or one-word entries that predominate in school log and punishment books suggests that either teachers considered misbehaviour so commonplace that it was unworthy of note or they were simply unaware of the deep undercurrent of resistance within the classroom. And, most important, since middle-class adult control over manuscript and printed evidence relating to schooling was absolute, on the few occasions when detailed accounts of disobedience were recorded they tended to condemn rebellious children with a torrent of abusive and value-laden labels. 'Insubordination', 'impertinence', 'defiance', 'wilfulness', 'obstinacy', 'conceit', 'indecency', 'irregularity', 'ill manners', 'ignorance', 'inattention', 'laziness', 'dishonesty', 'foul language' — these were some of the most common crimes for which children were often savagely beaten.[2] To redress the balance, we must listen to the testimony of those old working-class people who stand accused in the official records of acts of resistance against rational state instruction.

Working-class children's resistance in the classroom can be properly understood only when situated within the broader social context of the structure and development of the state schooling system from the late nineteenth century onwards. A brief sketch of the growth of educational provision is necessary, then, in order that

No.	Date.	Name of Child.	Age.	Offence.	Nature and amount of Punishment.	By whom inflicted.	Remarks.
304	3.10.34	RATHBONE Jack	8	Interfering with the gas aniel burner after being sent away	2 on each hand	A.T.Jn.	Reported by Miss Crabbe
305		MOULTON Harold	9				
306		DALE Raymond	8				
307		GLANVILLE Herbert	9				
306	10.10.34	McPHERSON Cyril	12	Breaking a ruler	2 on each hand	A.T.Jn.	A troublesome boy
303	19.10.34	GUEST Ivor	13	Tearing pages out of exercise book and lying about it	2 on each hand	A.T.Jn.	A troublesome boy
310	25.10.34	LIHOU Francis	10½	Rough play in yard	2 " "	A.T.Jn.	Punished 3 times in succession
311	8.11.34	COOPER Hugh		Persistent Idleness and Inattention	2 " " 2 on seat	A.T.Jn.	Reported WFB. Very troublesome boy
312	13.11.34	WELCH Percy	8	Running at school	2 on each hand	A.T.Jn.	A troublesome boy
313	19.11.34	LONDON Donald	8½	at 2.10 having been sent at 1.35	2 " "		
314	14.12.34	GUEST Ivor	13	Cheating in test	2 " "	A.T.Jn.	Exam papers cancelled for same.
315	14.12.34	SCOTT Fred	12¾		2 " "	A.W.Jn.	Reported E.R.T.
316	9.1.35	GUEST Ivor	13	fighting with rulers	2 " "	A.W.Jn.	Reported E.R.T.
317	9.1.35	REDMAN George	14	in N.J.'s absence	2 " "		
318	22.1.35	NICHOLLS Dennis	11	Eating and reading a comic during lesson	2 " "	A.J.Jn.	Giving a lot of trouble to Mr Aldman
319	30.1.35	NICHOLLS Dennis	11	having entrance during lesson	2 " "	A.J.Jn.	Punished every day since 22.1.35

the nature of pupil resistance may be related to the nature of deeply rooted class structures and relationships.

The state schooling system was conceived as potentially the most powerful instrument with which to inculcate in successive generations of working-class children values and attitudes that were thought necessary for the reproduction and reinvigoration of an industrialist-capitalist society. It was not designed to impart literacy, skills and knowledge as ends in themselves. Instead learning was conceived as a means to an end — it made the pupil more amenable to a socialization process, through which his or her character and future lifestyle might be shaped.[3] Yet it would be misleading to suggest that there was no controversy over the precise form that this socialization process should take. In fact, the development of the schooling system can most usefully be seen in terms of the conflict and interplay between two broad educational ideologies, the liberal and the conservative.

The liberal educational ideology was the dominant force, at both a national and a local level, in the initiating and moulding of schooling provision, particularly between 1870 and 1902 and during the inter-war period. This ideology was shaped by three central concerns. First, it sought to ameliorate important social problems — principally the demoralization and destitution of some sections of the working class, juvenile crime, street-gang violence, disease and drunkenness — through an infusion of bourgeois values such as hard work, discipline and thrift. Fundamentally, it attributed social deprivation to the ignorance and immorality of working-class culture rather than to capitalist structures and therefore proposed individual as opposed to political solutions to problems of class inequality.[4] The second, related aim of this ideology was the transmission of middle-class culture through the school curriculum in order to encourage the moral development and elevation of the working-class child's personality.[5] Third, the liberal ideology sought to extend the elementary and secondary school systems in order to provide limited opportunities for talented working-class children to achieve social success by climbing the educational ladder. The addition of this meritocratic dimension to the liberal ideology was governed more by economic and political considerations of national

---

Two pages from the punishment book of St Barnabas School, Bristol, in the 1930s. Apart from the two instances of cheating, the 'offences' suggest above all boredom and high spirits; the 'remarks' indicate the teacher's concern with conformity and suggest a highly repressive approach to classroom discipline.

efficiency than by any commitment to extend democratic rights and opportunities to the working class. For the major concern, which reflected the growth in international rivalry during this period, was that Britain's domination as a world power was threatened, particularly by German industrial and military expansion, and the liberal ideology saw schooling as a key factor in maintaining Britain's overseas power.[6]

The main concern of the conservative educational ideology was that state schooling should act as an agency of class control to enforce obedience to authority and resignation to one's lot and to create an orderly and efficient labour force in the next generation. Although these aims were also present to some extent in the liberal ideology, the conservative philosophy embraced such a pessimistic view of the social and intellectual potential of the working class that this concern with authoritarian control assumed a critical importance. The second key feature of the conservative ideology was its reluctance to accept changes that were proposed in the educational structure, such as increases in the school-leaving age, principally because it feared that the raised expectations that were likely to result from extended schooling might undermine deference and resignation. However, although conservatives were usually suspicious of liberal proposals for educational reform and often applied pressure to reduce increases in expenditure to a minimum, they gradually came to recognize that a limited extension of educational opportunities for working-class children was both economically and politically advantageous.[7]

Despite certain differences, then, there was a fundamental consensus between the liberal and conservative educational ideologies on the content, structure and form of schooling for the working class. They shared the crucial, common-sense limitation that schooling should seek to train young minds to fit into the existing social structure. Of course, this does not suggest that teachers were consciously involved in a manipulatory process, for indeed they often viewed themselves as missionaries bringing moral and cultural standards to a deprived and brutalized working class. However, the missionary ideology tended to reinforce structures of inequality because its adherents did not seriously question the constraints of the class-divided society within which they operated, and because the path to salvation they envisaged led children away from a distinctive working-class culture towards incorporation into the dominant middle-class culture.[8] This concern with socialization into the values of the dominant culture was clearly reflected in the curriculum content of the elementary school, which was suffused by three principal dogmas — those of religion, imperialism and competitive individualism — the key elements of which were shared by the liberal and conservative educational ideologies. These dogmas exercised a major influence on the school syllabus, school books and lesson content.

The imparting of religious knowledge and the implanting of religious sentiments formed an integral part of the teaching process during the period. Although there was great emphasis on religious instruction and catechisms in voluntary schools, board and council schools also insisted upon daily religious worship and study. But more important than specifically dogmatic instruction was the resolute attempt to create a religious atmosphere that would pervade all school activities and help to inculcate the gospel of deference, discipline and hard work.[9] However, both oral and documentary evidence suggests that school authorities met with widespread resistance to their efforts to shape the religious character of working-class children.

The most common criticism of this infusion of religion into the school curriculum recalled by interviewees was that it appeared irrelevant and incomprehensible to many children. The obsession of some teachers with the cramming of Old Testament incidents, names and genealogies, together with compulsory attendance at church services and festivals outside school hours, were clearly important factors in children's growing disaffection from religion.[10] Some pupils like Frank Thomas, who attended St Mark's school, Bristol, in the 1900s, truanted in order to escape from this tedious duty. 'It was church history all the time. And then in the season of Lent . . . every Monday, after school, four o'clock when we should be going out having our freedom, we had to go to church for an hour.'[11] Feelings of boredom commonly led to inattention and detachment from religious worship; as Ada Iles put it, 'at the end of school we 'ad a service to thank the Lord for the day. Well, we was that fed up with it all we'd take no blind notice, an' we'd be trying to shuffle off 'ome before they even finished the amens.'[12] Sacrilegious playground chants were perhaps the safest strategy available to children who wished to express their contempt for the Church, though a deeply ingrained religious awe prevented some from indulging in this type of symbolic revenge, as Ernie Till remembers: '"I one the Bible, I two the Bible, I three the Bible", us kids used to say that, an' I always got to the "hate" bit (eight) an' I'd go all funny like, I never said it until I got older.'[13] Occasionally, however, this disassociation from formal religious instruction escalated into a subversive challenge to school authority, when gangs of older boys refused to continue their lessons and fiercely resisted attempts made by teachers to reassert control through physical coercion. Jack Wolmersley, recalling his schooldays in Bolton at the turn of the century, describes how he provoked this type of conflict after being transferred to All Saints school, which placed much greater emphasis on religious instruction than had his previous school.

They used to have religious reading when you went in, and I said to myself, I'm not going to be a parson so why should I carry on with this rubbish? I says, 'I'm not bothering with this stuff, I've come from other school, we didn't have it there and I won't start it at this time either, I'm not going to do it.' He [the teacher] said nothing. They daren't have punished me because they used to gang, there used to be four or five in a gang and as soon as teacher come round, said to me, 'Wolmersley, get up,' there'd be four more gang up with me too, with their fists like that. And you'd say, 'Go back, you soft cakey.' Never hit anybody, they daren't touch us.[14]

It would be ingenuous to claim that such determined and violent resistance as this was motivated simply by a particular distaste for the formalized, solemn and sanctimonious nature of religious instruction and worship. In fact, the deep disaffection from religious values shared by many working-class boys and girls in their early teens derived from the feeling that religion was unrelated to the daily struggle for survival, which demanded a practical and opportunistic code of conduct that conflicted with the absolute moral dictates of the Bible. This contradiction between esoteric Christian dogma and a practical morality rooted in family and community relationships, is often hinted at, yet rarely articulated in a precise way by interviewees. However, it is clearly expressed by Charlie Miller, recalling his schooling in Bristol during the early part of the century:

We'd start the day with a religious ceremony, sing the hymns of the day, and then one of the sessions during the day would be on religion, taking a section of the Bible, the New Testament or the Old Testament, and this would be dwelled upon for some time. It wouldn't be dissected in any way but it was impressed upon you that you had to know something about it. It was part of the medicine you had to take going to school. . . . I thought that perhaps somewhere some people needed this sort of thing and they made it one of their obsessions of their life. But I could never bring myself to think about it as something which just had to be or was even in any way important. . . . I think it was put over to us to say our prayers at night before we went to bed, you know, thank the Lord for all the good things you nearly had. But I don't think this was kept to very much. I certainly didn't do so and I don't think I was any worse or any better than any of the other kids. The whole thing, the concept of religion . . . meant exactly nothing at all, it just meant another way of life. . . . I don't know as I've ever had any prayers answered. I know on occasions I said my prayers at night for some particular reason, for something that had gone wrong or something or other, and I thought that perhaps a prayer might help, but I think the help seemed to come from within myself rather than from some external source.[15]

The contradiction between religious rhetoric and the disadvantage and deprivation experienced by working class children lay at the heart of many acts of resistance. Interviews clearly reveal that this contradiction presented itself in a variety of different forms to different people and found unique expression according to the particular circumstances and experiences of each. For Edna Rich it was the tension between a life of grinding poverty and an inner yearning for freedom and beauty that fired her angry outbursts against the preaching of tired theological clichés that urged resignation to one's lot.

I was difficult, I think, as a child because I was restless and I realized that poverty was a stigma and I wanted nice things and at times I yearned for it. And it made me difficult as a child to have to live in this world that I had to. The world of poverty, that made me very discontented. . . . In the evening chapel for children, you would have these Evangelical Bible punchers and they would keep on, you know, about hell's fire and the loving God and judgement, and you wanted to shout and be naughty then. Well, I think I used to do that at times and then be told to go, then have to come back and apologize. And if it got to my foster-mother's ears, she would be very cross and angry.[16]

For Jessie Niblett, who deliberately arrived late at school each morning in order to avoid the religious worship and instruction she hated, the contradiction between comfortable rhetoric and personal anguish was compounded by a number of harrowing experiences. The callous and complacent treatment of her starving family by the workhouse authorities, their enforced separation and the brutal rape inflicted upon her by an uncle all combined to produce a deep resentment against her parents, who refused to believe she had been assaulted, and against religion, for she reasoned that no God would allow any child to endure such agony.

When I was twelve my father fell out of work. There weren't no work and my mother was ill. We had no money. If you wanted any help, you had to go in front of the doctor on the Board of Guardians. Then he'd come down and see what furniture you 'ad, an' if you 'ad a good home, you had to sell it. We was having dinner one day, he came, my mother had been to him for help, an' he said, 'You can make that do for twice, what's on that plate.' I always remember that because I went up to my grandfather and started crying, an' told him what this wicked man had said. After that it ran into weeks perhaps with no food, unless somebody send you on an errand and then give 'e a piece of bread and butter. If you had no food, you 'ad to sell yer furniture. If the Guardian man came here today and seen my little home, he'd tell me to sell it.

We had no beds, my father had to sell it all to give us food, and we ended up sleeping on the floor. Then he went to the Board of Guardians and they give him half a crown to buy groceries and two loaves of bread. And that was supposed to feed ten of us and pay rent. And it ended up my mother and father 'ad to go out the workhouse and my brothers and sisters went into the Downend Home for children. My uncle and aunt kept me. I used to go out every Saturday to — (it's called Manor Park now) and see my mother and father. . . . I had to go to the lodge gate and say who I wanted, and then the man used to stamp the card I had and I had to go through. Naturally enough, as a kiddy I used to cry when I went in and cry when I come out. The man at the gate told me he wouldn't let me in any more if I cried like that.

Then my mother and my father used to wait for me. My mother used to come in and I remember she had a little white thing on 'er head, little white apron, and all in black. My father, he was six foot and my mother was smaller than me. I can remember the first time I seen them, they didn't bother about me, they both caught 'old of one another, they hadn't seen one another for two weeks. 'Cos they used to part 'em when they went in, the men went on one side, the women went the other and they were not allowed to mix. The only time my mother and father did see one another was when I did go out and they used to let 'em both come into the room where I was. They didn't bother about me 'til I called out to 'em, I always remember that.

Then I used to leave my mother and father. I had to go from there to Downend to see my brothers and sisters. I'd be running across the fields. I used to take oranges and apples out to them, that was all they were allowed to have. . . . My brothers and sisters, they was alright 'cos they didn't understand too much, see, they thought they was on 'oliday. They enjoyed theirselves. I didn't, I wish I had gone. If I had gone, nothing would have happened to me, what did happen. My uncle raped me, my mother's brother, I was only twelve years old. Supposed to be bringing me up and looking after me. I've never forgot it. My mother laughed at me and my father gave me a good hiding. Said I told lies. But neither of them took me to a policeman or to a doctor. I've never forgotten it and never forgiven it and I never will 'til the day I dies. I was twelve then, now I'm old, I understand the meaning.

I think myself I was the most hated child there was. I've always said that. . . . That's why sometimes I think there can't be a God above to allow things like that to 'appen. . . . And scripture, oh, it was murder. I didn't like scripture. Instead of going into school at nine o'clock I used to go in at 'alf past. One morning the schoolmaster had me out in front the class. I thought, now what have I done? I thought I was going to get the cane. He said, 'Now then, Jessie, tell us why you don't get to school 'til half past nine. Your mother sent a note with your brothers sayin' you should be in school by half past eight.' But instead of that I didn't. I said, 'You makes me sick talkin' about Jesus.' He told me I was wicked an' told me one of these days I should speak me mind too quick, too much and that the policeman would have me.[17]

The combination of circumstances that culminated in Jessie Niblett's bitter opposition to religious instruction was in many ways exceptional. More commonly, resistance was inspired by the simple contradiction between religious rhetoric and religious conduct, principally the failure of most churches to display more than a nominal spiritual and compassionate concern for the local working-class community. This contradiction was most blatantly apparent in the class segregation and discrimination that was practised in many churches and chapels,[18] as Cliff Hills, recalling his Edwardian childhood in the Essex village of Great Bentley, vividly remembers:

One thing as a boy I didn't like and it sticks in my mind today. I came to the conclusion that churchgoers were something like railway carriages were at one time, first, second and third class. You see, my mother was a person of the lower class, was a poor woman, and she and her friends were all poor, but they were great churchgoers, regular churchgoers, kindly, gentle people. But they had to sit in the back pews. In the middle of the church were the local shopkeepers and people who were considered to be a bit superior to the others. And right at the top of the church, behind where the choir used to sit, were the local farmers, the local bigwigs, you see, posh people. And when people left the church, although, as I said, he was a nice old kindly vicar, he didn't seem to have any time for the lower classes. Mother and her friends would pass out of the church door, the vicar would stand near the church door, and he would nod and smile, perhaps not even that. But when the higher class people came out he would shake hands and beam to every one of them as if they was somebody far superior to my mother and her friends, the poor, the very poor. . . . And I didn't like that. I thought my mother was worth a handshake as well as the rich.
There was Captain Peele and other local farmers who were considered to be rich in those days. They were select, they had chosen seats, reserved seats. My mother's seat wasn't reserved. If there was something important on and the church was full of people, it wouldn't matter to anyone whether she got in the church or not, although she went so regular and did most of the work. They did all the cleaning [in the church]. . . . I must have been

perhaps twelve when it used to strike me. I said it wasn't right, it wasn't proper. I said she shouldn't go to church. She said, 'Nothing will ever stop me going to my church.'[19]

The hypocrisy inherent in this class division sowed seeds of resentment and rebellion that undermined the legitimacy of formalized religion among some children. Similarly, the Church gradually lost its credibility for perceptive pupils like Bristolian Vic Amey, who were acutely aware of the contradiction of its participation in Empire Day celebrations and the moral inconsistencies implied by the jingoistic enthusism of local church notables for military conflict.[20]

On Empire Day we used to all go to the parish hall, sing 'Flag of Britain' and all the rest of it. We had a vicar, I won't mention his name, I remember him keeping on to us about the German navy, the strength of the German navy, and why shouldn't our navy be equipped with bigger guns. And, as I say, I was pretty bright and I thought it was pretty cheap at the time for a man of God to talk to us about our navy not being armed with big enough guns.[21]

Another clear contradiction between moral rhetoric and reality sensed by many children was the frequent adult recourse to authoritarian methods in order to ensure regular religious observance among children. Catholic churches and schools were often the most severely authoritarian in their imposition of elaborate religious rituals and regulations that demanded absolute obedience and submission and made serious encroachments on a child's right to freedom of choice or privacy.[22] And although the Catholic Church was very successful at maintaining lifelong allegiance to the faith, its manipulatory and authoritarian techniques occasionally provoked minor acts of resistance from working-class children. Precisely because of the rigid, hierarchical nature of Catholicism, such minor transgressions were interpreted by the authorities as cardinal sins and were punished accordingly. But the anger and humiliation felt by some children who were unfairly reprimanded and punished gave them the strength to break free from religious shackles of deference and duty to superior authority, as Bill Harding remembers:

Being a Catholic and going to a Catholic school, we probably did take it more seriously than an ordinary school because the Roman Catholic religion is really a religion of fear, and we were afraid of committing sins and that sort of thing. Mass on Sunday, confession once a month, communion once a month, and it was a mortal sin to miss mass, you see. We were told that if you miss mass on Sunday, you go to hell for ever and ever. Therefore you didn't miss mass, not because you loved God or anything like that, but because you were afraid of going to hell. . . . And we had to go to Sunday School. A story that sticks out in my mind is that my father and his brother belonged to the Socialist Party then, and they used to encourage us to go along to the meetings. Well, every year on the Sunday nearest May Day, there was a procession from the centre of the city up to the Downs, and on the Downs they would hold meetings. In those days if you belonged to the Socialist Party it was like admitting you were a communist today — it was looked down upon. Well, on this particular May Day we and other children were on — they used to have horse-drawn lorries going up to the Downs and we had a ride on them up to the Downs. This is my father's idea, you know, and somebody must of seen me on this lorry and told the headmaster and he must have told the priest in charge of the church. Because on the Monday morning, Father Murphy, his name was, came into the classroom and called me up in front of the class and reprimanded me for being on this lorry going up to the Downs and for missing Sunday school. And he ended up by slapping my face and I can still remember the shame and embarrassment of that moment. I think that was the beginning of the end of the Catholic Church for me. It must of started some reaction because when I started work I gradually left off church. Of course, for a long time I had the spectre of excommunication hanging over me, because that was something terrible that would happen to anybody who abandoned the Church. But it gradually wore off and I never bothered with it since.[23]

All the people whose experiences have been quoted above on disassociation from religion discontinued their involvement in any form of religious worship or instruction after they reached their mid-teens and were no longer compelled by teachers or parents to attend church services. Despite their anger and resentment, only one, Edna Rich, was for a time politically active. The remainder rapidly became as disillusioned with the state and the possibility of progressive political change as they were with formal religion. In both these respects the people whose memories are recorded above are representative of two broader trends within working-class culture: first, the gradual decline in membership of religious organizations[24] and, second, the persistent non-participation of the vast majority in any form of political party or pressure group.[25] These trends have been popularly ascribed to working-class apathy, which itself is often viewed as an expression of the mediocrity, conformity and low intelligence of the 'masses'.[26] However, the discriminating and critical awareness that is clearly apparent in the reminiscences I have quoted strongly suggests that the charge of apathy can in some circumstances usefully be rejected in favour of the concept of resistance through withdrawal from, or rejection of, what is provided. Childhood and youth constituted a key period in the lifecycle of many working-class people, a time when religious detachment and disassociation crystallized. For the incorporation of formal religious instruction and worship into the school curriculum, its infusion with class prejudice and discrimination, its close association with imperialism and its authoritarian and compulsory nature all confronted the working-class child with a series of contradictions. And, as the individual matured and attempted to resolve these contradictions, he or she often came to the conclusion that formal religion was irrelevant, manipulative and hypocritical.[27]

The primacy of the Bible and religion was replaced by the growing influence of imperialism, which played a crucial role in shaping the changing school syllabus, especially from the 1900s onwards. The addition of subjects such as history, domestic science and games into the elementary school curriculum was conceived and justified in terms of the contribution that they could make to national strength and efficiency.[28]

History was widely viewed as a source of moral examples, good and bad, the study of which would encourage children to develop a sense of duty and loyalty towards national institutions. As a consequence, the history syllabus focused attention on military victories and imperial power, while history textbooks described a heroic national stereotype that was compared with stereotypes of inferior races and frequently contained homilies on the need for patriotic duty.[29] Imperialist sentiments were not restricted to history textbooks, for they also invaded and infused other school subjects and activities. Many English readers, for example, contained passages and stories that glorified the monarchy and celebrated Britain's commercial wealth and progress, and English teachers were increasingly encouraged to give instruction in the duties of citizenship. Domestic science subjects were included in the school syllabus after a series of alarming reports on physical degeneration and poverty had argued forcefully that the strength of the nation was being undermined by the ignorance of working-class mothers who, it was alleged, failed to manage their homes in an efficient manner. Subjects such as home economics, laundrywork, cookery and needlework aimed to instruct working-class girls in the correct performance of their future duties of motherhood, housework and domestic service, thereby promoting the reinvigoration of the nation and Empire through a sexist division of labour.[30] Similarly, the inclusion of games and sports in the school curriculum was justified in terms of their encouragement of a corporate spirit and their development of the physical strength and moral fibre of working-class youth — thus contributing to imperial success and stability.

The idealization of the 'muscular Christian' and the stress on sport as character-forming were transplanted from the public to the elementary schools, resulting in a rapid growth of competitive team games as a means of promoting desirable qualities such as discipline, courage and loyalty.[31] Sometimes the fostering of imperialism took a specifically militaristic form, as when rifle-shooting clubs and cadet corps were established for older children.[32] In wartime imperialist feelings sometimes escalated into the type of jingoistic manipulation recalled by Jessie Marshall: 'I always remember Empire Day. The war had just started before I left school and we mimed about the way the Germans treated the children, and I know one rhyme we had to repeat: "Vengeance is mine, I will repay."'[33] Most often, however, imperialism was associated in the child's mind not with racism, rifles and regimentation but with the flag-waving and colourful processions of Empire, Coronation and Jubilee Days, and with the chocolate buns and mugs that were distributed freely on such patriotic occasions. Indeed, for many children Empire Day was celebrated not as a patriotic occasion but as a holiday, on which they would pursue their own interests in the city streets and countryside rather than participate in formal ceremonies. As George Pavey, who remembers playing street football on Empire Day, put it, 'Empire Day, we used to have the day off. We used to sing then: "Empire Day, twenty-fourth of May, if they don't give us a holiday, we'll all run away."'[34]

However, interviews reveal that working-class children were generally much more responsive to lessons and activities that were inspired by imperialism than they were to any religious influence in school. In part this success was due to the stimulation of children's interests and energies by the introduction of an element of variety into an extremely restricted curriculum based on the three Rs. Many children clearly welcomed games lessons, colourful stories of heroism and national glory and imperial celebrations as relief from the monotony of the school routine. Most important, however, the ideology of imperialism made a direct appeal to working-class youth because it reflected and reinforced a number of its cultural traditions, in particular the street gangs' concern with territorial rivalry and the assertion of masculinity. Of course, the imperialist ethos was not simply grafted on to working-class youth culture, for individuals were selective and discriminating in their responses, often involving themselves in an activity for its own sake and rejecting any ideological trappings attached to it. Thus enthusiastic participation in school sports, for example, does not imply automatic development of the specific character traits intended by the school authorities. However, interviews clearly suggest that imperialist elements in the school curriculum, when combined with the jingoistic juvenile literature of the period, did exercise an important influence in guiding the thoughts and feelings of some working-class youths into conformist channels.[35] The memories of Bill Woods, for example, illustrate not only the internalization of the public school ethos by a working-class boy, but also the process by which the corporate and competitive spirit and the hierarchical control that infused school sports was reproduced in deference to social superiors.

They used to encourage us to be proud of the flag, salute the flag when we was at school. Yes, I was proud of being British. We was always taught to be proud of the Queen and King. We was the people of the world wasn't us? . . . I knew we 'ad to have somebody in charge, I knew, same as having a teacher or headmaster in charge of the school. You 'ad to have somebody up there, didn't you? I was proud of the school, I used to play football for the school. On Friday afternoons we would 'ave school assembly and whoever was picked for the team, their name was called out and you had to march to the front. The teacher would give you out your 'shirties' as we used to call them. No football knickers or nothing like that, an' we had no football boots. We used to play in our ordinary shoes! I used to 'ave an old pair of army boots, with holes in the bottom with a big toe cap an' I used to be able to kick the ball the length of the pitch when it was dry weather. But as soon as it was wet weather the boot got damp as there was a big hole in the bottom. They used to flop and I used to have to try and kick the ball in the air. We'd play in the park against Eastville Park and Victoria Park. Wherever the schools was, we used to go round to the parks. The teachers would arrange the teams. We 'ad a captain of the team an' positions. We had our own colours, green shirt, 'St Silas for honour, for loyalty, for courage, for courtesy. Play up, play fair, play the game.' When I left school they had one of the finest teams in England, yes, they won the Woodcock Shield.[36]

Although, as we shall see later, in conflicts at school Bill Woods was loyal to his classmates rather than to the school authorities, imperialism undoubtedly captured the hearts of some of the working-class youth.[37] We should not underestimate the range and depth of resistance it inspired, however. Just as resistance to formal religious provision was rooted in the contradictions between

religious rhetoric and reality, young people's resistance to
imperialism was most commonly motivated by the contradictions
between imperialist rhetoric and the bitter daily experience of class
inequality. For Edna Rich this contradiction was an important
factor in her subsequent conversion to socialism as a teenager in
Bristol in the early part of the century.

I loved poetry, and the school was assembled and they stood me on top of
the headmistress's desk and I had a Union Jack draped round me. And I
had to recite, 'Oh, where are you going to, all you big steamers? To fetch
England's own grain up and down the great sea. I'm going to fetch you
your bread and butter.' And somehow or other it stirred a bit of rebellion in
me. I thought, where's my bread, where's my butter? And I think it sowed
the first seeds of socialism in me, it really did.[38]

Sometimes the latent contradictions in imperialist rhetoric were
highlighted by socialist schoolteachers who increasingly infiltrated
the state education system from the 1890s onwards. In the following
extract Fred Mattock, a former tram and bus conductor, explains
how under the guidance of a politically conscious teacher he began
to realize that his imperialist beliefs had been crudely manufactured
and manipulated at school and how he came to reject them in
favour of an alternative, socialist philosophy.

Now we 'ad a man at Wick Road school . . . today you'd call 'im a
communist, but looking back, he didn't tell us history out of the books.
Now if you got hold of all those history books we had at the time, they was
all a load of flannel, about Edward the Peacemaker, Queen Victoria and
Elizabeth the First. When he did give us history the way he did give it, he
did show us that they wasn't as glorious as what they made out, how we
lost the American colonies and in India and places like that. He gave us a
truer picture because all the books were glorifying the monarchy and I
used to honestly think as a lad that there was nobody like the British. All
the rest, if he was a foreigner, that was it, he was like a load of rubbish.
Well, you can tell by the way they did call 'em 'Froggies' and 'Eyties' and
'Dagoes' and things like that. I mean, the only way you'd describe them
was they were beneath you. But he started me on the trail, that bloke, that
teacher. And later on, when I was getting on to fourteen, I started to read
these historical books an' I took an interest in 'em. And I thought to myself
at the time, well, what a load of rubbish we've been taught in the past. Well
then I thought to myself, 'Right,' so then I started reading all different
books, an' I read *Old Nobility* by Robert Blatchford, anything to do with
history, I started reading it. And I thought to myself, well, this is the type
of people we're supposed to look up to and respect and they'd 'ave been
turned out of a decent working street with the capers they cut. They'm on

about the morals and the behaviour of the working people, it's far superior than these other wallers. But you 'ad to respect 'em, see. You 'ad to look up to 'em, they were your betters. It was pumped on to them that they were our betters an' it was pumped on to we that we ought to be satisfied with our position in life.[39]

For Fred Mattock and Edna Rich there was no family tradition of radical political activity to offer them support and advice in their personal struggles to resolve the contradictions that confronted them. But it is important to remember that a number of working-class children did receive such an alternative political education at home from parents, relatives and neighbours. For large sections of the socialist and labour movement were extremely suspicious and critical of the inculcation of imperialism and militarism in schools and youth organizations and resolutely refused to allow their children to participate in Empire Day ceremonies.[40] Thus Jim Flowers's introduction at an early age to a wide range of radical literature by his trade unionist father provided him with class awareness, an idealistic vision and immunity from any form of imperialist manipulation at school.

The history as we were taught it at school, it was just what was sorted out for us as members of the British Empire. It was all dates and names and battles, the Spanish Armada, Nelson, Marlborough and all that. I mean, we only did the history of England just like I suppose the workers of France only read the history of France and the same with the Germans and everybody else. It didn't make much impression on me though. It went into my brain and I stored the facts because you had to, but patriotism never struck me as being very clever. See, I'd read Tom Paine and he'd had a big influence on my thought historically as well as on biblical teaching. His outlook was towards being a citizen of the world rather than of a little parish, and his view on republicanism, his abhorrence of monarchy, that gave me a broader outlook than the school history books, and that was when I was twelve years old. And through the war, every morning the headmaster used to read us the leading article in the *Daily Chronicle*, and that was always giving a rosy picture of the way things were going for the British troops. It struck me that if ever the British had to go backwards they wouldn't say it was a retreat, it was a strategic withdrawal so that they could swallow up the enemy later on. And whenever the National Anthem was played I wouldn't stand up. I always had a feeling that I didn't want to stand up for monarchy because of Tom Paine's views as a republican, it always struck me as being very sane and sensible and I still hold the same view today. I don't want to stand up for anyone.[41]

Although imperialism remained a powerful force in the school curriculum, it was gradually superseded by a growing emphasis on competitive individualism. Competition as a motive for learning and the incorporation of regular tests, reports and merit awards into elementary school life derived from a conscious imitation of the public school ethos and was particularly evident from the 1920s onwards. The establishment of the free-place scholarship system and the increasing faith that educationalists placed in psychometric intelligence tests led during the inter-war period to the development of rudimentary forms of streaming in order to prepare able pupils for competitive exams.[42] However, interviews suggest that the competitive spirit was internalized only by a talented minority, who were striving against each other to gain the limited scholarships and free secondary school places. Indeed, officials and teachers frequently complained that many children refused to take their work seriously and to compete with their fellows. Instead they often preferred to copy and cheat, unmoved by the prospect of bad results and reports. Yet although interviews tend to confirm this general lack of interest in competitive school work, which was attributed officially to ignorance and apathy, they suggest an alternative explanation. Fundamentally, interviews reveal a widespread disassociation from, and rejection of, the bourgeois ethic of rational and methodical striving for personal achievement and advancement. Consequently, in the absence of the competitive desire to defeat rivals, to win the praise of teachers or to further career ambitions, sustained concentration by working-class children tended to be maintained only on those occasions when teachers were successful in stimulating interest in a subject for its own sake. And because many placed little value on good school reports, even the most intelligent pupils, like Vic Amey, were tempted to seek revenge on authoritarian schoolteachers and relief from the monotonous school routine by disrupting lessons as soon as their work no longer held their attention.

I enjoyed every minute of my school days but I'm afraid my teachers didn't enjoy me. . . . All I thought of was getting my answers correct, never mind anyone else. What made me work was the thirst for knowledge. Anything mechanical, if it worked I wanted to know why or how. I always had that inquisitive turn of mind. . . . I lived for the day, I never thought of my future. I was always being punished at school. I'll tell you why. I absorbed knowledge so quick, I grasped the subject and while the others were still puzzling, especially sums like, look around, dip a little bit of blotting paper in the inkwell and put it on the end of a rule and flick it. I've weals on my hand from being caned. I can remember having a weal and it so frightened him [the teacher] that he got his pocket knife and let the blood out so he thought it wouldn't be seen when I got home, but it was still showing and I showed it to my father. My father went down and saw the headmaster but they hushed it up. Some of them were dogs. There was only one teacher that I really liked, and I really loved that man. He was one of nature's gentlemen. He made teaching interesting and made you look up to him.[43]

It is ironic that the tactics of copying and cheating that were often adopted by less able pupils as a strategy to avoid chastisement should themselves have led to the severe punishments that recur in the official school records. However, interviews reveal that copying was motivated not merely by shame and fear but also by a desire to share skills and knowledge in a co-operative way. For example, the caning that Arthur Burley received for copying at the village school of Perranwell, Cornwall, in the early part of the century might usefully be seen as a case of suppressed mutual assistance, in which one boy with an artistic flair helped another to master an intricate skill and to enjoy the satisfaction of drawing a difficult object accurately.

I remember one day the master put a kettle on top of his desk an' we 'ad to draw that kettle. Well, there was one boy there called Oswald Datsun an' he was a master boy for drawing. He could draw anything in a second. So I passed my paper down to Oswald an' asked 'un to draw very lightly the outline of that kettle. Well, he did 'un an' give it back to me, see. Well, I took 'un, see, an' I had a pencil an' went on it hard. Well, when the master come round now looking at our papers, my God, when he come behind me, he was taking a long time to go on. He said, 'Now turn that paper over and draw me another kettle like that.' Well, 'twas impossible wasn't it? [Laughter] 'Twas more like a cow than a kettle. Oh well, out the front I 'ad to go. I was cheating, wasn't I? He knew very well I never draw that, so I had to 'ave four cuts of the cane.[44]

Although the principle of competitive individualism was rigidly enforced in elementary schools, it was always within the framework of obedience and subordination to superior authority. Emphasis was placed on rather petty considerations, such as obsessive cleanliness and tidiness, thrift, good manners and sharp punctuality.[45] This curriculum concern with the formation of regular and orderly habits was to a large extent a consequence of the

A cleanliness inspection at a London elementary school in 1911. Poor children were sometimes condemned for their ragged appearance, a product of their families' poverty, about which they could do nothing.

dictates of central government, which fundamentally demanded the creation of a malleable and disciplined labour force able to perform simple manual and clerical tasks efficiently.[46] Also important in the imposition of elaborate rules and regulations governing every aspect of school life, however, was the teaching profession, many of whose lower-middle-class members tended earnestly to inculcate a puritanical work ethic and a fastidious respectability in dress, deportment and manners, to which they owed their own success.[47] Despite the adoption of a more liberal approach to the aims and methods of teaching by the Board of Education and by many local education authorities from the 1900s onwards, the elementary school curriculum remained virtually unchanged throughout our period, and instruction in many schools continued to be dispensed in a uniform and mechanical manner that neglected the childrens' developing interests.[48]

Although official handbooks increasingly stressed that, wherever possible, instruction should proceed from the interests and stages of development of the individual child, the impact of this concession to progressive child-centred theory was reduced to a minimum through its incorporation into the hierarchical education system of public school, grammar school and elementary school, which purported to correspond to three distinct types of intellect and personality, ranging from those capable of 'abstract' thought to those restricted to 'concrete' thought.[49] Thus because it was assumed that working-class children's thoughts operated on a narrow and mechanical 'concrete' level, the form of education considered most appropriate for them consisted largely of simple and repetitive tasks. In addition, creative or imaginative activities encouraged by progressive educational thinkers were often restricted to infant and junior classes and were thought to be unsuitable for older children, who continued to be taught by traditional 'chalk and talk' methods.

The conflict between the regimented school routine and the spontaneous and exuberant events that emerged from the children's own culture is vividly illustrated in Daisy Wintle's memories of schooling in Bristol in the 1900s. Her recollections clearly illuminate the stark contrast between formal and informal codes of conduct, and the characteristic refusal of both pupils and parents to accept the legitimacy of punishments for petty offences — which were ultimately sanctioned and enforced by the threat of legal prosecution.

Miss Dugdale, after we 'ad prayers in the big hall, she'd go round an' look at yer shoes, then she'd say, 'About turn,' we'd about turn an' she'd look at the backs of yer shoes. If you 'ad dirty shoes, 'No play. Stay in.' Well, very often our parents never 'ad enough money to buy boot polish so we used to spit on a brush to put on our shoes. Then she'd say, 'Hands out.' You'd 'ave to put yer hands out an' yer nails 'ad to be clean an' yer hands to be clean. She was a perfect governess, that one. If you only walked in front of 'er desk, you 'ad to say, 'Please excuse me, Miss Dugdale.' She'd nod and you were allowed to pass 'er desk.

One time, it was a girl's birthday an' there was three of us, like friends, an' one girl, she kept a fried fish shop, said to me, 'I'm going to give Lily Hopkins a present.' I said, 'Oh, how nice,' and thought to meself she didn't give me anythin'. So anyhow, we were sat one in front the other like an' she said, 'Lily, 'ere's a present.' So Lily caught 'old the present an' put it underneath 'er desk an' she looked back at me. 'I've got a present.' So she undone it, it was a raw plaice. So of course we started laughin' an' I used to laugh rather hearty, an' teacher said, 'Come out.' Lily Hopkins goes out with this fish behind 'er back an' of course all the class then started roaring laughin'. Well, governess was in the other room. She 'eard us laughin' an' out she came. 'What's going on here?' Teacher said, 'Lily Hopkins has had a present from Kate Simmons and she's brought her in this fish.' 'Oh,' she said, 'you horrible things. Go to my room.' We went to 'er room, we each 'ad two cuts with the cane an' it wasn't really nothin' to do with me. Then we 'ad to go out and put pinafores over our head. She'd stand us in the corner. We were shamed then. And of course when we 'ad our pinafores over our head we used to catch 'old an' peep out the corner an' make all the rest laugh. We were proper hardened at school, mind.

Anyhow, we all 'ad the cane for Kate Simmons bringin' the fish to school for Lily Hopkins, so Mrs Hopkins thought it wasn't right. Course, my mother never took no notice, she said, 'You ought to behave yerself. Serve you good right.' Didn't get no sympathy. But Lily Hopkins's mother goes up an' it was beltin' down with rain an' she 'ad an old pair of slippers on. She knocked on the door. She said, 'Which is Miss Waite? What do you mean by caning my girl?' Miss Waite was over in the corner. . . . She took off 'er slipper an' she slung that slipper across at 'er an' there was the mark of the dirty slipper on the wall. Well, governess said she'd send for the police an', oh, we 'ad a lecture. Some gentleman, I don't know who he was, came to the school an' gave us all a lecture sayin' that if anythin' happened like that again, we'd all get put in homes an' our fathers and mothers 'ud be summonsed. Frightened us to death. When we used to get the cane after that we never used to go home an' tell.[50]

Working-class children who, either through choice or poverty, failed to maintain meticulous standards of cleanliness and tidiness often experienced unfair treatment at school. For although a ragged appearance did inspire a sympathetic response in some teachers, many children who did not conform to school standards were condemned to segregated seating at the back of classrooms and were penalized by receiving less attention and encouragement than the respectable and well-dressed.[51] This discrimination often provoked deep bitterness, which occasionally exploded into minor acts of resistance, as Mabel Yeo, recalling her Exeter schooldays in the 1920s, remembers:

In they days the teachers 'ad just their favourites. They used to keep going to 'em, you could tell the difference. Now you take me, I wanted to learn to swim, but I was never picked out. There was only two or three picked out of the class to go swimming an' I never 'ad the chance. We was so poor we didn't 'ave no bathing costumes. We hardly 'ad much clothes to wear. We 'ad to wear everybody else's 'leave offs'. . . . The teachers were not kind to us, they were not nice. I remember going for a nature walk an' I 'ad a button out of me shoe an' she said 'Who's scuffing?' I used to like going on nature walks too, I liked that. And, of course, me button was out of me shoe an' I was trying to hold on to me shoe as well as I could an' she sent me back to school. So I thought to meself — 'twas only just after half-past two — I thought, 'I'm not going to sit 'ere all afternoon. I can be home.' Mother was in bed with a baby then, so I thought to myself, right, let's go home. So I went out the school an' then she 'ad a prefect come to look an' see if I was at home an' alright . . . An' she caned me next morning in front of the whole class, she really caned me, just for leaving school, because I wasn't going to sit there all afternoon by myself, just because the button come out of me shoe, I could've struggled on . . . I didn't cry. I wouldn't let 'em see me cry. Because she knew my mother was in bed with the baby, she knew my mother couldn't get at 'er.[52]

While teachers were able to exercise some personal discretion in the imposition of rules governing cleanliness and tidiness, educational authorities insisted upon regular and punctual attendance as an essential prerequisite for the efficient functioning of the school and the synchronizing of the intellectual and personal development of individual children.[53] It is extremely difficult to determine precise patterns of punctuality because to a large extent the official records reflect merely the variable standards of rigour with which different schools chose to document the evidence of this particular problem. However, there was a significant reduction in complaints concerning unpunctuality in inspectors' reports and log books between the 1890s and the 1930s, which suggests that the deterrent effect of severe punishment and the threat of legal sanctions established the norm of punctual school attendance among most working-class communities by the end of our period. But this regularity was achieved in the face of considerable resistance, for it placed an intolerable burden upon the many families in which children undertook domestic duties before school

in order to assist in the daily struggle for survival; although teachers
frequently penalized and punished children for what they considered to be a form of slothful and self-indulgent conduct, they
found it difficult to weed out the unpunctuality of older children in
large families, for their resistance was firmly rooted in the essential
contribution they made to the family economy.[54] Instead, the
teachers' vigilance planted seeds of resentment, as is illustrated by
Mabel Bennett's recollections of her Bristol childhood in the 1900s:

I had to take the children to school, and then I had to go nearly a mile to my
school, so I was late. I always came in for the cane . . . they'd lay it on so
that it would nearly cut your hand in half. I was sick of it one time, so I
played truant. I went all along the river past the market. I fell over some
logs, nearly broke me leg. Got back an' mother wondered where the bruise
came from. So I told 'er I'd fallen down the steps at school. I 'ad to tell 'er
something. It was a lie, but still. That's how I got out of that. The
schoolmaster didn't want to hear about it. It wasn't my fault, I couldn't get
there earlier.[55]

Lying was a common strategy adopted by children to protect
themselves from interrogation and punishment, and the instrumental
importance of untruths, clearly revealed by interviews, provides an
alternative social explanation to the pathological interpretations of
children's dishonesty that proliferated in our period.[56] In fact,
accusations of dishonesty were a ubiquitous feature of classroom
conflict, and teachers generally seem to have defined this particular
offence as not only a refusal to conform to school rules but also a
reluctance to admit or accept guilt once discovered. Any form of
devious behaviour usually received a ritual punishment, even when
the motive was genuine need and desperation, as Frank Vowles
relates:

We used to borrow books from the library an' there were free periods
where you could read your own books, an' I'd taken this book to school, an'
it was towards the end of the term before going on your month's holiday.
We used to get four weeks, an' we broke up an' I'd left this book at school.
Well, to a little boy, having to take that book back — you could keep it out
for seven days — having to wait a month to take that book back, you were
afraid. I was scared an' I thought, how am I going to get my book?
Remembering that all your belongings were tied up in these boxes an' put
up on top of the cupboard out of the way, I tried first of all to get the
caretaker to let me in an' he wouldn't. So I climbed over one evening — it
must 'ave been the same day, like about seven o'clock in the evening — I
climbed over the wall an' managed to get into the school an' was undoing
the box to take the book out an' I was caught by the caretaker. . . . And, of

course, he reported me an' when I went back to school I had this punishment from the headmaster. . . . I did have four in the headmaster's study an' they'd make a great show of giving you a real hard blow, you know. Oh, they'd waggle the cane an' bring it down. It hurted, of course, but you remembered an' you thought twice about doing that again, whatever it was you were punished for. He realized that I wasn't in there to pinch anything but, of course, it was the act. I should 'ave left it there and got my parents to pay the fines or whatever.[57]

The inculcation of an individualist ethos was further encouraged by the incorporation into the curriculum, from the late nineteenth century onwards, of new subjects such as cookery and crafts which were intended to promote independence and industriousness.[58] In addition, the development of school savings systems such as 'penny banks' sought to induce thrifty habits among working-class children. However, although such instruction was to some extent useful and beneficial, there was considerable resistance from both parents and children to attempts to impose bourgeois values of self-reliance upon communities that were accustomed to seeking and offering support and assistance in times of hardship. The process by which formal schooling severed individual moral development from collective loyalties is clearly illustrated in Frank Thomas's bitter recollections of how a street collection for a school trip among family, friends and neighbours was confiscated and punished as the reward of 'common begging':

I loved botany. I can give you an incident about that. Every year we used to make a collection for a children's hospital. Well, the headmaster said that the boys that brought the most money in would have half a day through the Frome Valley, studying, see. Well, I was all for that. I don't know exactly how much I collected, about one and six I suppose it was, and I collected off the neighbours as well, you see. Well now, I took the money to school and the headmaster said, 'Very good, that's very good.' Well, then one of the boys there told him that I'd been from house to house, collecting. An' I had a hiding for begging, and I did not go on my day. And I never got the money back to give to the people. I thought it was real spiteful.[59]

So far we have looked at the opposition of working-class children to the content of schooling and their resistance to the ideologies of religion, imperialism and competitive individualism that infused the curriculum. Next we will examine the way in which this profound alienation from school work led to a general disassociation from the entire structure of the state schooling system. To begin with, however, it is necessary to situate this disaffection within the class structure of the educational system. Just as there was a general consensus between the liberal and conservative educational ideologies on the content of schooling for working-class children, so there was broad agreement that the education they received should be of a limited quality and duration. This consensus found concrete expression in the development of a three-tier educational structure, based on the public school, the grammar school and the elementary school, which mirrored the inequalities and privileges of society.[60] There was an enormous gap between the state education system, which served the working class, and the public and grammar schools, which enabled middle-class parents to buy a superior education for their children and thereby to perpetuate the class system and to reduce social mobility to a minimum. However, despite considerable pressure from the labour and trade union movement for an extension of educational opportunities, reform proposals — for example, for increases in the school-leaving age and for compulsory continuation classes up to the age of eighteen — found little sympathy or support among many working-class people.[61] Furthermore, although the working-class demand for secondary education exceeded the limited number of free places that the scholarship system could supply, most working-class parents and their children were not attracted by the prospect of an extended education. Thus secondary education continued to be dominated by the middle class, and the labour movement was unable to exert sufficient pressure to threaten to undermine the tripartite educational structure.[62] Instead liberal and conservative educational ideologies were able to maintain a hegemony by absorbing and incorporating in a diluted form some of labour's demands (for increased opportunities, for improving the quality of elementary education, for a comprehensive school welfare system and so on), yet always within the limits and imperatives of a capitalist system. And, through a complex fusion, the liberal educational ideology came to be embraced by many members of the labour movement, so that, paradoxically, the organized working class failed to offer an oppositional challenge to the grammar and public school systems.[63]

The lack of interest in, or rejection of, state educational provision by large sections of the working class has sometimes been explained in terms of the inadequacy of their income to support the continued education of their children. More commonly, however, it has been seen as a consequence of cultural deprivation, with its associated characteristics of apathy, ignorance, anti-intellectualism, deference, immediate gratification and low expectations, all of which, it is claimed, indirectly reproduced and reinforced class inequality. But oral interviews reveal that this widespread unconcern with educational provision can to a large extent be seen in terms of class resistance through withdrawal from the state schooling system, the cultural and economic contradictions of which prompted pupil opposition.

The fundamental cultural contradiction experienced by working-class children was that state schools were essentially middle-class institutions, which embodied official values, and that commitment to schooling required a rejection of the distinctive styles of speech, thought and behaviour characteristic of working-class culture. The process of class-cultural conflict in which schools were involved is forcefully expressed in the influential Newbolt Report of 1921, which became the standard text for the teaching of English during the inter-war period. Its moral condemnation of working-class styles of speech deserves to be quoted at length.

Speech training must be undertaken from the outset. . . . Teachers of infants sometimes complain that when the children come to school they can scarcely speak at all. They should regard this rather as an advantage. . . . It is emphatically the business of the elementary school to teach all its pupils who either speak a definite dialect or whose speech is disfigured by vulgarisms, to speak standard English, and to speak it clearly. . . . The great difficulty of teachers in elementary schools in many districts is that they have to fight against the powerful influence of evil habits of speech contracted in home and street. The teacher's struggle is thus not with ignorance but with a perverted power. . . . A child with home advantages hears English used well and grows up to use it well himself. He speaks grammatically, he acquires a wide vocabulary, he collects ideas. The English which he has learnt at home may suffice, independently of any school teaching, to keep him well ahead of his classroom neighbour. The latter's English may be a negative quantity, requiring great pains on his teacher's part to cancel out before any positive progress can be made. . . . The real difficulty will be found, our witnesses assure us . . . in combating the causes which prevent production of the correct sounds such as habitual lip laziness. . . .[64]

The pupils' experience of this type of cultural conflict in the classroom was a key factor that led to disassociation from the structure of the schooling system, with its promise of extended education and entry into the ranks of the middle class for talented children who accepted the rules of the game. Much of the school routine was experienced as an imposition, with little relevance or application to the world of the working-class child. In the words of

Bill Bees, reflecting on his schooling in the south Gloucestershire village of Hanham in the 1920s:

To myself I used to think, well, they're not teachers really, they're just 'ere asking you a lot of silly questions. I used to think, What's she asking I this for? What's she asking I that for? But you 'ad to try an' give a straight answer.[65]

For those who viewed the school routine as essentially meaningless, the long-term educational goal of progress and achievement through attention, concentration and hard work was rejected in favour of the short-term goal of making each boring school day pass as painlessly as possible. The most common strategy used by children to overcome boredom in the classroom was larking about. Interviews reveal that some children would defy attempts to classify and segregate classmates in terms of their ability by making deliberate errors and sacrificing success in school work in order to be allotted seats close to friends with whom they wished to lark about.

If you wanted to 'ave a bit of fun in class it was important to be sitting next to your mates. Girls 'ud sometimes get their work wrong just so that they could sit next to their mates. You see, the class was divided up in rows, one row of bright children, then the not so bright, then the average ones, then the dunces. If you were a bit brilliant and yer mates was only average like, you wouldn't want to be moved up the class, you'd want to stay with them, so you'd deliberately get some of your spellings or your sums wrong.[66]

The experience of schooling as a monotonous and pointless chore often intensified as pupils became older, so that, for many, attainment of the school-leaving age and entry into the world of work was celebrated as a moment of joyous release and liberation. For the majority of working-class youths, like Dick Cook, who 'felt like a greyhound let loose',[67] and Frank Thomas, who 'ran all the way home, thanking the Lord',[68] although the exhilaration of escaping from the confines of the classroom was short-lived and quickly replaced by the drudgery and discipline of manual labour, they never regretted leaving school at an early age. This commonly felt desire to escape from school, at whatever cost, was not merely a consequence of boredom; more important, it was a response to the school's attempt to shape the working-class child's morals and manners into a conformist, middle-class mould. Jane Taverner's memories of her Exeter schooldays in the 1920s vividly illuminate the experiences that led to this disassociation from school. As well as illustrating the monotony of the school routine, her recollections reveal the lasting effects of subordination and rigid discipline on the working-class child's confidence and independence.

It was the same thing, day after day. The main education was twice one is two, an' twice two is four, an' so on. I was that browned off in school . . . I didn't care if I learnt anything or not. I would look at the clock an' think to myself, you know, I'll be glad when it's dinner time. . . . The teachers in them days, they didn't know a lot about education themselves, I didn't think so. I was highly delighted when I left, to tell you the truth. I couldn't get out quick enough. . . . They were your teachers and you were taught respect. Mind you, its something which has kept us back all of our lives that, because you lost the confidence in yourself which I love to see in this generation. We were kept down too much and all through our life it's been a drawback, it's something in you. And perhaps me going into service 'twas the same thing because, believe you me, they kept you down. But I would imagine it was just ingrained in you and I know, although I'm a fairly free mixer and can mix, and have mixed with all classes and gone into places of all classes, but I've always felt that bit of something in me, which I attribute to that. . . . I tell you a funny incident, I went to have a slight operation in Baltimore Nursing Home and I was sat up waiting for my husband to come in and, I don't know, I didn't have my attention on the door, then I looked and coming through was two of my old schoolteachers. And I automatically got down under the clothes [laughter] and I don't know why, but automatically I just sunk down. And I'd been left school a good many years, 'twas more or less middle-aged. . .[69]

It was only a minority of working-class children who felt angry and resentful when their schooling ceased at an early age. The hostility that was generally directed against working-class boys and girls who succeeded in entering grammar schools was motivated not so much by envy as by contempt for those 'snobs' and 'poshoes' who appeared to have rejected their own culture in exchange for social advancement. Certainly, working-class children who were obliged to wear grammar school uniforms did not inspire the respect of their peers, for as Cyril Willis put it, recalling his schooldays in Stoke-on-Trent in the 1930s:

You'd always be careful to avoid the town boys on your way to the grammar school. They'd recognize your school cap, your school tie and your school socks and they'd let you have it, pelt you with stones or try to start a fight.[70]

The cultural contradictions that led to opposition to the entire structure of schooling were compounded by equally important economic contradictions. There was, of course, a multiplicity of restraining factors rooted in poverty and deprivation, such as disease, hunger and exhausting part-time and domestic jobs, that placed difficult barriers in front of working-class children who attempted to make the steep climb up the educational ladder to social success.[71] Even more demoralizing for children with a genuine thirst for skills and knowledge was the constant awareness that any form of secondary education, or in some cases an apprenticeship, was likely to be financially beyond their reach because of the necessity of earning a wage at the earliest possible age in order to assist in the family's struggle for survival. This contradiction between the elementary schools' promise of secondary education for the most talented and the harsh reality of enforced withdrawal from school through economic hardship was most frequently and bitterly experienced by children from large and unskilled families.[72] Like Bristolian Tom Partridge, such children became aware of the hollowness of the rhetoric of equality of opportunity at an early age, when they discovered that pupils whose parents could afford secondary education were favoured by teachers.

I loved school. I loved writing and composition, where you put a story on paper. I would loved very much to have gone on from when I left school at fourteen but I knew at the time that there was no chance. . . . We knew as children, we knew that we weren't going to go on in school. The parents couldn't maintain us in any way at all on their income to carry on at school after fourteen and we realized that. And we all left in turn at fourteen, left school, found a job of some sort, and started money coming into the family, that was the main object. There was no question of parents wishing us to go on, no matter what abilities we had. They just couldn't afford to maintain us at school. They didn't have the money, that was all there was to it. . . . I think there was a little bit of class distinction there [at school] because I remember a lot of the boys that were in my class, the teachers used to walk along the road where they lived and they knew the parents, they'd stop and talk to them. And they were people with two in a family and they could afford to dress them properly and they got all this sort of help indirectly. Yes, I think it made a lot of difference. They were encouraged because they were potential secondary school children, really. See, they had all the advantages there.[73]

Although there was a gradual increase in the numbers of working-class children attending secondary schools from the late nineteenth century onwards, they remained at an enormous disadvantage in securing any form of extended education. For example, whereas the proportion of children of semi-skilled or unskilled parents attending grammar schools increased from approximately 1 to 10 per cent between the 1900s and the 1930s, children of professional and managerial parents attending such schools increased from 37 to 62 per cent during the same period.[74] It was frequently commented by social investigators that working-class parents refused scholarships or withdrew their children from secondary education after only a short period.[75] Thus in Bradford during the 1920s, despite the fact that fees for grammar school education were abolished, the numbers of refusals of free places exceeded the number of acceptances.[76] Even though education officials were often aware that poverty influenced the withdrawal of children, interviews suggest that official opinion grossly underestimated the extent and significance of material deprivation in accounting for working-class children's failure to take advantage of the limited educational opportunities available to them. Also the recollections of old people illuminate the important role played by young people themselves in rejecting secondary education in favour of family and class solidarity. For in many cases children were not simply compelled by parents to leave school after winning scholarships; they would often take the decision to opt out of the education system themselves when they felt that the grim struggle for family survival was becoming an intolerable burden to their parents.[77] In such circumstances a feeling of moral duty to the family was the key factor that led to withdrawal from the grammar school and the sacrifice of any opportunities for educational advancement, as Cyril Willis remembers:

My father was an invalid for ten years after the pit explosion. I remember he told me he was slowly dying. It was his heart slowly packing up, you could tell. His face and skin were going bluer and bluer. The only time I saw him when he looked like a normal human being was when they brought him back in the coffin from the hospital; that was the only time he had a normal complexion. I'd won a scholarship to the grammar school in Hanley, but my mother was having to work like a slave to keep the family. And I think subconsciously it was getting me down, because from the time I came home from school to the time I went to bed, I wouldn't see my mother, and from the time I got up in the morning to the time I went to school, I wouldn't see her. I wouldn't see her from one day to another, she was working that hard. Nobody said anything to put pressure on me to leave but I desperately wanted to earn some money to make it easier for her. I was aware I was sacrificing my education when I left, and I valued education. In fact, I started going to night school the same winter. But I wanted to leave to hand my wage packet over to her so it wouldn't be such a struggle all the time. And I wasn't the only one. My friend Freddie Potts, he left, and several others did as well that term, because they felt their families couldn't support them any longer.[78]

But the most remarkable form of resistance to the scholarship system revealed by interviews was the deliberate failure of examinations by some talented working-class pupils to make certain that they did not obtain an extended education that they felt would threaten the family's economic survival. In these cases fierce pride, a refusal to acknowledge to teachers the desperate poverty of their families and fear that the education authorities might force them to take up scholarship places should they discover the deliberate mistakes all combined to ensure that children would tell nobody of their secret acts of sabotage in the examination room. For example, Sam Emberey, recalling his schooling and scholarship examination at Preston village, near Yeovil, in the 1920s, remembers that his teacher never discovered the real reason for his unexpected failure to progress to the local grammar school.

My mum was wonderful. She was always on to me to read Dickens and all the good books, you know. She said, 'You must read these, these are good literature, you must read them.' . . . She was always encouraging me to learn things. She said, 'You can never learn too much, you'll never regret it,' and I never have. She was very, very wise in her little way. . . . I liked school really, especially I liked writing and composition and reading. In fact, I asked for a new book this particular day and then we had to write a story of a boy who left home to make his fortune, and I filled the book up and he still hadn't made his fortune.

There was a fund that was laid down by some rich Lord of the Manor in the area. This was left, this lump sum, so that the best boy of eleven years of age each year could go to the County School in Yeovil and I was mad keen to go. The only reason I wanted to go really was the fact that they had a football team there and I was football-mad, you see. I didn't want to go for academic reasons. And I was telling mum all about this, saying, 'Oh, I can be in the team, might even be captain,' and she said, 'All I hope is that you don't win it.' And I looked at her in surprise and I said, 'Why on earth not?' She said, 'Well, they only pay for you to go there. We've still got to clothe you and get all your uniform and books.' And my father was out of work. He was out of work altogether twelve years during the Depression, and although I was only young, I realized that what she said was true because we went through such hard times then, with my mum working and taking in washing and doing sewing — she was a great needlewoman — and going out scrubbing, doing a bit of charring here and there. We'd never have survived. I mean, she used to make our shirts, dresses for my sister and things like this. It was only on her work that we survived because dad couldn't get no work because there was no work to be had and he used to go busking in the street because he was a musician. . . . As I said,

I wanted to go to this high school but when I realized the futility of that and how poor we were, then, of course, I wanted to go out to work and though I only had one pound eight shilling a week, that was a great help. . . . So I made up my mind that I wasn't going to pass the exam and I didn't either. Teacher called me out afterward and said, 'What have you done with your mathematics paper?' And I said, 'Nothing.' She said, 'No, I can see that.' She said, 'Well, why not? You could do any one of them on there.' And I wouldn't tell her. She never knew why I didn't do anything on that paper. I was afraid to do them in case I passed, so I just fiddled a few figures down and left them all unfinished, you know, so of course I got nought.[79]

Where acts of resistance at school involved personal sacrifice such as this, they were likely to lead to deep feelings of resentment and subsequent politicization. For Jane Taverner it was her moral obligation to fail her scholarship examination, combined with subsequent experiences of discrimination and inequality, that, in her words, 'turned me red Labour and I've been Labour all me life'.

I was put in for the scholarship. I remember the rating I got because I didn't pass. I was fully expected to pass, but I didn't try because I knew that if I passed, I couldn't go. I wanted to pass, but you see it was no use, because although there was help, it wouldn't have been enough for our family. Actually, I didn't try and I was hauled over the coals. Headmistress had me in, didn't she? 'Why didn't you pass? What did you do?' And I suppose I didn't answer. 'I don't know,' I said. . . . To this day I see her [the schoolmistress]. We have a chatter and she'll tell me at times, 'And I'll never know why you didn't pass that scholarship,' and I've never told her. . . .

I would have liked to have been a teacher but, you see, I knew what I was going to do and it was something I wasn't going to like. I had to go into service, for one thing to make room for the boys to sleep as they got older. And I had to go into service at fourteen. . . . I did every dirty job there was — what did they call you? scullery maid — and when I was in service I wasn't allowed to drink out of the same cup as the family. I had to have my own cup, saucer, plate, knife and fork and everything. You weren't allowed to use their things . . . you were dirt. . . .

I go by the majority. The majority is the working man who keeps the country going, because I know it's what they do with their hands that is the main thing. A pen pusher isn't going to survive. . . . And I'll tell you one thing, some of these that I met during my life in service that went into these jobs in the banks and all that sort of thing, our boys could have jumped over their heads as far as anything was concerned. I mean, how they ever got their jobs I don't know. I was sure the biggest boobs got in. You know what happened, they were always on somebody's back and I think there was a lot of that. When you look back you realize that the silly boobs that went in and got such good jobs, I know now they couldn't possibly have kept them in any other way. I know it, I'm no fool.[80]

It is difficult, in conclusion, to estimate the precise significance of schooling as an agency of socialization and to assess the impact that the content and structure of the state education system had upon the working-class children who were incorporated within it. What is clear from listening to old people's recollections is that the legislators and bureaucrats in central and local government who often assumed that working-class children would automatically absorb the values encouraged by schools severely underestimated the extent and intensity of resistance to provided education. This opposition was rooted in the values and modes of behaviour that were learned from the family, the neighbourhood and street culture. Indeed, it is likely that agencies of socialization operating outside the school exercised a much more profound influence upon the morals and manners of the working-class child than the school-teacher in the classroom. The working-class child would probably have left school at the early age of twelve, thirteen or fourteen, and much of the time spent there would have been wasted through inefficient teaching methods, inattention and disobedience. In fact, it was not so much within the schools as within the capitalist system in general, and especially the experience of work, that the real education of the majority of the working class could be acquired, an education based on a shared experience of an unequal distribution of income, opportunity and control in all spheres of life. The experience of class relations in everyday life — although these relations were not necessarily articulated in class terms — was of far greater significance in shaping the consciousness of the working class than was the experience of schooling. Indeed, it was the complex cultural and economic contradictions between the rhetoric of bourgeois ideology and the reality of class injustice and inequality that lay at the heart of much of the resistance we have examined in this chapter. Despite this opposition, though, schooling did to some extent achieve its purpose of reproducing and reinvigorating a class society. This was probably due more to coercion, lack of opportunity and the absence of any alternative mode of education, however, than to the inculcation of any positive identification with, and loyalty to, the dominant culture and its institutions. It is this key element of coercion in the classroom, and resistance to it, that must be examined at length in the next chapter, for widespread resistance to the content and structure of the state schooling system meant that the external constraints imposed by its authoritarian and bureaucratic form were of critical importance in controlling and shaping the behaviour of working-class pupils.

CHAPTER 3

Challenges
to Classroom Coercion

Fred Mattock: I think myself, the Education Committee was thinking all the working classes was a lot of rogues an' the more beatings they 'ad, the better citizens they'd make. That was the attitude they adopted. . . . The teachers, you 'ad to address them as 'sir'; you did look up to them as a class above you. Old Blacklock, he used to whack hell out of us with a ruler, a long foot-ruler. It's a wonder he didn't break people's hands, the way he did clout them. . . . They wouldn't actually say you wasn't doing the work right; they'd say you wasn't paying attention. Like when I was drawing, teacher said, 'Have you ever seen a vase like that?' And he used to carry the cane round with 'n an' he gave me a whack, hit me across the shoulders for not doing the work properly. . . .

Elsie Mattock, Fred's wife: My mother 'ad 'er little house next to the school an' she'd say, 'That's my Freddie' — my brother, that was — 'he's crying out.' She got up, jumped that [school] wall, went right into the class an' she took the cane out of the teacher's hand an' she hooked 'n with it. She'd say, 'I give 'n what for. I hit 'n across his ass.' She was put in court ever so many times for that.[1]

By listening carefully to the memories of elderly working-class people like Fred and Elsie Mattock, we can begin to understand that their experience of schooling bears little or no resemblance to the rhetoric of educational providers, who have invariably celebrated the development of the compulsory state schooling system in Britain as a flower of democracy planted by a benevolent middle class. In fact, schooling was widely experienced by both children and parents as an oppressive constraint, and this hostility towards state coercion provoked a strong undercurrent of resistance, which occasionally exploded into acts of violent revenge. This chapter will explore the nature and extent of resistance to the distinctive bureaucratic and authoritarian form taken by the schooling system. It will deal first with resistance to compulsory attendance regulations through truancy and, second, with the various forms of opposition to authoritarian control in the classroom. Such opposition deserves detailed attention, for the hidden school curriculum of compulsion and constraint constitutes perhaps the most important element in the learning process during the period under study.[2]

In Britain as a whole the average attendance rate rose from approximately 60 per cent in the 1880s to over 80 per cent from 1906 onwards.[3] This gradual increase, however, does not represent a smooth extension of educational opportunity to the underprivileged, for increases were only achieved after a prolonged struggle to overcome the resistance of working-class children and their parents to compulsory attendance. This resistance found expression in three principal forms of irregular attendance, which I will term opportunist, retreatist and subsistence truancy. Despite their interrelated and overlapping nature, it is possible to make fairly clear distinctions between these different types of truancy.

Opportunist truancy was an occasional form of resistance practised by many working-class children who, several times each year, would attempt to abscond from school to play in the fields and on the beaches, to poach, to go to fairs, markets and processions and, later, to swimming baths and picture palaces. Although detection meant certain punishment from both parents and teachers, many children like Frank Vowles were periodically lured away from the classroom by the promise of adventure, excitement and food for free in the surrounding streets and countryside.

If it was a glorious day, a great thing us kids used to do, we used to go out into the countryside. Bristol was smaller. There weren't the environments like Knowle and all these built-up areas — that was all fields. So from the school to the fields was half a mile and you were out in the country. Well, of course, we used to go into the orchards pinching apples and that kind of thing. Or you and another boy would say, 'Well, we won't bother to go today' (always remembering that you were for it at home and at school), and we'd think, we'll do the jumping on the carts. In those days, most of the vehicles were horse-drawn and mainly flat, trolley-type on four wheels, and what we used to do was wait for one to come along and jump on the back and go wherever that was going for a nice old ride. The majority of the drivers didn't take any notice. They would let you ride on it. Well, you might land up at Kingswood, then you'd get one to come back. Or you would go wandering round the dock and try to get on the barges and pinch the monkey nuts that used to come in on the boats. That's what used to get you going on the mooch. I mean, you didn't do it very often because the punishment was fairly severe (that was off the headmaster, obviously) and a wigging. I mean, if your parents believed in clouting you, well, you got a clouting, but with my father it would be stopping of a little bit of pocket money or something like that.[4]

In cases such as this, truancy must be seen as an expression of a conflict between working-class recreational demands, which were based on personal impulses and community traditions, and the rational and bureaucratic organization of school and work, which reduced and regulated leisure time.[5] This type of truancy was widely viewed as a form of larking about, which I will examine in more detail in chapter 5 as one of the most effective means of opposition available to working-class children to resist authoritarian control. However, officials and criminologists often assumed that it was motivated by primitive childish or adolescent instincts that the working-class family had failed to socialize and suppress.[6]

In contrast to the occasional and spontaneous nature of opportunist absenteeism, retreatist truancy tended to be incessant and deeply ingrained, inspired by a profound aversion to various aspects of school. The precise nature and extent of retreatist truancy is extremely difficult to discern, but oral and documentary evidence reveals that some of the most important motives influencing non-attendance were a desire for independence and adventure, fear of a particular teacher or lesson, victimization because of poverty, difficulties with learning as a consequence of poor health (especially defective eyesight or hearing) and a search for freedom and solitude away from the regimented school routine.[7] Of course, these motives were also influential in prompting opportunist truancy; however, while the opportunist could tolerate school for long periods, the retreatist experienced such deep-seated feelings of discontent that regular attendance became an intolerable constraint. Indeed, when this antipathy was reinforced by severe dislocations in the child's family life, arising from the separation or death of parents or unfair treatment at home, the persistent truant was likely to attempt to run away. Further, retreatist truancy was characterized not by one single desire or dissatisfaction but by a convergence of alienating factors that estranged the child from school. This particular form of resistance was often a solitary activity engaged in by lone individuals as opposed to the groups of friends normally involved in opportunist truancy. It found a unique expression in each individual child, as is illustrated by the moving recollections of Winnie Ettle, whose poor eyesight led her to experience severe difficulties with lessons, especially needlework, for which she was reprimanded and punished. These powerful disincentives to attend school, together with the alternative attraction of a serene Jewish cemetery nearby and the awe-inspiring funeral processions entering it, encouraged her to employ one of the favourite strategies of the retreatist truant — the fake infectious illness.

I did go on the mooch sometimes, generally on a Friday afternoon. Well, Friday afternoon was sewing and I couldn't see to thread the needle. You'd 'ave to stand on your seat, then you'd thread the needle, then you'd sit down. Well, I'd be up all the time, trying to thread me needle. Well, then you'd get the cane on the end of that, because you'd hadn't 'ave thread your needle an' done your work. . . . Perhaps she would thread the needle sometimes an', of course, I would do great stitches nowhere near the end where it ought to be. And, of course, they never thought of 'aving your eyes tested or anything like that, 'til the nurse came round an' tested my eyes an' said I wanted glasses. . . . 'Course, I'd be on the mooch on the Friday afternoon, then I'd go into the school on Monday. They'd say, 'Why is it you never came to school on Friday?' Well, once — I can never forget this — I said, 'Please, teacher, mother thinks I've got mumps.' And she said, 'Oh, you'd better go home.' So I goes 'ome, an' my mother says, 'What have you come home for?' And I said, 'Teacher thinks I got the mumps.' Well, she wrapped me round in flannel an' I was home for about four months. Never went, until my mother got fed up. She took me up to school. 'Here,' she said, 'I brought Winnie up. I don't think she got the mumps at all.' An' I walked round with this flannel on, you know. Of course, I never 'ad the mumps, I was just making out. . . .
    Now, at the bottom of our street, at Birken Street, St Philip's — it's still there — a Jews' burial ground, all the rich Jews used to be buried there. It used to be beautiful. . . . I used to love going into cemeteries. When we knew there was a Jew's funeral, we used to go an' see it. They used to wear little black caps on their heads. I used to love going into cemeteries an' sitting down and reading. I didn't think there was a more peaceful place than a cemetery. I used to love going round looking at all the monuments, all the verses, an' I'd sit hours in a cemetery rather than I would in a park. I used to say to my friend 'Let's go to the cemetery' and it would be all locked up because nobody was allowed in there, only the caretaker. . . . It was most interesting to go in there an' to see different names an' their ages an' where they came from, some came from abroad. I used to think it was the only Jewish burial ground and it wasn't very big. They had a nice little porch inside, two seats each side, then they sit in there and have a little service, shut the door. And you could hear them all singing like, an' I used to stand outside and hear them singing.[8]

The hidden and deviant nature of retreatist truancy makes any attempt to assess its extent largely speculative. It is likely, though,

that gradual improvements in the standard of living, the introduction and development of minimal standards of health care in
schools and the increasingly rigorous enforcement of attendance
regulations all contributed towards a reduction in the incidence of
ill-health and poverty as major factors producing this type of
truancy.[9] However, the persistence of severe deprivation and disease
among some sections of the working class ensured the continuance
of retreatist truancy into the 1930s, and although there was a
gradual liberalization of some aspects of the elementary schooling
system, state education retained an authoritarian and bureaucratic
character, which continued to alienate pupils to such an extent that
some felt impelled to escape from teachers whom they feared and
lessons that they disliked intensely. Despite the liberal rhetoric that
legitimized compulsory state schooling, this form of resistance met
with an increasingly coercive response from the authorities, which
involved the commital of persistent truants to reformatory
institutions that were often brutal and manipulatory, as we shall
see in chapter 8.

In the case of subsistence truancy, non-attendance at school was
provoked essentially by poverty and social deprivation. This was
the only form of truancy sanctioned by parents, principally because
it was instrumental in ensuring the family's continued survival.
The need for children to take part-time or full-time employment to
supplement the family income and to assist overworked mothers
with domestic chores and child-minding duties were both characteristic features of subsistence truancy.[10] Another expression of this
fundamental need to protect and provide for the family's members
was the reluctance of parents to send children to school with
inadequate clothing, footwear or food, especially in the extreme
cold of the winter months. Working-class children's awareness of
the necessity for subsistence truancy in order to provide for the
family's basic needs inspired a fierce solidarity in opposition to the
school authorities and a collective resistance to the inflexible
imposition of attendance regulations. The depth of this class feeling
is clearly illustrated in the recollections of Bill Woods, who despite
his conformist and deferential views — which we encountered in
chapter 2 — deviously concealed his classmates' illegal Friday
afternoon coal-picking expeditions from the eyes of the school-
teacher.

Friday afternoon was the afternoon that most of the kiddies did all go up
'the Neck' — that was what they called the electric light factory [dump]
down Feeder Road. They used to go over through Raggy Tucker's field

Children and parents working side by side in the preparation of reeds for thatching on the Fenland marshes near Spalding, Lincolnshire, in about 1890. Economic necessity often forced children to help their parents with work like this during school hours.

(that was clay pits); they used to dig the clay there for the pottery. We used to go round these an' over the electric light place to pick up ashes or cinders, where they used to chuck the coal after it 'ad been burned making the electric. They used to chuck it all down on the floor an' we used to sort it over an' pick out the coal or coke. Then you used to take that 'ome, see. That was for burning. And we was at school one Friday an' there wasn't many children there. They was all out from school, truanting on the afternoon. So the teacher turned round an' said, 'Anybody know where the children is, or where they're going or gone?' So somebody must've turned round an' said, 'They'm over the Neck, picking up coke or cinders.' 'Alright,' he said, 'we want somebody to go over and take their names. What about you, Woods?' I said, 'I don't mind, sir'. So anyhow I walked down through the school, over Raggy Tucker's clay pits an' over to the dump, an as I was looking over I see a hell of a crowd of people there. I couldn't discern them because I was so far away. So I got up over the railway line, over the other side of the railway lines, then all at once I hears someone shout, 'Oh, 'ere he is.' And when I looked to see where they was to, I could see nobody. And I thought, that's funny, they can't 'ave gone anywhere but I can't see 'em. And I was walking round — there was a big hut there, he was built about two foot off the ground — and I hears somebody say, 'Shut up, you, 'ere he is.' So I thought, they're hidden under there. So I got some clinkers an' I throws them in under an' I hears somebody shout out because I must 'ave hit them. And I said, 'Come out, whoever you are.' I told them who sent me — a teacher, Mr Newton — an' I said, 'I'll have all your names.' So I wrote all their names down an' I said, 'I'm going back to school now.'. . . . And I ripped it up after. I ran back an' said there was nobody over there. I said there was somebody but he was gone. I said I couldn't put on him. Had no names. . . . The next week there was a lot of kids not in the school again, so the teacher said, 'I want somebody to go over the Neck and find out who goes over.' And all the kids in the class shouted out, 'Let Woods go, sir, let Woods go.' Then any Friday he wanted anybody I was the one who 'ad to go over looking for 'em. When they knew I hadn't reported them, then it was alright . . . because I said there was nobody over there. I told lies.[11]

Subsistence truancy was most prevalent among older siblings, but their degree of commitment to the family economy — for example, whether they were required to absent themselves from school for days, weeks or months at a time — was determined by the complex and changing nature of the working-class household. The precise form and extent of subsistence truancy was shaped by such factors as the size of the family, the level of economic hardship experienced, the employment opportunities for children available in the locality and the vigilance with which the authorities enforced attendance regulations. It was particularly prevalent among large families in which the father was either dead, unemployed or unskilled and in country districts where there was a huge demand by farmers for seasonal labour in the fields.[12] Subsistence truancy steadily declined as a consequence of the enactment of legislation to prevent child labour and to increase the school-leaving age but persisted well into the twentieth century, especially in country districts where attendance regulations were rarely rigorously enforced.[13]

    Both retreatist and subsistence truancy have invariably been condemned as expressions of ignorance, immorality and cultural deprivation, and the history of child welfare legislation celebrated as a history of progress inspired by liberal ideals to extend social rights and opportunities to working-class children. State intervention to provide for the care and protection of destitute children, to prevent the exploitation of child labour by ruthless adults and to establish the individual child's right to a minimal education do, of course, provide some evidence to support this view.[14] However, this orthodoxy tends to obliterate any positive element in the resistance we have examined, particularly the alternative conception of learning and work that some of it implicitly contains. Admittedly, retreatist and subsistence truancy cannot be seen as evidence of a clearly articulated and evaluative working-class resistance to compulsory schooling, as they were both to a large extent determined by poverty and deprivation. But both of these types of truancy offered an implicit challenge to the state schooling system, which sought to reproduce and reinvigorate a developing industrial-capitalist class society. For, crucially, they were in some situations task-orientated rather than time-orientated, as was the organization of work imposed by schooling; they often offered a degree of independence, responsibility and personal freedom in contrast to the dependent and submissive forms of behaviour demanded by schools; and they frequently permitted work and character development to take place informally in the heart of family and community rather than in the formal, depersonalized and authoritarian context of learning in the classroom.[15] It is only when we comprehend the problems that truancy posed for the smooth functioning of a class society that we gain a true perspective on the systematic and coercive efforts made by the state to control and eliminate it from the late nineteenth century onwards. The monitoring of truancy through attendance registers and attendance officers, the issuing of summonses on a massive scale to the parents of children whose attendance was irregular and the incarceration of persistent truants in reformatory institutions were not primarily humanitarian in intention and effect, as is commonly assumed.[16] Instead, they must be seen as part of a broader process of class control in which the bureaucratic apparatus of the state was deployed to ensure uniformity and regularity of habits among the working-class younger generation.[17] Many children and parents viewed the truancy laws precisely in this way, as a form of class oppression, and as a consequence considerable resentment was directed against the attendance officers and the police who reinforced them. In the words of Bristolian Tom Radway, who occasionally truanted from school in the 1900s: 'We'd always be on the look-out for coppers on the beat or attendance officers on their bikes. They really put the fear of God in you 'cos they did the dirty work that had you sent to the industrial school.'[18]

Although there was deep-rooted resistance to the imposition of compulsory attendance regulations, the most potent and persistent opposition of working-class children to schooling occurred in the classroom itself. Their enforced confinement in institutions that had little to offer apart from rote learning, rigid discipline and training in manners and morals that were often alien and meaningless led to a constantly antagonistic atmosphere. Most commonly, the pupils' resistance took the form of acts of disobedience, disorderly conduct and a reluctant and apathetic attitude towards learning. The unco-operative and sometimes openly hostile behaviour of many children, together with the large classes and the inadequately trained or equipped teachers, combined to produce friction. Elementary schools attempted to resolve the conflict by regulating learning strictly and by resorting to the traditional authoritarian methods of fear and punishment. The ultimate sanction of authoritarian teaching methods is, of course, the resort to harsh physical means of control, and even though there was a gradual decline in the recorded numbers of canings from the 1900s onwards, there is much oral evidence to suggest that corporal punishment continued to be a routine and sometimes everyday occurrence in most elementary schools throughout the period under study.[19] The frequent infliction of canings by teachers was, in a minority of cases, motivated by a sadistic disposition or the desire to dominate children.[20] However, the principal justification for corporal punishment, from the teacher's point of view, was the need to exercise control over large classes of disenchanted pupils. The accumulated experience of the struggles of several generations of elementary schoolteachers to establish and maintain control over children crystallized into a distinct professional tradition, which embodied a number of well-tried strategies for survival and success in the classroom. The fundamental assumption upon which the teachers' perception of their authority was based was that an initial period of coercive and rigid control, a cold and formal presentation of one's personality and a willingness to cane disobedient children were all essential ingredients in the recipe for the successful domination of pupils. This recipe was itself rooted in a number of broader values and attitudes that infused middle-class culture — the evangelical belief in the fundamentally sinful and selfish nature of children, the traditional conception of the development of personality and intellect as a process that involved restraint as opposed to self-expression and the hostile denigration of the 'rough' sections of the working class as ignorant and immoral. This recipe for success was also of enormous practical importance, for it safeguarded the teachers' own careers, which depended upon the ability to control and instruct large classes, for if a teacher failed to command obedience, he or she would be despised by pupils, parents and colleagues alike and would be forced to resign from the teaching profession.[21]

Manuals of teaching methods provide the most precise evidence of the rigorous standards of discipline expected in elementary schools. Most handbooks written prior to the 1900s urged teachers to demand that all instructions and tasks be obeyed with military precision, promptness and regularity.[22] However, from this period onwards progressive, child-centred theory gradually began to win acceptance in official reports and training colleges, and a deep rift emerged between the theory and practice of teaching, which widened during the inter-war years. For while the liberal theory embraced by some college lecturers and education committee members, many of whom had little or no teaching experience, stressed the development of individual personality and potential, teaching practice was concerned essentially with problems of control and domination.[23] Many teachers, who laboured in harsh conditions that made progressive experimentation practically impossible even had they wished to attempt it and who were daily confronted with the harsh reality of controlling large classes of hostile working-class children, firmly believed that corporal punishment was essential for the efficient functioning of the school.[24] Consequently, they fiercely withstood pressure from education authorities, parents' associations and the labour movement to restrict or abolish the use of the cane. During the pre-1914 period education authorities that sought to restrict the right to cane children to headteachers met strong resistance from assistant teachers, who protested that classroom control would be undermined unless they were permitted to administer corporal punishment freely.[25] And although by 1939 over two-thirds of local education authorities had issued regulations that limited the use of corporal punishment to a certain extent, these controls were often achieved in spite of the opposition of teachers' associations.[26] An indication of the frequency with which canings were sometimes inflicted is provided by the report, made shortly after elementary schools were compelled to keep punishment books in 1900, that 378 cases of corporal punishment had been recorded at one infants' school within just three months.[27] However, many working-class children and their parents refused to submit passively to this harsh treatment, and interviews reveal a broad range of resistance to authoritarian control.

Perhaps the most moving and most unusual tradition of resistance that developed in response to the widespread use of corporal punishment in state schools was the emergence of an elaborate children's folklore, which celebrated the magical power of various substances such as salt or orange peel either to snap the cane or to immunize the victim from any sensation of pain if they were applied to the skin in the correct ritualistic manner. Although most children's beliefs — for example, faith in the power of a hair, when placed across the palm of the hand, to snap a bamboo cane — were clearly mythical, it is possible that other practices, such as the regular rubbing of resin into the hands, did in fact toughen the skin to such an extent that it occasionally broke the cane on impact. Like a number of other old people, Bristolian Winnie Ettle, recalled:

Sometimes when I knew I was going to get the cane — we always 'ad a bit of resin — we be rubbing this resin on our hands. 'Hold your hand out.' They'd give you the cane, but it would snap the cane an' you never felt it.[28]

But as children grew older, they gradually became aware of the unreliable and imaginary nature of much of this resistance and resorted to more practical strategies, such as hiding or stealing the teacher's cane. However, they often discovered such devious tactics to be equally ineffective, as Reg Summerhayes, recalling his Bath school days in the early part of the century, remembers.

Sometimes we used to get hold of the cane an' we used to hide him. We used to push 'n up the chimney or put him behind the cupboards. He used to say, 'Well, I can't find my cane nowhere.' I remember one day he said, 'Summerhayes, do you know where the cane is?' 'No,' I said. 'Well,' he said, 'here's a shilling. Now go down the road an' buy a new one.' I done that several times where he couldn't find the other one. He didn't mince no matters about it. He did give it to you hot 'n holy, right up over his shoulders, you know, an' right across that thumb an' it don't half hurt across there, mind. We used to put all sorts on us hands. We used to put our hand in our hair an' put a hair on it so the cane would break. It never did though. Or we'd rub a bit of sugar on there or a bit of resin, you know. None of 'em worked.[29]

Interviews reveal that some children resolutely refused to submit to the infliction of corporal punishment, especially if they considered the caning to be unfair and undeserved. The frequency and distribution of this resistance varied widely according to the age of children involved and the nature and location of different schools, but it clearly predominated among older, physically well-developed children who lived in notoriously 'rough' city neighbourhoods and who were taught in grossly understaffed or rigidly authoritarian schools. There were three different types of pupil resistance — opposition to the form of punishment chosen by the teacher, opposition to the excessive nature of the punishment and opposition to the right of the teacher to administer any form of physical punishment whatsoever. Each type will be briefly dealt with in turn.

Assistant teachers who were prevented by education authority regulations from using the cane often developed their own range of painful and humiliating punishments. Many children resented the casual infliction of these punishments, which for boys commonly included raps with wooden objects such as blackboard rubbers or rulers, the boxing of ears and the slapping of faces or legs, while girls were frequently ordered to hold their petticoats or slates above their heads for long periods.[30] But the most determined resistance to particular punishments that teachers attempted to impose occurred when boys refused to remove their trousers to be beaten on their bare bottoms. There is little doubt that this peculiarly British, middle-class flagellomania contained a strong sado-masochistic sexual element, and the prevalence of flagellant prostitution and pornography, especially during the late Victorian and Edwardian periods, suggests that erotic pleasure was frequently derived from inflicting or observing these ceremonial beatings. However, although these ritual humiliations were for many years an integral part of public school life, teachers from such a background often discovered that working-class parents and children were resolute in their resistance to this type of punishment.[31] Boys like Joseph Maddison, who grew up in South Shields in the early part of the century, would stoically endure traditional punishments of the sort that their parents might inflict but refused to submit to the more degrading disciplinary measures favoured by some middle-class schoolteachers.

We're out in the schoolyard drilling, and it was hips bend and all. Well, somebody at the back of me give me a shove. Of course, I half fell down and I shoved somebody in front of me. He's seen me. He says, 'Get inside! Get inside!' And, of course, I had to go inside. They came back in school and he says, 'Come out the front here, Maddison.' He says, 'Undo your trousers and get your trousers down.' He said, 'I'm making an example of you.' I says, 'Look, Mr Herman,' I says, 'my father's never told me yet to get my trousers down,' I says, 'and don't think you're going to get my trousers down because I'm telling you you're not.' He says, 'Do you know who you are speaking to?' I says, 'Certainly, sir, I'm speaking to my teacher.' I says, 'And do you know what my teacher's told me?' I says. 'My teacher's telling me to do something my own parents don't do.' He says, 'Come out here. I'll

take them down.' So I was a big lad when I was at school and I went out
the front. But he was the first on the floor — I had him down easy. The lads
thought it was great, this. 'Yippee! Go on, Maddison!' they were shouting.
Just then Mr Carter next door, he heard. He came in, and I had to go and
see the headmaster, Mr Philipson, and he says, 'What happened?' And I
told him. But he says, 'You've got to learn discipline.' I says, 'That's not a
case of discipline to me.' I says, 'In school you get a cane and it's either on
your hand or else it's across your bottom but never a bare bottom.' I says,
'That's the difference with me.' 'Well,' he says, 'will you take a punishment
from me?' I said, 'That all depends what it's going to be, sir,' I says, 'the
hands or I'll lie across a desk, but not me trousers down.' 'Well,' he says,
'I'll give you the normal cane on your hands.' And I got, I think, six off him
and it never worried me. So I went back to me class. 'Maddison, out, out of
this school,' he says. 'Don't come back here any more.' So I went out. Next
morning I came back — on a Friday morning. I just came and sat at me
desk. He said, 'I thought I told you to leave school?' I says, 'You have no
authority to tell me to leave school sir. You're only my teacher.' I says, 'My
headmaster hasn't told me to leave school and I don't finish school until tonight.' I was fourteen. I says, 'I finish tonight. I won't be back on Monday.'
'Well,' he says, 'I'm not having you in this class today.' 'Well,' I says, 'that
be up to you and the headmaster, but my education doesn't finish, not
unless the headmaster sends me home.' 'Well,' he says, 'I'm not going to
have you. I'll give you a job.' And he give us all insurance cards for the
teachers, every school in South Shields. And I had to go round giving the
new insurance cards out. Aye.[32]

Although children might occasionally succeed in having
humiliating punishments commuted to more acceptable forms after
appeals to headteachers, they received little sympathy if they
claimed that the number of canings the teacher was preparing to
administer was excessive. Indeed, such behaviour was likely to
lead to further retribution as a penalty for the child's failure to
acknowledge his guilt and for his insolent challenge to the teacher's
authority, as Marie Smith remembers: 'If she was going to give you
two whacks for something where you thought you only deserved
one, you'd complain sometimes an' try to take yer 'and away, but it
only made it worse 'cos she'd give you an extra one for being so
cheeky.'[33]

However, the most brutal scenes of authoritarianism occurred
when pupils refused to accept any form of physical punishment
whatsoever.[34] Proud and unrepentant children would either snatch
the cane from the teacher's grasp and attempt to snap it or, more
often, they would remove their hand at the last second before
impact and the cane's momentum would occasionally drive it
painfully on to the teacher's own legs. In this situation other

teachers would be called into the classroom to restrain the victim physically and to grip his or her arms rigidly while another administered the beating, as Charlie Dallimore recalls:

I tried to grab the cane. If you could grab that cane, you could snap 'im across your knees, but you would suffer afterwards 'cos they'd get another teacher in to come an' hold yer hand — one teacher to hold yer, while the other hit 'im proper. Many a time. They'd say, 'Hold yer hand out,' an' I'd pull 'im back an' they'd bring 'im down an' keep hitting their legs an' they'd get nasty an' say, 'Go and fetch Miss So-and-So.' And she'd come an' hold yer hand an' that was that. You didn't struggle then 'cos if you did, you was for it. That was a regular thing.[35]

When classroom conflict escalated to such a potentially subversive level most rebellious working-class children grudgingly acknowledged defeat, for, like Charlie Dallimore, they knew that further resistance would court the risk of expulsion, official designation as 'beyond control' and subsequent committal to an industrial or reformatory school. But while these deterrents were sufficient to ensure that most boys and girls who resisted the cane would eventually succumb to the teachers' dictates, a small minority of children loathed school to such an extent that they adopted an intransigent stance, even in the most serious situations.[36] For example, although aware of the brutal and oppressive nature of the local reformatory institutions to which rebellious children were committed, Herbert Shill felt so deeply resentful about the worthlessness of the education he was receiving that he continually disrupted lessons and refused the cane. Many such children, as we shall see in chapter 8, received long sentences in reformatory institutions, but Herbert Shill was saved from this fate by a paternalistic gesture from the headmaster at Hanham School, south Gloucestershire, which he attended in the 1900s.

If you was bad, they sent you to the reformatory school. Now Kingswood Reformatory by us, they did birch the boys on a Sunday an' they used to get the Boy's Brigade band in to play out in the school yard that day, an' everyone always said 'twas to drown their screams. All the kids knew that. . . . Even though you knew there'd be trouble, you played up in school. Because we 'ad nothing in our school days. We 'ad no opportunity whatsoever; we simply went. Now people that could pay for their children to go on to secondary education, that's where they scored, look, but we 'ad no chance. 'Twas all boring. I was only too pleased to get out because I was recognized as a good carpenter an' I wanted to do that. . . . And I can remember once we 'ad a drawing lesson an', 'course, naturally, you was leaning over the desk like, leaning into someone else. So what I did, I dropped a rubber down Inkwell's neck. [Inkwell was the nickname for Grenville Godfrey, the class swot.] 'Course, this chap started grumbling, like. The teacher — we used to call'n Snotty Lewis to tell you the truth — he said, 'What's the matter Godfrey?' 'Shill's dropped a rubber down my neck, sir.' 'Come out here, Shill.' So I come out here, and he want to give me the cane and I refused it, look. He said, 'Right.' He said, 'When you go home, you write a hundred times "I must not drop a rubber down Grenville Godfrey's neck".' . . . Now, I refused the cane several times actually, and he couldn't do anything with me, so I refused'n once an' he said, 'Go out to the headmaster, Shill.' So I went out to 'n — Mr Wicksey, his name was, a nice old chap. He said, 'Shill, I have not heard very good reports of you in your class.' He said, 'The best thing I think for you to do is to come out here with me,' and for the rest of my time I went out with 'n in the great hall, and he'd give me a few lessons and I'd go round the classes with books, things like that. And one day he did say to me, 'Look, Shill, I've heard you're a very good carpenter from the woodwork teacher. Should you like to go down and put up some fencing for my wife?' 'Course, I was in my glory. I says, 'Thank you.' I went down there an' I had cups of tea an' all this. 'Twas a grand time, 'cos I was out of school.[37]

Interviews clearly indicate that girls were as likely to resist authoritarian control as boys. This may seem surprising in view of the orthodoxy that portrays working-class girls as much more passive, subservient and deferential than their male counterparts,[38] yet although boys were undoubtedly responsible for a large portion of crime and delinquent behaviour outside school, there is evidence to suggest that inside schools girls were as disobedient as, or even more disobedient than, boys. This defiance was occasionally reflected in higher expulsion rates for girls as compared with those for boys,[39] but because girls often employed more subtle and devious techniques of resistance than boys, much of their misbehaviour has remained hidden and unrecorded in school log and punishment books.[40] Clearly, no rigid distinction can be made between the behaviour of boys and girls, as this varied to some extent according to character, temperament and age, but it does seem that the resistance of girls tended to be of a different nature from that of most boys. Among boys disobedience usually took the form of spontaneous and volatile outbursts of physical aggression, and they would disrupt lessons or seek immediate revenge on authoritarian teachers by throwing inkpots or by kicking or punching them. For example, in the following extract Henry Teague, a street gang leader in Bristol in the 1890s, recalls his angry response to a petty and brutal punishment inflicted on him by his teacher.

I didn't try hard and I couldn't concentrate. But it was more in fear of the teachers than anything else because they was brutes in them days. I'll tell you, on one occasion there was a big strapping man, over six foot, a teacher. And I was sat in my desk one day with the copy book in front of me, writing what the teacher had dictated. And I was conscious of a blotch on the paper, but I couldn't do anything about it. And all at once, and I wasn't aware of it, and it was very cruel, I felt a hand [he makes a slapping sound] like that. Right across my ear. Well, it stung me for a minute, but what I did, I got up out of my seat and I kicked him right in the shin. Then after that he sent me out to see the headmaster. He gave me a good bang in the face and I gave him a good kick in the shin. But to come behind a child and wham! You could ruin the drum of a boy's ear, and a big man, he was twice the size of me.[41]

Girls, however, tended to rely less on physical strength than on trickery and evasion to resist authoritarian control. They would often gain temporary relief from the unremitting and regimented organization of school work by claiming falsely that they were unable to understand the teachers' instructions, as Flo Mullen, recalling her schooldays in the village of Bitton, south Gloucestershire, in the 1900s remembers:

The girls weren't no angels. Some of 'em wouldn't do the work. Teacher would say, 'Flo, you do so and so,' and I'd say, 'No,' and she'd say, 'Why?' and I'd say, 'Because I can't.' You could but you didn't want to. [Laughter][42]

Similarly, while boys often openly defied petty and bureaucratic school rules, girls, possibly because they were more frightened of corporal punishment than the boys, were much more practised in the arts of concealment and subterfuge.[43] Winnie Ettle, for example, remembers how she successfully defied a rule that forbade children to bring skipping ropes to school.

We used to buy a skipping rope [for] a ha'penny. . . . We would put that round our waist under our dress an' take it into school, then come out an' play skipping with it. We were frightened of the teachers. What the teachers said was right. That's why we done that.[44]

When girls were drawn into conflict with authority, they were much more likely to resort to verbal rather than physical abuse, often making loud and sarcastic comments about the teacher's personal appearance. And if, as a consequence, teachers caned girls for insolence, pupils would often call upon their considerable reserves of artfulness in order to convince their parents that the punishment was unjustified. Many working-class parents refused to acknowledge the teachers' right to punish their children physically for acts of minor disobedience,[45] and by giving a slightly distorted version of the events that preceded the caning, girls were often able to win the sympathy of their parents, who would arrive angrily in the classroom and threaten teachers with retribution — as Jessie Niblett remembers:

We girls were caned more often than the boys, I should think. I used to have more 'old buck' than they, more mouth, answer back. My father once went up the school to complain. He was going to pull old Ginger's hair off her head 'cos she hit me so hard. Then when I got home on the night time, he said, 'What did that teacher hit you for really?' I said, 'Because I called her Ginger,' and, oh, he knocked my face. He said, 'And you made me go all the way down that school because she hit you like that?' I said, 'Yes.' He went down and went for her because I'd told him how hard she'd set about me, but I didn't tell what I done.[46]

Parental protests concerning the unfair punishment of girls were far more frequent than was the case with boys, and although education authorities in some localities responded only by pressing for the prosecution of parents guilty of trespass and interference in the classroom,[47] in some schools teachers were forced to make concessions to the combined resistance of parents and children. For example, in the following extract Hilda Williams, recalling her schooldays in London in the 1900s, remembers how persistent canings for petty misdemeanours ceased after she advised a friend to scream incessantly when caned, thereby frightening the teachers and alerting the local community to the brutal punishments inflicted in the school.

We had one girl there, Cissy Buckingham, and the teacher was so spiteful to her, Miss Hallett, she used to slap that girl across her face for nothing. They were spiteful to you in those days, you know. You only had to be late or give a cross look, and I remember this teacher, she caned this girl for something. And I said to her, 'If she hits you again like that,' I said, 'scream at the top of your voice and don't leave off. Scream, scream, scream!' Well, she got a whacking after that and the teacher hit her across the wrists. Well, all the faces come out the street, out the class doors. She never stopped screaming. Mind you, she was in pain. And then the caning stopped. After that you only had your name put in the punishment book.[48]

Although the disobedience of girls was most frequently expressed in artful, subtle and devious ways, nevertheless, when severely provoked individual girls' feelings of resentment occasionally exploded into violent acts of resistance. Alice Comelay's recollections of such an incident from her Bristol schooldays in the 1900s illustrates vividly a number of characteristic features of these outbursts — the short-tempered teacher labouring under great pressure to control and instruct large classes, the sullen and bitter attitude of children who suffered the agonies of malnutrition and poor health, the fierce solidarity of classmates with victimized children, and the desperate struggles of headteachers to maintain some standards of professional integrity and to protect the reputation of the school.

[Our teacher] was a little maiden lady. She used to suffer a lot with headaches. . . . And one day we had a girl there, the girl wasn't feeling very well and she upset the girl . . . she brought up the word 'consumption'. I know, something went wrong with the lesson we were doing, and the girl evidently wasn't doing it right. She said, 'What else can you expect when you're suffering with consumption?' And that upset the girl. She said, 'You say that again,' and with that she picked up the inkwell and threw it at her. It all went down. She had one of these blouses, white silk blouses with a lovely frill — it was a marvellous blouse — 'course the ink went down. So, of course, she went for the girl, and we shouted out, 'Leave 'er alone!' 'Course, the headmistress come in and she said, 'What's the trouble?' Teacher told her, and she asked the girl, and we all shouted out, 'She shouldn't 'ave said what she said to the girl.' The headmistress took the girl's part, sent the teacher home. She said, 'If you knew you had a bad head, you shouldn't have come in this morning. You could've sent a message to say you wasn't going to be in. You'd better go home now and come back when you've got rid of your headache.' She apologized to the girl but, of course, about six or seven months after, the girl died with consumption.[49]

Interviews reveal that one principal way in which elementary schoolchildren protested against the worse abuse of authoritarianism was through the destruction of school property, and oral evidence suggests a clear correlation between acts of vandalism and particularly brutal school regimes in which corporal punishment was used indiscriminately. Vandalism tended to be committed by older boys, was usually of an unpremeditated and spontaneous nature and often occurred in response to the infliction of a punishment that was considered exceptionally unfair either by the victimized child or by his classmates. All these characteristic features are present in the following description of vandalism by Bill Harding, who suffered permanent physical damage as a result of savage punishment by his teacher. He recalls how one boy took revenge on the authorities at Barton Hill school, Bristol, which was for many years notorious for its militaristic standards of discipline, and in which unprovoked punishments of children were frequent occurrences.

Why I've got my bad ear is because I went to sleep sat at the desk, where I was half-starved. Didn't get enough food when we was children. I went to sleep in the class. The teacher called me out. He said, 'Harding!' Made me jump when he shouted. Had a terrible loud voice. I went out an' he give I the piece of chalk an' I had to put where the apostrophe 's' should be. An' I put 'n in the wrong place. I put it at the beginning of the word instead of at the end of the word. And he caught me, crash! And before I fell to the ground, he hit me on the other side, hooked me up again. He said, 'You weren't paying attention, were you?' I always remember that 'cos it bled an all an' I went home an' told me mother, but mother never bothered with it. She said, 'Oh, you must've been misbehaving yourself.' I wasn't, but she didn't believe me. Anyway, I didn't take any notice. It healed up, sort of business, until I 'ad to join the services in the last war, an' that's why they turned me down. He said, 'Do you know you've got a perforated eardrum? Your ear's gone. It's no good at all.' And if I covered the other one up now, I couldn't hear a damn thing. . . .

And I had the cane once from the teacher, I think it was very unprovoked. There was a bit of a skirmish in the classroom an' he came through the door an' I was nearest, so he collared me and belted me. I always reckon it was because he didn't like me, an' I'm sure there was a personal feeling behind it, an' he vent his feelings on me with the cane. I 'ad six strokes an' I didn't know what it was for. And because he said, 'Do you know what that's for?' an' I said, no, I didn't, he give me another couple, ended up six strokes altogether. He said I was insolent. But I still stand by it today. I wouldn't do anything wrong. I was too scared to do anything wrong. . . .

Well, we used to go to woodcraft once a week an' we'd 'ave to march from Barton Hill to St George, march in the gutter, while the teacher walked on the pavement. And it was the time of the First World War an' the wood was very very scarce. They was using it for munitions, an' schools 'ad to be very careful what wood they used. All the wood was kept in the back room. Well, this kid, he didn't behave himself this morning an' our teacher (his name was Mr Oliver), he clouted this boy. Now he was a devil for carrying this big fat ruler. He didn't hesitate. He'd pull 'n out of his pocket an' he'd give you one. If he thought you was holding one of the tools in the wrong way, he'd hit you right across your hand. He didn't hesitate, didn't ask any questions. 'Course, this kid squeaked out that particular day, an' he went for 'un. Well, he was a big, strong man, this Mr Oliver. He caught hold of 'un chucked 'un down over the stairs [into the back room] an' he turned the key in the door. Oh, it was silent for a few minutes, then all of a sudden we could hear this saw going down there. He sawed all the damn planks up down there. It was murder. He said, 'Serve you right for sending I down there. You chucked me down there.' He sawed all the planks of wood up.

'Course, we laughed, an' he wanted to belt all of we then, but old Mr Oliver, he was caught that time, wa'n 'ee? [Laughter][50]

Some acts of vandalism were instigated not by children who were themselves persecuted by teachers but by classmates, as a protest against the unfair punishment of children who were particularly poor, delicate or sick. In the following extract, for example, Bill Bees, whose family experienced appalling poverty in the south Gloucestershire village of Hanham during the 1920s, recalls how his friend was committed to a reformatory after smashing school desks in anger at the teachers' persistent victimization of Bill.

I've been to school with my sister's clothes on, an' you couldn't tell whether I was a boy or girl sometimes. My mother put what I thought was a nightgown on me, an' he'd come right down to yer toes an' you couldn't see yer boots hardly. And they used to say at school, 'Have you just got up, Master William?' 'No, teacher, why?' 'Well, what have you got on?' 'Well, I don't know, my mother put it on me. She said, 'That'll do for today.' We didn't comment because we didn't know what it meant. And I had to go to school with two odd boots for shoes on, an' wore patches in my trousers that were in a patchwork quilt. I used to wear the lace-up boots with buttons done up with a hook. Now, as the years went on, I found that women did wear 'em. Anythin' that come along, we 'ad to wear it. There was no such a thing as put it away; it 'ad to be worn. And we all 'ad our hair cut like convicts. Yes, it was cut by a horse dealer with clippers every month. . . . Our teacher, the children was beginning to hate 'im. You couldn't think how cruel he could be. He 'ad no sympathy for you. Once you went up to that desk an' stood there — he wouldn't come an' talk to you — an' he'd say, 'Well now, look, William, I'm sick and tired of punishing you. Now you be a good boy, now go back and sit down and listen to the sermon.' He did love punishin' you. . . . Once I did threaten the master with somethin'. He said somethin' 'bout my parents, an' I was goin' to let the inkwell go at 'im, full of ink. I would 'ave. And he called me over an' I said, 'If you ever hit me again, you'll know it.' But he did thrash me all the same for that. Because sometimes I really did feel that he was taking the mickey out of me. 'Course, the other boys, they 'ad a nickname for me. They used to call me Dinky, owing to me being late every mornin'. They used to call me 'Dink, the missing link'. And they'd say, 'Old Dink'll be alright in a minute. He'll be going up for his medicine.' And I used to say, 'Shut thee row up,' an' they didn't punish they; they'd punish me, see. 'Course, we didn't talk posh, like they do now. 'What's the matter with thee?', 'course, proper Hanham.
    My friend that was put away on the training ship, he did stand up for me once or twice. He said, 'You want to stop hittin' Bill. Why pick on Bill?' But I think the master was really afraid of 'im because he 'ad a very violent temper an' I think that's why they 'ad 'im put away. He did have a bit of

sympathy for me one day. He drove his boot right into the desk an' kicked the top right off. He kicked hell out of the deak an' all the inkpots were flyin' up. Everybody was going berserk. Yes, he went mad that day, an' I think that's why they had 'im put away on this training ship. It wasn't through not going to school, because he did go to school regular. He was a nice chap. I liked 'un. He was put away for so many years.[51]

Such was the severity of retribution for individuals found guilty of deliberately damaging school property that if a teacher failed to catch the child in the act, it was extremely difficult to identify the culprit subsequently, for he or she would generally be stubbornly defended and protected by classmates.[52] Occasionally, whole classes or even entire schools were summarily caned after children had refused to betray the guilt of those accused of such offences as smashing lights and windows or damaging toilets.[53] This fierce solidarity was based partly on fear, for children who informed on offenders were sometimes excluded from group play and street gangs or were threatened with violence. More often, however, it derived from genuine bonds of comradeship, for some children would make considerable personal sacrifices in order to protect friends from detection. This intense solidarity is illustrated in the recollections of Bill Woods who, despite his deferential views, chose loyalty to his classmates rather than loyalty to his school when it came to the crunch.

I had six strokes of the cane once — that was three on each hand — because somebody went in the toilet and flushed the tank an' wasted so many gallons of water, an' I was blamed for it. I didn't do it. I knew who done it, but I wouldn't tell on 'em. So I took the punishment instead . . . six strokes of the cane in front of the whole school. Well, they lost thousands of gallons of water when he turned this pipe or something on in the toilet. No, we never used to tell 'em things like that. They was hard in those days.[54]

The infliction of severe and indiscriminate corporal punishment in many schools, especially during the late Victorian and Edwardian periods, though designed to instil obedience and crush resistance, was in fact often counter-productive in its effects, further aggravating the tension between the working-class community and the school. For while parents usually accepted and approved of mild and occasional punishments for their children, the injuries inflicted were sometimes so severe that incensed parents summonsed the teachers involved. However, court cases were invariably dismissed, and irate parents were frequently tempted to seek immediate verbal or physical retribution in the classroom and street.[55] The parents who caused these disturbances cannot simply be dismissed as the 'rough' elements of the working class, who, it is often assumed, were themselves guilty of brutality and harsh authoritarianism. To illustrate this point I wish to quote at length from Arthur Burley's recollections of an incident that occurred at Perranwell village school in Cornwall, during the early part of the century, in which he was savagely beaten by his teacher after rescuing a terrified classmate from a caning. Arthur, a huge boy for his age, was nicknamed Gi (for Giant) by his friends, but, like his father, a quarry labourer who never physically punished any of his children, he was extremely sensitive and opposed to the indiscriminate use of corporal punishment at school. His memories are particularly interesting, for they reveal the strategies available to a threatened teacher and his wife to contain the resistance of an angry working-class father and his son.

The cane, you're bloody right it hurt. He had these bamboos as big as your finger and 'bout three foot long, and when you hold your hand out and the stick come down, you'd think he'd cut your fingers off. I'm telling you, when you'd 'ad the first one, you'd nearly jump off the floor. Well, that's only one — you 'ad to have three more yet. Well, time you'd had four of they, two on each hand, I'm tellin' you, my God, for about an hour you was rubbing your hands because they was that painful, you had a job to write afterwards. Boys'd cry, my God, and scream. When they got only one cut of the cane, they used to start crying but by the time they had three, well, the tears now was running off their cheeks with pain.

   There was one little boy at school, he didn't have no father, and there was three children, and their mother never had no money. She used to take washing in. She used to wash clothes for people, and she would be there, outside her back door, from when I go to school, washing clothes; she'd be there when I go home for dinner at twelve o'clock; she'd be there when I go back to school, washing clothes; and she'd be there when I come home from school, hands in the water, washing clothes all the time. And I don't suppose she had very much for it, and she had to keep three children on that. Well, her son was a very little fat boy, you know. So it was summertime, and she made him a little suit, a little jacket and little short trousers, naked knees, you know. Anyhow, he was talking, and the master was watching him. Well, in the end, he shouted to him and told him to come out the front. Well, this little boy, he had to put his little fat hand out, and when the master brought the cane down across that little fat hand, well, he screamed an' he wouldn't put his hand out no more now. He was afraid, you see, and the master was trying to pull his arm out straight, an' the little boy was screaming. Well, I couldn't stand it no more, so I jumped up, pulled the cane out of the master's hand, put 'n across me knee an' broke 'n in half, an' put 'n in the fire. Oh, my God, well, he wrote a letter and I suppose about half-past three he called this girl an' he said, 'Mildred Tellick, come to the front.' He said, 'Now, on your way home from school I want for you to carry this letter in an' give it to Mrs Burley.' So when I come out of school I said, 'Mildred, you've got a letter for my mother. You give me that letter.' 'Oh, no,' she said, but I made 'er hand it over and tore it up. So anyway, the next mornin' at school after prayers he called Mildred Tellick to the front and he said, 'Did you deliver that letter last night I gave you?' And she was looking at the master, then she was looking at me, like. I was putting me fist up like this to her, see. Well, she didn't answer the master, so the master said, 'I've asked you a question. Did you deliver that letter?' Then she started to cry. 'Oh,' he says, 'you haven't delivered the letter.' She said I took the letter from her and, oh dear, oh dear, he said, 'Well, you go back and sit down.' So he lifted up the desk cover and he took out a bamboo which 'ad a handle on it like a walking stick, and he came back in a temper, and he put that stick across my back so many times until he got tired of doing it. I held myself so that the cane would go right across my back for I wanted him to mark me back, you see. Anyway, playtime come, and we went in the toilet and I said to the boys, 'Pull up my shirt. Have a look at me back. See what it's like.' So when they pulled up me shirt the said, 'Oh dear, you've got great weals across your back, like a finger.' Oh, I thought, that's alright, though my back was stinging all the time.

Anyway, I went home from school and my mother, she always used to stand in the gate, looking up the hill, every night when I was comin' home from school. An' when I come down, mother said, 'What's the matter with you, Arthur?' 'Well,' I said 'I've got a bad back, mother.' So I went in. Mother took my jacket off an' pulled me shirt up and when she seen these great weals on my back, she says, 'Who done that?' I said, 'The master.' Well, mother then was going round the kitchen working like twice her ordinary speed, like. And then, every now an' then, she was going out to the gate, looking up the road to see if father was coming. Well, eventually father came, and it was very seldom mother was out the gate when father come, an' seeing mother out there — father always used to call my mother 'dear'; 'Yes, dear,' 'No, dear,' he wouldn't speak to her otherwise. . . . So he said, 'What are you doing out here, dear?' Mother said, 'I've been waitin' here an hour for you to come 'ome from work.' 'Well, what's the matter?' 'Well,' mother says, 'when you come in, you'll see.' So mother showed father my back. Father said, 'Who done that?' 'The master up the school,' she said. Well, mother had father's supper cooked, like. She always used to have it on the table waitin' for when he came in, and father said, 'You put that in the oven, dear. I'll go up and see 'un before I 'ave me supper. Come on, Arthur,' he says, 'you go with me.' So we went up to the master's house. Father knocked on the door, and the master's wife come to the door, and she said, 'Hello, Mr Burley. How are you?' Well, father said, 'I haven't come here to inquire about health, I've come here to see your husband.' So she went in and told him he's wanted at the door. So when he came out he said, 'Good evening, Mr Burley.' Father said, 'While I've been waiting here for you to come out, I've noticed in your passage you've got a hall stand with walking sticks and umbrellas in there.' Now father said, 'I could break all they walking sticks and umbrellas around your back, but I aren't going to. But outside your gate is the king's highway, and when you go out there — it may not be tomorrow mornin', it might not be the mornin' after, it might yet not even be this week, but one mornin' when you go out — and you get down to the village, I shall be waitin' for you with a stick.' And he said, 'I'm going to beat you with a stick right up through the village and the women in the village'll all see me doing it.' So the master's wife come and said, 'What's the trouble, Mr Burley?' Well, father turned me round and showed her my back, and when she saw my back with all the weals on 'n, she said to her husband, 'You're not fit to have animals, talk about children.' And she went for her husband, hammer and tongs.

Anyway, the next night I was coming home from school and the master's wife was there waiting for me, and she asked me to come in. And when I went in, there was a gentleman there, an' he had a tape in his hand and she said, 'This gentleman is going to measure you for a new suit.' So he measured me, and then another night when I was comin' home I went in to try this new suit on, and 'twas the first suit I ever had with long trousers. It was a brown suit, and when I showed it to mother she said, 'This is far too good, Arthur, for you to wear to school. You'll have to keep this for going to chapel and Sunday school.' So, of course, I never wore the suit to school the next day. When Mrs Brown saw me in the ordinary things, she said, 'Where's the suit I bought you?' 'Oh,' I said, 'mother said he's too good for me to wear to school and I've got to keep it for Sundays and wear it to chapel and Sunday school.' So the following night coming home from school she called me in again, an' this gentleman measured me for another suit, and this time when I had the suit he was navy blue. So when I carried 'un home an' give 'un to mother, she said, 'This is better for you to wear on Sundays, navy blue.' She said, 'You'll look lovely in this one,' so I tried 'un on, and mother said, 'Oh yes, we'll keep that one for you to wear to Sunday school and chapel and you'll wear the brown one to school.' So I went to school the next day. Well, you'd think I was the schoolmaster, new white shirt on an' a tie, this lovely brown suit and a new pair of boots, like. And when I came into school, the master called me over to the desk. 'My dear Arthur,' he said, 'you're looking like a gentleman.' He said, 'I'll tell you what I'm going to do. I'm going to give you a class of boys to look after now every day.' And I never done no more sums, nor anything no more, all the time I went to school. All I had to do was to look after these boys.[56]

Children and parents were often themselves forced to resort to violence in order to resist some of the excesses of authoritarianism in schools. It must again be stressed that this resistance was not an expression of the intolerance and violent passion that many supporters and apologists of state schooling ascribed to working-class people but was instead the only immediate and effective means of opposition available to them and was rooted in family and neighbourhood loyalties. The most dramatic acts of resistance occurred when brothers, sisters and close friends attempted to protect each other from canings and struggled to restrain teachers in the classroom, while other children ran out into the streets and neighbouring houses to alert mothers and to rally reinforcements, as Bob Adams remembers:

Well, we 'ad one [teacher] an' he was a big pig, a sadistic pig. He delighted in rapping kids' knuckles if you weren't paying attention, daydreaming instead of writing. [Respondent bangs on the table.] 'Wake up, boy! Wake up, boy!' Anyway, one of my pals there, name was Been, he 'ad a younger brother, Arnold, in a lower class. And a kid rushed into our class an' said, 'Eh, Tommy Burrows i'n't 'alf 'itting your Arnold, Wilf.' So Wilf Been and Wilf Williams and me got out of our seats an' rushed into Tommy Burrows's class, and he was doing little Arnold. And we jumped on him and we had 'n down an' we was going, 'We'll have you! Leave our Arnold alone.' In the meantime someone had rushed round the next street, Walter Street, an' my mother was doing 'er washing. She was a tiny woman. She always wore my father's cap and a sack apron. She rolled 'er sleeves up, round the school, into the classroom, 'I'll kill you if you hit my son.' He'd hit both of us, marked us, wealed us, marked all our legs with the stick. We could 'ave sued the 'Education'. She sparred up to him. He was about five ten, six foot. [He] got behind the desk, out the way — he was ever so brave. And they kept us away from school for four days, both of us, because we were marked. It made me the worst boy in the class for hitting the teacher.[57]

Occasionally, this type of violent resistance exploded into sudden riots in the classroom or playground, which were quickly suppressed by the authorities, who summarily prosecuted any parents involved, as Ada Iles, recalling her schooldays in Edwardian Bristol, remembers:

The mothers used to come up an' play merry 'ell with the teachers for caning us. Another thing mothers'd go mad about was when we weren't allowed to go to the toilet an' we ended up wetting ourselves. Our Aunt Sally'd be up there all the time, 'cos she was poor but she never used to lay a finger on 'er girls, never. Once she came up and pulled 'er [the teacher's] hairpins out. Then she caught hold of 'er hair an' started to drag 'er out of the classroom and into the playground. Of course, we kids was enjoying every minute of it, shouting an' cheering, 'Go on, 'ave 'er!' And the kids in the other classes saw what was happening, an' they pushed their teachers aside an' ran out to join us. It was a proper riot. We was all shouting and screaming. Anyway, they got us back in eventually, an' Aunt Sally got summonsed, fined five pounds for that.[58]

Although parents faced certain arrest and prosecution for assaulting teachers or inciting school riots, explosions of resistance were often celebrated as moral victories and the assailants proclaimed as heroes by the local working-class community. Street collections would be made to pay the fines, and rosettes were worn by sympathizers in court or on the day of release from prison. Similarly, while children could expect severe punishment for their involvement in subversive activities, this was a small penalty to pay for a momentary triumph over school authority, which not only released deeply felt hostility but also was likely to make teachers more circumspect in their use of corporal punishment in the future. Mary Melhuish's memories of her Bristol schooldays in the 1900s vividly recreates the profound rift that developed between the working-class community and state schools.[59]

One day my sister got to school late and this German governess hit her. She fell on the pipes and had to have three stitches in her lip. Of course, the kids went home and told my dad. My dad went up there and he lopped her one. My dad had seven days' imprisonment for it. She had it out on me after when I used to go to school. Hit me across the legs with a cane and all like that. So anyway, we moved away from there and we went to Moorfields. And lo and behold, who do you think we've got for a governess? This bloody old governess. And I thought, no. I goes hom to my dad. I said, 'Dad, who do you think we've got for a governess?' He said, 'I don't know'. I said, 'Miss Davey.' He said, 'Now, don't you say anything to her. Take no notice of her. Don't do anything.' So anyway, the woman next door has got a boy going to the same school. This governess picks this little boy out. Of course, this woman drinks a lot. She goes up to the school; she hits her; she pays her blind. She got fined twenty pounds for assault. All the women made a collection, then went and fetched her out of prison with rosettes and white hats on. One morning it was snowing and it was ever so cold. And she hit one little kid right across the legs. So we couldn't stick that. So I says to all the kids, 'Come on, let's have a go at her.' And we did. We snowballed her and all. And she had a wig. We ripped her wig off, rubbed her head in ice balls and threw her into this big bin and we shut the door up. And, of course, the school head, or whoever it was, comes down and he says, 'What's going on here?' I said, 'She's been so cruel to us all that we chucked her in the bin.'[60]

To conclude, the intensity of resistance to schooling recollected by old people whose reminiscences have been cited in this chapter cannot be explained merely in terms of a volatile anti-authoritarianism, characteristic of rough sections of the working class. Instead, their testimony must be seen as evidence of a violent class conflict over the form of education that working-class children should receive. Opposition to the authoritarian and bureaucratic form of rational state schooling was rooted in three principal grievances. Its compulsory nature threatened the domestic economy and survival of many families; its regimented and repressive form abused the fundamental personal liberties that most working-class parents accorded to their children; and its removal of character development and work from the community to a depersonalized and bureaucratic setting was widely felt to be an infringement of the customary rights of the family. The form of education preferred by parents is clearly illustrated by the local networks of dame schools, common day schools and private adventure schools that persisted throughout the nineteenth century and, by the 1860s, were providing an alternative education for approximately one-third of all working-class schoolchildren.[61] This enormous demand for private as opposed to public education is perhaps best illustrated by the fact that working-class parents in a number of major cities responded to the introduction of compulsory attendance regulations not by sending their children to provided state schools, as government inspectors had predicted, but by extending the length of their child's education in private schools.[62] Parents favoured these schools for a number of reasons: they were small and close to the home and were consequently more personal and more convenient than most public schools; they were informal and tolerant of irregular attendance and unpunctuality; no attendance registers were kept; they were not segregated according to age and sex; they used individual as opposed to authoritarian teaching methods; and, most important, they belonged to, and were controlled by, the local community rather than being imposed on the neighbourhood by an alien authority. This community control sometimes took the form of mutual aid, whereby the more affluent parents voluntarily paid higher fees in order to subsidize the education of poorer children. The threat these schools posed to the state was to a large extent overcome by the harassment and enforced closure of many of them in the late 1870s and 1880s, on the grounds that they provided an inadequate education.[63] The closure of these private schools not only illuminates the form of education demanded by many working-class parents; it also provides further evidence that the altruistic rhetoric that legitimized state schooling in fact disguised a repressive process of class control. It is not suggested that there was a simple conspiracy engineered by the ruling class, in which teachers and attendance officers acted as the NCOs of the state, to use schooling as a weapon to mould the minds of the subordinate class and to bind them to existing structures. Indeed, the teaching profession was from its inception dissatisfied with a mere child-minding or control function and strongly supported an extension of educational opportunities for the working class within the state system. However, what is at issue is not a conspiracy but the logic of a particular set of social relations and social structure. The authoritarian and bureaucratic form taken by the emerging state schooling system was clearly instrumental in perpetuating, reproducing and legitimizing capitalist social relations. Some of the key elements in this process were the enforcement of a time-oriented and depersonalized organization of work, regular and punctual attendance, obedience to authority and the severe punishment of any form of behaviour that did not conform to the demands of the regimented school routine. When viewed from this perspective, the occasional or persistent truants, the children who disrupted lessons and protected classmates from punishment and the parents who threatened or assaulted teachers must be seen to have been involved in a fierce class-cultural struggle over the form of social relationships that were to prevail in schools. Their resistance was rooted in a powerful residual tradition that found expression in the small private school and clung to the belief that learning and work should spring from the needs of the individual, the family and the community, not the authoritarian demands of an essentially bureaucratic institution.

CHAPTER 4

School Strikes

Pupils and Parents Protest

When I was a lad of ten I used to work after school hours as a lather boy in my elder brother's barber's shop. Now, the barber's shop was a real meeting place for men, where they'd talk about all aspects of life, and sometimes they'd have a big laugh talking about the school strike that they had in their school days. I know the genuine story because I used to hear it from all the different men that were in it. My elder brother was a very popular young man, real extrovert, and it was him who was the ringleader of the strike at Southall Street school, along with two other lads who were brothers. They used to say it began at first as a mischievous adventure, but deep down they were very serious about the abolishment of the strap and cane. You see, the teachers at that time, without any doubt, were sadists. They ruled with fear. They firmly believed in the adage that kids were to be seen and not heard. All they needed was the least excuse — if you were one minute late, if you weren't sitting upright, or if you had dirty hands, they'd cane you without mercy. Now when the boys went on strike, they demanded the abolition of the cane, and they also wanted a shilling a week to be paid to the monitors, because they were just used as lackeys. On the big day they met outside the school, over three hundred of them, and they marched to a field opposite the gaol walls of Strangeways. Then they marched along the main road, singing their battle parodies, and threw some stones at the school windows. The strike lasted for three days, but eventually they gave up and returned to school, and all the classes were lined up in the main hall to witness the punishment of the ringleaders as a lesson to them. My brother said they were held over a desk by their outstretched hands and caned on their bottoms. Now, one of the brothers put a plate inside his trousers, and the blow of the cane broke the plate into pieces, badly cutting the lad's bottom. But they come unstuck with my brother. He was a really big chap and fearless. When it came to his turn, he took the teacher by surprise, wrenched the cane from his grasp and started hitting him with it, then, like lightning, he ran out of the school and home. In the evening, when father came home from work, my brother told him

90

about the canings, and the next morning he went up to the school with him. He was an exceptionally strong man, my father, over six foot tall, and he told the headmaster he didn't approve of the beatings that were carried out at the school, because a lot of the parents were angry when their children told them about the punishments. And he gave the headmaster a strict warning that if anyone dared apply any punishment to his son Jack, then he would go up and mete out far worse to the one responsible. If his lad did anything that required punishment, they were to send a note and he would deal with his son by his own disciplinary methods.[1]

The most dramatic and subversive act of resistance to schooling was the pupils' strike. Larry Goldstone's memories of the revolt of Manchester schoolchildren in September 1911 illustrate a number of recurring features of children's strikes, which periodically disrupted the elementary school routine in many parts of Britain from 1889 onwards. This form of pupil protest was a collective response to severe provocation by teachers or education committees and was characterized by demonstrations and meetings to enlist both the support of children in neighbouring schools and parental sympathy and to encourage solidarity; harsh repressive measures were taken by the education authorities to crush further resistance. Recently, a few of these strikes have been rediscovered; for example, the nationwide protest of schoolchildren in 1911,[2] the wave of Herefordshire school strikes[3] and the creation of an alternative strike school at the village of Burston, Suffolk, in 1914.[4] However, because such strikes were a source of acute embarrassment to teachers and education authorities, they were often conveniently forgotten and omitted from the pages of punishment books, committee minutes and official school histories, and it is only by listening to the reminiscences of people involved that we can discover the true nature and extent of this type of resistance. By scanning the press and by speaking to and corresponding with elderly people, I have discovered strikes at over a hundred other schools between 1889 and 1939, a few of which continued for periods ranging between several weeks and eighteen months. The memories of former participants are especially valuable, for they reveal a much more complex set of motives than is indicated by contemporary press reports, which normally dismissed school strikes as expressions of ignorance, indiscipline and precocious childish misbehaviour. Although most of the strikes were quickly suppressed, they were not quickly forgotten by the participants. Photographs of the strikers were often displayed in local pubs; stories of strikes such as the one remembered by Larry Goldstone were for many years recounted in families, shops and workplaces;

and this powerful oral tradition occasionally inspired further acts of resistance against authority.[5] For the school strike was essentially a defiant gesture of protest by working-class children and their parents against the authoritarian, bureaucratic and centralized structure of schooling that increasingly wrenched control of education away from the local community and geared its organization to the demands of a capitalist state.

To understand the dynamics of these strikes, it is useful to distinguish the several important features of school organization over which local working-class communities struggled to assert control. Opposition focused upon the key issues of corporal punishment, regulations concerning school hours and holidays and the school-leaving age, the provision of free education and welfare services and the payment of scholars, the appointment of teachers, the location and organization of the school itself. The underlying conflict on these five issues was occasionally liable to explode into strikes of pupils and parents against the education authorities. Although school strikes were sometimes motivated by a combination of grievances, it is necessary, for the purposes of analysis, to deal with each broad area of contention separately.

First, we will examine school strikes that were protests against the irregular or excessive infliction of corporal punishment. Such strikes were invariably instigated by pupils and tended to be of extremely short duration, rarely persisting for longer than a week and more commonly collapsing after only a few hours as a result of the coercive action of a combination of schoolteachers, attendance officers and police. This militant activity originated either as an isolated protest against the brutality of an individual teacher or as part of the nationwide wave of school strikes demanding the abolition of corporal punishment that occurred in 1889 and 1911.

Sporadic strikes are extremely difficult to document because teachers, anxious to protect their school's reputation for efficient instruction, often refused to acknowledge the existence of strikes and instead recorded them as instances of extensive truancy. Usually these isolated strikes failed to achieve their aims and resulted only in the severe and summary punishment of the participants, as Les Kenyon, recalling a strike provoked by the caning of an older boy at Gaskell Street school, Bolton, in 1914, remembers:

I remember going on strike at school . . . over Mr Fenhall giving one of the lads stick, and round fourteen mark then, you see — I were getting ready for leaving. And he were cock at school. He were boss at school. And he'd had stick, he said, for something, for nothing, so he got us all to go on strike. And we went back to school at dinnertime, and then when whistle blew were about a dozen of us went on Mere Hall Park, and we stayed there till Mr Fernhall, Mr Smith and Mr Roshill came to school and brought us all in, and we all got four raps apiece and our name in black book. . . . Soon as they knowed we weren't in class they were all up for us. And soon as we saw 'em, well, we were all shaking. Wonder what we're going to get at t'other end. . . . We got four raps, and we got 'em off Mr Smith in his office, and they were real corkers. You blew your hands when you'd had 'em.[6]

Occasionally, however, strikes such as the following one, which occurred in Manchester in 1924, succeeded in bringing the assaults of assistant teachers on children to the attention of sympathetic headmasters, who subsequently exercised more rigorous control over the irregular forms of corporal punishment inflicted in their schools.

One of the boys had been sent out into the corridor for misbehaving, and this teacher come along. 'What are you doing here Hannam?' 'Oh,' he said, 'Mr Smith has sent me out 'cos I've been misbehaving myself.' He said, 'Oh, well, you'd better go to the headmaster then, hadn't you?' Well, it wasn't his place to tell him to go to the headmaster, 'cos he wasn't his pupil. Well, this lad wouldn't go, and he [the teacher] thumped him in the stomach, said he was being cheeky. And he was seen by one of the boys in the classroom, and we all went on strike over it. First, at lunchtime we went up to the headmaster's office, but he'd gone for lunch, so when I got back (I used to go home for my lunch), the boy that was organizing the strike, he come up to me and said, 'Spence, we're going on strike. Are you with us?' I said, 'Yes, I'm with you, I'm with you.' And we went on the hills. . . . we played all sorts of games up on the hills and kicked a ball about, and we were out for over two hours. . . . And anyway, eventually we agreed to go back, providing there were no repercussions, providing nobody was to get caned or anything. And we went into the headmaster's office. He said, 'Well, I appreciate you boys standing together and working for one another, but you shouldn't take the law into your own hands. You should have come to my office and told me about it.' So I said, 'We did do, but you weren't available. You weren't there.' I remember when we got back into the classroom the teacher said, 'Who was on strike?' So I put my hand up and one or two more. 'So you were one of the heroes, were you, Spencer?' But that teacher never used the cane again. He got admonished for it.[7]

Whereas these isolated protests often passed unrecorded in the official records, the nationwide waves of school strikes in 1889 and 1911 aroused widespread public interest and concern. The 1889

Key
▲ 1889
● 1911
■ 1889 & 1911

■ Aberdeen

Dundee   Montrose
   Alyth   ▲ Forfar
Blairgowrie ▲
Dunfermline Pitlessie ■ Broughty Ferry
Clydebank Kirkaldy
Dumbarton ● Cowdenbeath
Greenock   Broxburn Leith
Port Glasgow   ▲   Dunbar
Stevenston   ● Edinburgh
Ayr   West   ▲ Berwick
Kilmarnock   Calder Galashiels
   Airdrie   Hawick
Paisley   Glasgow

   Blyth

   Newcastle Jarrow
Dearham   Gateshead ■ Sunderland
Workington ▲   Hartlepool
Harrington ▲   ▲ Stockton
Whitehaven   Bishop Auckland ▲ ■ Middlesborough
   Darlington

Barrow ●

   York
Blackburn Bradford ●
Oswaldtwistle   ● ■ Leeds   Hull
   Halifax   Goole
Bolton   ● Barnsley
Holyhead   Manchester ▲ Oldham   Grimsby
Birkenhead ■   ● Sheffield
Liverpool Runcorn Hyde Shirebrook
Stockport   Ashton-under-Lyne
Stoke-on-Trent ●   ● Nottingham
   Derby ●
Burton-on-Trent ●   Grantham
   Leicester ●
Birmingham ●   ■ Peterborough
Coventry ●
   ■ Northampton

Llanelli ●   ■ Colchester
Swansea ●   For details of London
   Cardiff   see separate map
   ■ Bristol   London

Southampton ●   Portsmouth ●   Folkestone ●

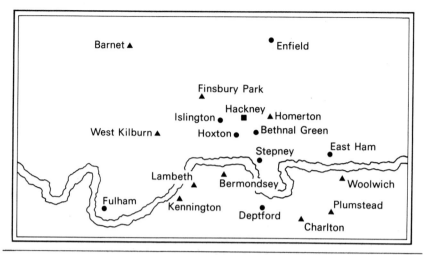

Nationwide school strikes, 1889 and 1911, London area.

school strikes originated in Hawick, Roxburgh, at the beginning of October and rapidly spread throughout the Scottish lowlands, the Tyneside area and as far south as London, Bristol and Cardiff.[8] The 1911 strike began at Bigyn School, Llanelli, on 5 September, when pupils deserted their classrooms and paraded the streets after a boy was punished for passing around a piece of paper urging his friends to strike.[9] During the following two weeks the strike spread to schools in over sixty major towns and cities throughout Britain. (For details of places affected by the 1889 and 1911 school strikes, see the maps.)[10] It is illuminating to contrast the explanations of the origins and nature of these strikes offered by educationalists and journalists with the accounts of old people who themselves participated in them. For while the caricatures and condemnations that recurred in strike reports were merely crude, common sense simplifications of the mass culture and cultural deprivation theories we examined in chapter 1, the memories of former participants clearly suggest a class-based explanation for the strikes.

The rapid diffusion of strikes in both 1889 and 1911 was viewed by most commentators as a consequence of the conformity, gullibility and unlimited capacity for blind imitation of working-class children and youth. This claim was substantiated by the fact that most major school strikes tended to occur at times and places at which parents were engaged in either local or national strike action and by the sensational publicity given to the children's

Nationwide school strikes, 1889 and 1911, excluding London.

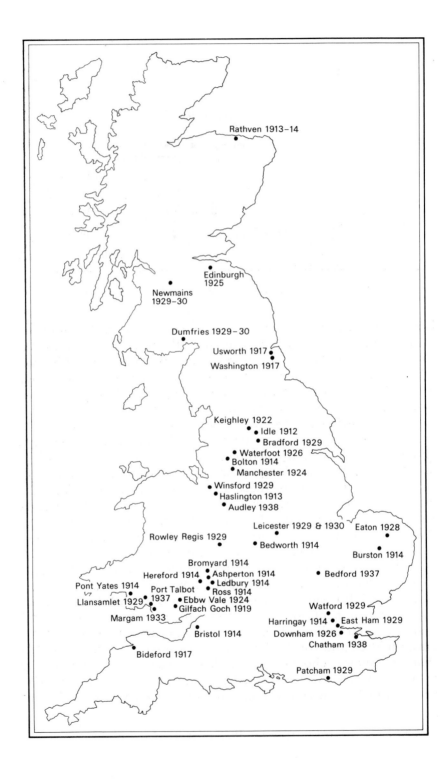

Rathven 1913–14

Edinburgh 1925

Newmains 1929–30

Dumfries 1929–30

Usworth 1917
Washington 1917

Keighley 1922
Idle 1912
Bradford 1929
Waterfoot 1926
Bolton 1914
Manchester 1924
Winsford 1929
Haslington 1913
Audley 1938

Leicester 1929 & 1930   Eaton 1928
Rowley Regis 1929
Bedworth 1914   Burston 1914

Bromyard 1914
Hereford 1914   Ashperton 1914   Bedford 1937
Pont Yates 1914   Ledbury 1914
Port Talbot   Ross 1914
Llansamlet 1929   1937 Ebbw Vale 1924   Watford 1929
Margam 1933   Gilfach Goch 1919
                                    Harringay 1914 East Ham 1929
Bristol 1914   Downham 1926
                                    Chatham 1938
Bideford 1917

                         Patcham 1929

activities by the popular press. Thus, the editor of the *Educational News* in 1911, for example, confidently assured his readers that

the cause . . . is easy to find. Men tired of work . . . strike. 'Striking' conversations are meanwhile carried on in their homes to the detriment of all else. Naturally, children are possessed of powers of . . . imitation, waiting only to be called into play. . . . Hence 'strikes', being the fashion with adults, become likewise that of the juveniles. The daily press has done much to spread the epidemic; for instead of paying little heed to the pranks of the scholars in one or two towns, has published full details . . . and a real game of 'Follow the Leader' has been the result.[11]

However, oral evidence indicates a more subversive explanation for school strikes, one that is related to deep-rooted class conflict. The characteristic features of both these major strikes — notably their nationwide scale, the widespread use of pupil pickets and street marches and demonstrations — were all derived from the practices of the emerging labour movement. Interviews clearly reveal that working-class children learned strategies of collective bargaining and resistance from the parent culture and practised them at moments when they seemed most likely to succeed — moments when the local working-class community was locked in industrial conflict.[12] And although sensational press reports did indeed act as the principal agency of transmission for information concerning the strikes, most of the participants were inspired by more serious motives than the infantile foolishness and frivolity attributed to them by journalists. For, as Joe Hopwood remembers, the bitter experience of regular canings led many children to resort to strike activity in the hope that it might prove to be as powerful a weapon in the hands of pupils as it was for parents in securing fundamental rights, such as the abolition of corporal punishment.

The teachers was hard in they days. They did cane you just for a little mistake in your work, you know. I've still got a mark on me finger where the teacher caned me. Well, there was a lot of fathers out on strike in Bristol in 1911. And on my way to school I saw on the content bill outside the newspaper shop: 'The London Schoolchildren on Strike For No Cane.' I run down the lane into the playground an' started it. 'Come on, out on strike! Come on up the top an' see the bill.' And they all see'd it an' there was forty or fifty of us, and we all marched out of St Silas round the other schools to get the others out, singing an' shouting. We were going to get

Localized outbreaks of school strikes.

everyone out, then bide out 'til they says, 'No more cane.' But they locked
'em in by the time we arrived. It didn't work, so then we said, 'Come on,
we'll go back.' That was the only time I remember playing truant, on that
strike. We thought it might have done good, but it didn't. It done worse.
They were just more determined. We got back 'bout twelve an' the
headmaster lined us all up, 'Come on, hold 'em out!' an' we 'ad three of the
best on the hand.[13]

A misconception closely related to that of the gullibility and
conformity of working-class youth, which we have seen recurring
in the literature on the culture, was the assumption that many
young people were precocious and amoral because of inadequate
adult control and guidance. As a consequence, school strikes were
frequently viewed as an expression of anti-social, adolescent
rebelliousness, aggravated by the pernicious influence of delinquent
ringleaders. The rising tide of rebellion against school authority
was associated with a deterioration in the manners and morals of
the younger generation, which in turn was often attributed to the
increasing moral laxity of working-class parents, improved social
conditions and 'progressive' teaching methods. These charges were
widely interpreted, particularly in moments of industrial crisis
such as 1889 and 1911, as a threat to the preservation of social
order, necessitating an immediate reassertion of authoritarian
control. Such fears are vividly expressed in the following extracts
from a series of editorials on school strikes in the *Educational News*
of October and November 1889, which clearly illustrate how social
concern with the morals of the younger generation can be
reformulated as class-cultural control and how the ubiquitous
concepts of disobedience and rebelliousness can be reformulated as
class resistance:

Schoolboy strikers . . . are simply rebels. Obedience is the first rule of
school life. . . . School strikes are therefore not merely acts of disobedience,
but a reversal of the primary purpose of schools. They are on a par with a
strike in the army or navy. . . . They are manifestations of a serious
deterioration in the moral fibre of the rising generation. . . . It is a matter of
grave moment to the community that those about to join its industrial
ranks should enter on the duties of life with habits of mind adapted to the
requirements of the social hive, where obedience, zeal, and devotion to

*An illustration of schoolchildren on strike, marching through the streets of
London to demand the abolition of corporal punishment. The picture appeared in
the* Graphic *in October 1889. This clash with the school authorities was not as
peaceful and good-humoured as the drawing suggests.*

duty are indispensable to the success of the individual as well as to the welfare of the public. School strikes . . . are the direct result of that sickening sentimentality which has of late become the fashion. . . . Corporal punishment by anyone below the highest rank is now practically an assault. . . . It is difficult to believe that parents, as a body, are wholly innocent in the matter. In any case, the movement is one that bodes their authority no good. If the children are setting their teachers at defiance with the connivance of their elders, they are learning a lesson that may, ere long, prove as inconvenient at home as it now does in school; and if they are acting in disregard of their parents they are displaying an absence of home discipline that is but another proof of the folly of sparing the rod. The rod is the sure cure for strikes. . . . The ringleaders are probably few in number — not more than half a dozen in any school. It should be the business of the teacher to find them out and expel them. They will prove dangerous centres of moral contamination wherever they have the opportunity of posing as heroes. . . . Freed from their presence, their erring dupes would speedily forget their folly and settle down to work.[14]

This type of alarmist fear that strike action to abolish corporal punishment was genuinely subversive did have some foundation, for, as we have seen in previous chapters, the cane was an instrument of crucial importance in the battle to maintain control in the classroom. In 'rough' neighbourhoods the school strike was merely an extension and escalation of pupils' day-to-day resistance against school authority, and when rumours of local strikes were circulated, it required only a minor triggering incident for disaffection from school to explode into militant action. This intense conflict is illustrated in Len Etherington's recollections of his involvement in the Hull school strikes of 1911, when children enjoyed their momentary freedom (from school) and expressed their disregard for respectable manners and morals by bathing naked in the River Humber.

Lord only knows what present-day parents would say about the punishments of those days. Six of the best on each hand wasn't uncommon for some of the bad lads, and we really had some bad ones in that school. It was very rough. I was a pupil at Scarbro Street school and would have been twelve years old when the strike started. Someone said that the kids at West Dock Avenue school were on strike about canings and that we

---

The 1911 school strike in London. Young ringleaders prepare to picket the entrance to Bath Street School under the surveillance of two policemen and a photographer.

ought to join them, so we did. Our class had been to woodwork at Constable Street school that morning, and we were always allowed to return to our school a little later in the afternoon. As a result, we — about thirty of us, all boys, of course — were outside the school gates while the rest were already in class, and it was then that our strike started. We started shouting, and I remember one of the teachers coming to the gate and telling us to behave and get into school, and when nobody responded, he made a sudden rush and grabbed a couple of lads by the scruff of the neck and marched them into school. That did it. Somebody said, 'Let's go on Humber Bank,' so off we went to the river bank, where there was a stone slope to the water between St Andrews Dock and the old Riverside Quay. . . . How we got there, a crowd of thirty or so unruly lads, without being stopped beats me! Our school was always great on swimming because it was largely made up of trawlermen's families, and though we had neither trunks nor towels, being just a bunch of uninhibited kids, we just stripped off and in we went. Then it happened. Someone had spilled the beans to a local news reporter, and he and a photographer arrived on the scene and took our picture, which we thought was great fun. We went home about four o'clock as usual and all went well till after tea. Then a nosey neighbour walked in with a copy of the evening paper, and there, as large as life, was yours truly in the middle of the picture, completely starkers. That was really awful in those days, and I got a belting and was sent straight to bed without any supper.[15]

The final and familiar concept frequently used to explain school strikes was that of the aimless and gratuitous violence of working-class children and youth. The vandalism, the violent attacks on school property and the street battles with the police that were a common feature of many strikes were attributed by the press to delinquents, truants and street gangs, who, it was assumed, instigated the militant action.[16] According to the investigators of the *School Board Chronicle* in 1889, this violence was inspired not by any strongly felt grievance but by a sheer joy in destructive, anti-social activity, for it was claimed that 'on inquiry the strikers do not seem to know why they are on strike and they assign no reason whatever for their uproarious conduct.'[17] This blissful ignorance of the purpose of the strike was explained in the same journal as a consequence of the violent recruiting tactics of the strike leaders — 'the coercion used by the ringleaders, by means of sticks and whips, have brought considerable numbers to their ranks.'[18]

Although oral interviews confirm the official view that the majority of militants comprised truants, delinquents and street-gang leaders, they give no support to the widespread opinion that the strikers indulged in aimless violence and brutality. It was understandable, of course, that those children who were the principal victims of corporal punishment in schools should form the bulk of those who protested most strongly for its abolition. And in these circumstances the ritual smashing of school windows in many localities by the stone-throwing of the assembled strikers was clearly of profound expressive significance, releasing the victimized children's hostility and desire for revenge against the authorities. But more important was the instrumental value of violence, for interviews reveal that the strikers were forced to resort to threats, intimidation and physical force in order to recruit children to the cause, to maintain pupil solidarity, to assert their demands and to resist physically the coercive strike-breaking methods of teachers and the police. The strategic importance of violence is clearly illustrated in Bernard Dennison's recollections of his involvement in militant activities during the Hull school strikes of 1911:

I think St Charles, my school, was the first school to strike against the cane. They teachers were strict disciplinarians. They had to be with a school full of tough lads. My brothers and I went to school in the morning, but on going back at twenty past one, four of the older big lads were standing at the top end of Prynne Street and threatened to punch our faces in if we dared go back to school. So we didn't dare go in. All the boys hung around together until after half-past one, then the militants went in with their demands. Some of the boys started kicking on the wood door, but we got no response. So we marched off and went to the Girls' Christ Church School, John Street, and we flung the hats and coats hanging in the doorway on to the pavements. Then we marched to Fountain Road school and got into the playground just as the boys and girls were coming out to play, and we tried to bring them out on strike, but the teachers realized what was happening, so they rushed out with their canes and started belting into the strikers. Then we marched off to attack Adelaide Street school. The school door was near to the pavement but it was locked, so we thumped and kicked it and eventually the headmaster appeared. But nobody would listen to him speak and somebody threw a stone at him. Then he slammed the door and bolted it tightly. After that we marched off to the Humber foreshore and had a paddle in the Humber, then I made my way back home.[19]

Although children who despised school work enthusiastically joined the ranks of the strikers, interviews suggest that some strike leaders were in fact successful school pupils or were the sons and daughters of socialists and militant trade unionists. This socialist presence in school strikes was also detected by the popular press — for example, in October 1889, when a correspondent of the *Pall*

Mall Gazette noted that the 'four or five hundred boys who marched through the streets in the neighbourhood of Bethnal Green making the street echo with their cries of "No more cane" were headed by a couple of boys carrying . . . red flags and wearing scarlet liberty caps.'[20] Indeed, in Dundee, which experienced the most prolonged and disruptive school strikes in Britain in both 1889 and 1911, involving several thousand pupils, the local press suspected that the children's uprising was part of a wider left-wing conspiracy to subvert the social order — a fear clearly expressed in the doom-laden warnings of the *Dundee Advertiser*:

It has not yet been ascertained through what medium schoolboys received the signal for united action. . . . Such movements as this do not spring up spontaneously. They are always evidence of a deep conspiracy against social order. . . . It is perfectly evident that the schoolboys from Land's End to John o' Groats could not without organization arrange to strike simultaneously. The doom of the Empire must be near at hand if the country is honeycombed . . . with Secret Societies of schoolchildren. . . . It is not astonishing to find the leaders of the Jacobite party expressing sympathy with the schoolboys in revolt, and it would not be a matter for wonder if it should turn out that the separatist press has been made the medium through which the signal for the strike has been carried over the length and breadth of the land.[21]

Of course, these fears were grossly exaggerated, yet although there is little evidence of adult socialist involvement in school strikes, the young militants did receive some trade union support. For example, on 11 October 1889 the chairman of the London school board received an urgent demand from the Street Masons, Paviors and Stone Dressers' Amalgamated Union informing him that

a meeting of the schoolboys of Kennington and Lambeth met on the Albert Embankment today. Unless the demands are granted they will keep away from school: — free education; one free meal a day; no home lessons; no punishment (by caning). The boys and girls will meet at the same place later on and parade the streets and extend it to the whole of London. A speedy answer will oblige.[22]

In fact, the letter was 'received amidst laughter', and the London strikes, like those in other parts of Britain, were quickly suppressed.[23] The violent response of the authorities, which in 1889 included public birching or committal to the workhouse for some strike leaders, serves to emphasize the value of situating school strikes within a context of class as opposed to generational conflict.

For the majority of working-class parents did not share the school authorities' moral condemnation of the strikes. Many parents viewed them as a fairly innocuous form of larking about, while in some areas, especially where the strikers combined other demands such as the abolition of school fees and the payment of monitors with their opposition to the cane, the militants received enthusiastic support from mothers in the streets.[24] And although the angry mothers who escorted strikers back to school enjoyed considerable publicity, their action was often prompted by fear or by threats of summonses against parents for the non-attendance of their children.[25] The contrast between the severe retribution administered by schools and the relatively lenient approach of parents can be seen in the memories of Bernard Dennison, who escaped punishment at home, despite the fact that he was discovered to have concealed his involvement in the strike from his disapproving mother.

Several women, including my mother, were out in the street talking about the strike, and they asked me if I'd been one of the strikers. I said 'No.' My mother said, 'I thought he wouldn't be a striker.' It seemed I was safe because my mother could give a good hiding if it was necessary. Now the funniest part of the story is that about a fortnight after the strike one of my older brothers, who was a lemonade salesman, served the Rose Bush House and saw a photograph of the strikers which had been taken by the pub landlord, and he had had it enlarged. And there, slap bang in the front row, was one of my brothers, with his head and shoulders almost into the camera, and I was in the middle of the group. Well, we were cross-examined about the strike, but my brother and I still denied being in it, then my older brother produced the photograph. We were stunned. We couldn't keep our lie any longer, so we had to admit being out on strike. So all our family had a good laugh about how we'd been caught out. But it was different at school. The day after the strike the headmaster had us out one by one and gave us a rap of the cane on each hand, and he had the ringleaders out bent over the desk, and they had to have four strokes across their backsides. And, strange as it may seem, after our sentences were meted out the strike was hardly ever mentioned again.[26]

Interviews suggest that brutal canings acted as an effective deterrent and that the memory of these savage reprisals helped considerably in discouraging any future attempts to stage a nationwide strike. Even Clyde Roberts, a West Indian youth with a local reputation for physical strength and tenacity who led the 1911 school strikes in Cardiff's dockland area, was frightened into submission by the beating he received from his schoolmaster.

Somalis National [School], in Bute Terrace, I'm going there. And I led 'em out on strike. I led the school out on strike. I was supposed to be the ringleader. So we marches down to North Church Street school, trying to get them out. Anyhow, when we got back, we had a schoolmaster, name was Mr Hobbs, so I got singled out. And he said to me, he said, 'I'm going to put the fear of God into you.' He did. There was a boy [on] each of the arms, legs, over the desk, and he didn't half whack me. . . . He was the only schoolmaster that I can say I was frightened of. I was dead scared of him after that lot.[27]

So far we have focused on school strikes that sought to abolish corporal punishment. There were also a number of strikes that aimed to reduce the amount of time that children were compelled to spend attending to their lessons by agitating for reduced school hours, extended holidays or a lowering of the school-leaving age. Often these demands, the most common of which were a shortened school day from 10 a.m. to 3 p.m., one free afternoon a week, an eight-week summer vacation and no homework, emerged as subsidiary claims of militants during the nationwide anti-caning strikes of 1889 and 1911.[28] But in a number of instances strikes were staged specifically to achieve a reduction in school hours, and although such demands met with repressive measures similar to those administered to children who wished to abolish the cane, a well-argued case for moderate reform occasionally received a sympathetic hearing. For example, Joseph Proctor, who together with some other members of the St Paul's school football team in Oswaldtwistle, Lancashire, went on strike in 1911, remembers that despite severe chastisement, his headmaster was impressed by his written statement that sport should be played in school hours.

We read about the strike of schoolboys in the paper, so at dinnertime the elder boys amongst us decided to strike in sympathy. After dinner about twenty of us went parading the streets with a home-made banner that we made out of a placard from a newspaper shop fastened to a broom handle we borrowed from a hardware shop. We never got the chance to go to other schools, though that was our intention, because we were rounded up so quickly and returned to our teacher, Mr Wilson. He gave us three of the best on each hand. Also, we had to stay after school and write an essay on it and our views on strikes. The cane was rarely used at our school and our strike was really for time off lessons twice a week to train for sports. It was mainly the sporty types in the football team who were involved. We would have liked to have an hour off in the afternoon because it was after school hours that we played our football matches with other schools. I remember in the essay I had to write I was strongly in favour of sport in school time instead of after school. The headmaster read it and saw me next day, and I had to rewrite my essay on separate pieces of paper. These were pinned up along the corridor of the school, so my essay must have been pretty good.[29]

The campaign for shorter school hours and the abolition of homework was not simply an expression of the perverse and wilful nature of children, as was assumed by some journalists and educationists. In fact, they can be seen as reasonable and justifiable claims, for homework was often impossible in the gloomy and overcrowded conditions that prevailed in most working-class homes, and the rote learning and regimentation that dominated the school day placed an intolerable burden on many children, already exhausted by the domestic chores, child-minding duties and part-time jobs that were necessary for family survival. Indeed, although most commentators insisted that the strikes should be ruthlessly suppressed, some admitted that they were perhaps a symptom of the psychological 'over-pressure' on children produced by the system of payment by results, whereby pupils were 'crammed' with facts by teachers in preparation for the annual inspection, so that their school would qualify for a government grant. The disruption caused by the 1889 school strikes was one minor factor that led to the abolition of this iniquitous system in the 1890s.[30]

Official regulations concerning school holidays were also a source of conflict between education authorities and the working-class community, which occasionally exploded into strike action. For state schools sought to impose increasingly standardized and uniform holiday periods throughout Britain, thereby reducing and regulating traditional festivals such as wakes, fairs and revels, which until the mid-nineteenth century were celebrated by different localities at different times of the year. These customary festivals not only posed a threat to the efficient functioning of local schools and industry; more seriously, the drinking, dancing and uncontrolled contact between the sexes that characterized them were widely viewed by the authorities as a corrupting influence on the children and young people who participated.[31] However, although these leisure traditions gradually became more restricted and more rigidly controlled, some working-class communities struggled to maintain local customs and traditional entertainments. For example, the attempt of the Bradford Education Authority to regulate local feasts in the area in the early part of the century met with resistance in the form of a school strike in the village of Idle, where pupils and parents wished to preserve the time-honoured Idle Feast. It was reported in *Education* in September 1912 that

Some time ago the Bradford Education Committee decided to discontinue the practice of closing the schools in the Idle and Thackley districts for two days at Idle Feast which commenced yesterday. This was much resented by the children who organized a strike. On Monday morning more than three-quarters of the scholars were absent from school, and those on strike, many of whom were supported by their parents, joyously paraded the district. When those who had gone to school came out for the play interval the strikers assembled outside and tried to persuade the blacklegs, as they were termed, to join them.[32]

While bureaucratic regulations such as these aroused widespread resentment, statutory increases in the school-leaving age were viewed even more seriously as a threat to the domestic economy of the working-class family. The desperation of poor families found expression in April 1914, when children and parents in Bedworth, Exhall and other villages in north-east Warwickshire resorted to strike action in order to resist the local authority's attempts to raise the school-leaving age from thirteen to fourteen. The struggle to assert community control over the duration of children's schooling persisted for several weeks and involved protest meetings, a petition signed by almost 6000 local people and a parentally supported pupils' strike. Militant action occurred in this particular area primarily because there was a huge demand for seasonal child labour in the locality, and to terminate the protest the education authority was forced to make a number of minor concessions, assuring parents that no children aged over thirteen from large families would be immediately prosecuted for non-attendance.[33] However, this type of strike was not always characterized by the clarity of purpose evident in the Bedworth revolt. For example, in October 1920 several hundred schoolchildren engaged in strike activity in the streets of Northampton after misinterpreting a local by-law prohibiting street trading among children under sixteen, which the pupils, together with their parents, believed would force them to remain at school until the age of sixteen.[34]

Another expression of poor families' dissatisfaction with compulsory attendance regulations was the demand, stressed in a number of school strikes, that parents and children should receive financial compensation for their extended education. Thus one of the claims made by some Scottish strikers in 1889 was that school fees should be abolished, and in the 1911 strikes many pupils argued that monitors should be paid small weekly sums.[35] There was much justice in this latter demand, for interviews reveal that in many understaffed schools older and more responsible pupils received little or no tuition themselves but were simply required to instruct and discipline groups of younger children. Charlie Dallimore remembers how anger at the exploitation of monitors led to a strike demanding their payment in St Jude's School in Bristol in 1914, which was repressed with such brutality that even his own stringently disciplinarian father was shocked by the inhumanity of the punishments.

Sam Brick, he was the ringleader. . . . He was a quiet chap, must have had trade unionism in his blood, got it from his father, I suppose. Well, it was a Friday. We was talking in the playground: 'We ought to go out on strike, threepence a week for monitors — we ain't doing this for nothing — and 'alf a day Wednesdays.' Well, in them days they used to carry news placards. Magic — find some of them. We turned them over and done writing on them. We agreed that when the Monday morning came we'd strike. Well, we was all outside the school on strike. It was mostly the older ones — I should say up to about a hundred of us. We then chased along to Hannah More school. We climbed up there, calling the kids to come out, like: 'We're on strike!' Anyhow, the teachers started chasing us away, so we chased from there up to St Barnabas, and they was all out in the playground. We got a couple of them to climb over, but that's all. It got round in the morning. The School Board and the Minister of St Jude's had gone round to tell the parents that the children's on strike, and as soon as I 'ad me dinner, me mother said, 'Come on back, you, come.' And when I were going down the street there were other kids coming along where their mothers had got hold of them. 'Course, they was threatened with summonses. It belonged to the church at that time, St Jude's Church, and they had a curate there, a great big strapping chap, Higgins his name was. . . . The next morning there was Higgins stood in there and the vicar. So the vicar gave a lecture about this striking business, how wicked we was and everything else, and ''Course, you can't go unpunished for a thing like that.' So he read out Sam Brick was the ringleader. 'Come out, Sam Brick.' He walks out and he was a big chap. Along comes this Mr Higgins. He had a cane, he was a beauty, oh, he was a proper one, and wallop! He had three on each hand. Now Sam Brick fainted on his last one. You could tell how he laid it in. They brought him round and sat 'im back. I come out in the next group, two on each hand. He'd catch you across the wrist and it swelled up immediately. Anyhow, my brother was in the next group, and when our Robert went up, Higgins looked at him and says, 'Did your Charlie take you out? Did you want to go?' 'Course, our Robert says, 'No, I didn't want to go out. 'Twas our Charlie, he made me go out.' 'Oh, did he? You go and sit down. Charlie Dallimore, come out again.' I had another one on each hand. I went home. Now, my father was a genuine bloke. Now, when he heard all about it, he started undoing the buckle of his belt 'cos that's what you 'ad in them days, the buckle on you. I said, 'Oh, God, don't hit me, dad,' I said. 'I've had enough.' He said, 'What do you mean? You haven't had enough by far. They ought to have taken thee down and birched thee.' I said, 'Look at my arms,' and he looked at it, me hands and me arms all swelled up. He said, 'My God, I'd like to have him here now, and I'd put the buckle into him.' He said, 'That's cruel.'[36]

Closely related to the widespread feeling among working-class people that compulsory schooling should not impose severe financial hardship upon families was the belief that free school meals should be provided, particularly in times of economic distress.[37] To achieve this aim a school strike was declared in the villages of Washington and Usworth in County Durham, where in 1917, because of prolonged half-time working in the local pits and high unemployment, many families were reported to be on the verge of starvation. A mass meeting of local miners held on 18 November 1917 unanimously resolved to instruct the children not to attend school until the local authorities implemented the Feeding of Necessitous School Children Act, whereby children suffering from malnutrition were entitled to free meals.[38] The following day over a thousand children from nine local schools responded to the strike call, thus risking corporal punishment, in a spirit of class solidarity that was remarked upon in the local press.

Those few children who did attend school — mostly the children of officials, shopkeepers and soldiers — were the subject of no little contempt and abuse. Yesterday the writer observed an incident near Usworth station illustrative of this attitude. A group of ragged boys was sitting on a fence, languidly throwing stones at a telegraph post across the way. Down the road came a more respectably dressed youngster across whose shoulders was slung a dilapidated satchel. As he drew near the lads on the fence he crossed to the opposite side of the way and with face half-averted and his hands stuck deep in his pockets, he began to whistle with affected nonchalance. The boys on the fence ceased their assault upon the telegraph post and when he came abreast of them they burst into loud, shrill shouts of abuse. 'Yah!' they cried. 'Blackleg!, Blackleg! Scallywag!' The object of their abuse proceeded onwards at a slightly accelerated pace and the boys on the fence with bewildering rapidity hurled a series of questions at his retreating figure. What did he mean by going to school? Hadn't he heard of the Lodge resolution? Was he afraid? Did he think he'd get wrong? Then altogether, 'Cowardly, cowardly-custard!' they yelled.[39]

Confronted by the fierce resistance from parents and children, the authorities conceded defeat on the second day of the strike, and miners' families were awarded increased financial assistance and relief from the Durham County Prince of Wales Fund.[40] Another way in which pupils and parents sought to assert community control over provided education was through strikes to support the retention of teachers whose position was threatened by local authority interference or to press for the dismissal of unpopular or incompetent teachers. The most prolonged and powerful strike action brought by pupils occurred in Herefordshire in 1914, when children supported the county's National Union of Teachers members' militant demands for salary increases. The children's resistance began at the beginning of February, when, in response to the union's strategy of mass resignations, the local education authority appointed new teachers, many of them unqualified, to replace those involved in the dispute. Pupils in towns and villages throughout the country expressed sympathy for their former teachers, who were among the lowest paid in the country, by refusing to be taught by the new members of staff, and seventy schools were forced to close. The most violent scenes occurred at Ledbury Girls' School, where a riot developed in which desks were overturned, and the new headmistress was chased off the premises by a crowd of girls chanting 'Blackleg'. And at Ross, although boys demonstrating in the town in favour of the strike were captured and locked inside the school, they retaliated by vandalizing the classrooms and escaping through some open windows. A bitter conflict ensued, in which the former members of staff enjoyed the enthusiastic support of pupils, parents, school managers and the press, and in the following weeks the Board of Education was forced to intervene to settle the dispute, successfully applying pressure on the Herefordshire education authority to reinstate the teachers and to award substantial salary increases.[41]

Another situation in which pupils and parents occasionally resisted education authority dictates was when economies in local government spending were made by dismissing members of staff considered to be superfluous. Married women were often the prime victims of these education cuts and were discharged indiscriminately on the grounds that they would suffer least personal hardship from the termination of their employment.[42] However, these measures aroused considerable resentment, and a strike was staged at Eastwood Council School, Keighley, Yorkshire, in September 1922 as a protest against the local council's decision to dismiss Mrs Belfield, the headmistress of the girls' department, who had taught in the town for over twenty years. Mrs Belfield had inspired the admiration and affection of the local community through her success in capturing children's interest in learning and through her involvement of parents in a variety of social and educational activities that revolved around the school.[43] The strike was the culmination of several months' agitation by the parents and pupils, who petitioned the local education committee and their Member of Parliament, then, receiving no satisfaction, resolved to strike on the day that the newly appointed headmistress was due to replace Mrs Belfield.[44] Although Mary Slater was just nine years old when the strike occurred, and was therefore only vaguely aware of its precise purpose, her recollections vividly recreate the militant atmosphere, with picketing girls threatening blacklegs with doffers' bumps — an initiation ceremony for young doffers practised in local worsted mills, in which the victim was lifted up by two assailants and banged on her bottom several times.

It was a well-run school at that time. It was considered one of the good schools, and Mrs Belfield was such a lovely headmistress. She was one of those kind, gentle sort of women. Everybody liked her. . . . Well, there'd been this talk about Mrs Belfield having to leave, but I was too young to bother about what it was all about, and that we'd be going on strike. All I can remember is going to school this particular morning, me and two more girls that I went with. We turned the corner into the street where the school was, Marlborough Street. It was absolutely chock-a-block with scholars, just crowded in the street. All the length of the school was thick with folk, pretty solid, and parents intermingled, mothers not fathers. We got right up to the front, us little ones. We all stood outside, and at the school railings there were quite a few boards tied on, 'We Want Mrs Belfield Back' and things like that, about not coming back 'til Mrs Belfield returned. Then I've just the vaguest recollection of seeing the school door open and somebody push somebody out, and then somebody said, 'What happens if anybody goes in?' And they said, 'Oh t'prefects are in there and they'll give 'em t'doffers bump and shove 'em out.' So this must have been somebody that had gone in that they'd shoved out.[45]

The strike collapsed on the second day, principally because of Mrs Belfield's strong disapproval of the action, the refusal of any boys or members of staff to participate in the protest and the promises made by the new headmistress that she would ensure that her staff did not inflict corporal punishment upon girls for acts of disobedience.[46] A similar strike occurred at Cwm Mixed School, Ebbw Vale, in March 1924, though in this instance direct action was taken as a protest against the decision of the local education committee to appoint an outsider as headmaster rather than promote Mr Bower, an extremely popular member of staff, to the vacant position. On 6 March pupils tied up the school gates, organized pickets and formed a procession. They wore badges and carried streamers bearing the inscription 'We want Mr Bower when

Mr Bedford leaves.' However, the protest proved to be ineffective.[47] Strikes that demanded the resignation of unpopular and despised teachers were more likely to succeed, for the prospect of prolonged hostility and harassment from pupils and parents was a source of acute embarrassment and concern to both the teacher and the local education authority. Ada Iles recalls one such strike in Fishponds, Bristol, in 1911, which resulted in the transfer of a teacher who was accused of inflicting unjust and unnecessary punishments upon pupils.

The strike started because of a teacher who was always down on the boys. When one of 'em was messing around in class, instead of finding out who it was an' making that person stop in 'alf an 'our, he'd keep the whole class in day after day. Well, there was a miners' strike on, an' George Hesketh said, 'We'll 'ave a strike. We won't go to school.' George was the ringleader, an' 'im an' about six other boys stopped by the gate an' stopped everybody from going into school for two days. Everybody was standin' outside the school refusing to move, an' they 'ad some talks, an' the Education Committee moved this teacher to another school . . . so we'd won an' everyone went back.[48]

The strikers' aims were not always radical, however; in 1917, for example, mothers and children in Bideford, North Devon, embittered and distressed by the deaths of their relatives in World War I, refused to accept a conscientious objector as a teacher in the Old Town School. Wilf Gammon recalls how the unfortunate schoolmaster was forced to leave after press reports of a tribunal that condemned his pacifist beliefs provoked a hostile response from the local community.

Most of the kids' fathers and brothers were away in the war — some had them killed — and we had this teacher, a Mr Guard, and he was a conscientious objector. And, of course, the kids didn't like it, and we went out on strike. We wouldn't go to school. We stayed out for about three days. He had to go before a tribunal, and when he was interviewed at the tribunal they asked him if in the case of the Germans coming to his house and attacking his wife and children, what would he do? Would he defend them? And he said no. And it must have got into the papers, and that's how it came about. Everybody knew about it. It was probably mothers who had husbands killed started it and it grew. . . . We had these pickets with boards up and it happened for three days. . . . Mr Guard left the school. The strike pushed him out.[49]

The final area of conflict with education authorities was the important issue of the location and organization of schools. Most of these strikes occurred during the inter-war period as a protest against the process of centralization and rationalization promoted by the Hadow Report, by which elementary schools were re-organized into age-segregated units, redesignated as infant, junior and senior schools.[50] The fundamental grievances that provoked these strikes were the local authorities' failure to consult parents or to consider their needs prior to the implementation of reorganization plans, the removal of children from schools situated within the local community to centralized units and, most important, the threat to the health and safety of children who were forced to walk long distances to their new schools, for in areas of economic distress, where many children were deprived of adequate food and clothing, parents were reluctant to allow them to walk several miles to school each day.

Many of these strikes occurred in rural districts, where the new centralized schools drew pupils from broad catchment areas. For example, for several weeks in the winter of 1938 parents in the village of Audley, north Staffordshire, prevented their children from attending the reorganized senior school at Halmerend, situated almost two miles away, a distance that required some children to set out at 7.30 a.m. each morning and to arrive home at 5.30 p.m. The parents concerned were summonsed by the local education authority, but the county magistrates dismissed the charges and ordered free transport to be provided after making investigations following a statement by one of the parents, Mr G. Swann, who appealed on behalf of all the strikers.[51] An extract from a report on his speech captures the feelings of resentment, rooted in the experience of poverty and inequality, that infused many of these strikes:

Mr G. Swann said the parents had gone on strike as a means of obtaining justice from the Education Committee whose attitude was unreasonable. There were many unemployed and poverty-stricken parents in Audley, which was a distressed area, and they could not afford to provide their children with proper clothing and boots to travel over bad roads in wet weather. They could not afford even the threepence a day which was required for a mid-day meal for the children, or to pay bus fares. The evidence of the parents was to the effect that they objected to the total distance of nearly four miles which the children had to walk to and from school, and also the dangers they had to encounter in the road. Some parents complained that their children were not sufficiently strong physically to make the double journey.[52]

Although most of these strikes originated as protests against decisions to remove children from their former neighbourhood schools, a few were motivated by more complex grievances. For example, the Rathven school strike, during which parents withdrew pupils from school for three weeks in the autumn of 1913 and four weeks in the spring of 1914, was provoked by the local education committee's refusal to build an elementary school in the village of Portessie on the Banffshire coast. Instead it merely agreed to make minor improvements to the dilapidated and overcrowded school that Portessie children attended in Rathven two miles away, which was in such an insanitary condition that Portessie parents believed it was responsible for the ill-health and premature death of their children.[53]

Whereas the pupils played an important role in staging many of the strikes we have discussed, parents normally assumed responsibility for the organization of protests concerned with the location and accommodation of schools. As a consequence of determined parental support, this type of school strike tended to continue for several weeks or more — much longer than those in which children were the main instigators. During these strikes working-class men and women who had no previous experience in public affairs were elected to sit on strike committees, raise funds, stage demonstrations and plan devious ways of avoiding attendance regulations without openly defying the law.[54] For example, the village shoemaker who organized a school strike at Eaton, Norfolk, in April 1928 devised the cunning strategy of escorting two different children to school each day in order to register their names, thereby ensuring a minimum attendance, which protected parents in the village from prosecution.[55] Strikes like this one, which ingeniously evaded the law, became so frequent that in September 1929 an editorial in the *Schoolmaster* commented:

for the last year or two the school strike has been always with us; it can almost be regarded as an inevitable by-product of reorganization. The earlier strikes were neither numerous nor particularly serious, and the exercise of reasonable firmness and patience was generally sufficient to enable the Authority concerned to overcome the difficulty. But with the passage of time and the general and intensive operation of the Local Authorities' programmes we are getting week by week more reorganization. As a consequence we appear week by week to be getting more strikes and, as their number grows, their difficulty also appears to increase.[56]

To estimate the exact number of strikes that occurred in response to reorganization plans would be a formidable task, for there were no general Board of Education investigations into the problem, and only an intensive search through local press and education committee reports throughout Britain would reveal the precise extent of the resistance. Although this is, of course, beyond the scope of the present study, I have so far managed to trace school strikes in which parents and pupils opposed reorganization and accommodation plans to the following village communities: Rathven (Grampian) and Pont Yates (Dyfed) in 1914; Gilfach Goch (Mid-Glamorgan) in 1919; Waterfoot (Lancashire) in 1926; Eaton (Norfolk) in 1928; Winsford (Cheshire), Llansamlet (Dyfed) and Patcham (Sussex) in 1929; Newmains (Strathclyde) in 1932 and 1933; and Audley (Staffordshire) in 1938.[57]

This type of school strike was not restricted to rural areas, however, for a number occurred in various towns and cities, where the main issues that provoked militant action were the excessive distances and danger from traffic to which children were exposed in attending reorganized schools. In addition, the transfer of pupils from neighbourhood to centralized schools disrupted the domestic arrangements of the working-class household, as long distances made it difficult for children to return home for a midday meal and restricted the time and energy available for child-minding duties and part-time jobs. As a result, strikes were organized in Harringay, London, in 1914; Edinburgh in 1925; Downham, east London, in 1926; East Ham, Watford, Bradford, Rowley Regis in 1929; Dumfries and Leicester in 1929 and 1930; Margam in 1933; Port Talbot and Bedford in 1937; and Chatham in 1938.[58] Although the number of parents and children involved in these strikes often dwindled when local education committees commenced prosecutions for non-attendance, direct action in both urban and rural areas often won concessions from the authorities, such as the provision of free dinners and bus services, and occasionally resulted in official submission to the strikers' demands. Many of the strikes deserve detailed case studies, which cannot be attempted here; however, one important point that emerges from these protests must be emphasized again. Strikes instigated by parents provide further evidence that children's resistance within schools can best be understood in terms not of generational conflict but rather of a broader class conflict, in which the working-class community became increasingly alienated from, and antagonistic towards, the bureaucratic state schooling system. Indeed, the contemporary press viewed these strikes precisely in this way, as expressions of a growing conflict between the local community and the school authorities, and there was widespread concern that the militant action of working-class parents would encourage children to follow their example of determined resistance to authority, which might have disastrous consequences. Thus, for example, the East Ham dispute — which extended from July to October 1929, involved hundreds of parents and over a thousand pupils and was only finally resolved through central government intervention — provoked Everybody's Weekly to comment:

There has never been a more iniquitous thing than the toleration of strikes by school children. This deplorable practice was begun a few years ago and now, at the least real or fancied wrong, out come the children. . . . At present the kids treat it as a rare lark. They get an extra holiday, they play at holding meetings, gain notoriety, enjoy hero worship from other children and get their photo in the newspaper. But what of the future? In the unmoulded minds of these children have been sown the seeds of discontent and the idea of active resistance to discipline which will lead to no end of trouble. In most cases they occur at the instigation and with the approval of the parents . . . who . . . should be made punishable by law.[59]

So far we have examined the origins, the nature and the consequences of several interrelated types of school strike. The final form of defence available to parentally supported strikers in their disputes with the education authorities was the formation of an independent strike school. Although this option was theoretically open to all dissatisfied parents, it was rarely attempted or achieved in practice, principally because of the enormous legal and financial difficulties that such action involved for people whose overriding concern was economic survival. However, in two strikes, those at Newmains and Burston, the local working-class community did manage to overcome these formidable obstacles and to establish alternative strike schools; its resistance must be briefly described here, for in many ways the schools represented the most subversive achievement of the school strike.

The Newmains strike began in January 1929, in opposition to the Scottish Education Department's policy of centralization, which in this instance involved the Lanarkshire Education Authority in transferring senior pupils from the mining village of Newmains to Beltanefoot school, Wishaw, over three miles away.[60] For eighteen months over 150 senior pupils and their parents stubbornly refused to comply with this directive, claiming that the long walk was a hazard to health and safety, that it undermined the domestic arrangements of many families and that it was an essentially bureaucratic measure that could easily be avoided by adapting the available space at Newmains school for the purpose.[61] There was a strong feeling that, as one protestor put it, 'the whole basis of the scheme was to provide highly paid posts for specialized teachers.' The professional classes were becoming the 'moochers on the industrial classes'.[62] The strike aroused the support and solidarity of the entire local community. Regular protest meetings and demonstrations were organized; sympathetic strikes of junior pupils at Newmains school and in the surrounding villages of Morningside and Cambusnethan were staged; and senior pupils, acting on parental instructions, occupied their former school after being refused admission.[63] Despite harassment from the local education authority and successful prosecutions against six parents, the villagers remained resolute, and their protest was finally vindicated in July 1930, when an inquiry by the Scottish Education Department recommended severe modification of the original scheme for the area and permitted first- and second-year senior pupils to remain at Newmains school.[64] One important strategy adopted in the dispute, which enabled parents to evade attendance regulations, to ensure a basic education for their children and to maintain militant action for a long period, was the formation of a strike school, staffed by five volunteers, in the local church hall.[65]

In contrast to the Newmains dispute, the Burston school strike and the pupils' and parents' formation of a strike school has been documented in much more detail. The strike originated as a protest against the dismissal of Annie and Tom Higdon from their teaching posts in the Suffolk village of Burston in the spring of 1914. The rector and school managers fabricated a number of charges against them, which included the brutal infliction of corporal punishment on two orphan children, who were pressurized into incriminating their teachers. This conspiracy was engineered by a group of local notables who sought to remove the Higdons from the village, for they were socialists and trade union activists, deeply involved in politicizing and unionizing agricultural labourers in the area.[66] However, both pupils and parents in the village were incensed by this victimization, and a strike, in which schoolgirl Violet Potter played a prominent role, was planned for the day on which the Higdons were due to be replaced by new members of staff. In an account written at the time one of the young militants, Emily Wilby, vividly recreates the local community's intense solidarity, its resistance to harassment by the authorities and its determined efforts to create an alternative strike school.

We came on strike on April 1st, 1914. We came on strike because our governess and master were dismissed from the council school unjustly.

The parson got two Barnardo children to say that our governess had caned them and slapped their faces, but we all knew she did not. . . . Governess did not know we were going on strike. She brought us all some Easter eggs and oranges the last day we were at the council school. Violet Potter brought a paper to school with all our names on it, and all who were going on strike had to put a cross against their name. Out of seventy-two children, sixty-six came out on strike. . . . The next morning the sixty-six children lined up on the Crossways. We all had cards round our necks and paper trimmings. We marched past the Council school. . . . Mrs Boulton, the lady at the Post Office, gave us some lemonade and sweets and nuts. She also gave us a large banner and several flags. . . . Mr Starr, the Attendance Officer, sent our mothers a paper saying if they did not send their children to school they would be summonsed, but our mothers did not care about the papers; some put them on sticks and waved them. . . . One day a policeman went round to twenty houses with summonses because we had not been to school . . . at Court the fine was half-a-crown each. . . . The next day our mothers thought we might begin school on the Common while it was fine weather. We had school on the Common a little while, then we went into the very cottage that the Barnardo children had lived in for a year and a half. Our mothers lent stools, tables, chairs, etc. Mr Ambrose Sandy said we could have his [carpenter's] shop for a strike school. Sam Sandy came and whitewashed it out and mended the windows. He put a ladder up so that we could go upstairs. Our mothers were soon summonsed again. . . . Our parents did not have to pay a penny of the fine. It was all collected on the Green and in the streets.[67]

The villagers' struggle attracted national publicity and became a celebrated cause of the labour and trade union movement, which contributed funds for the building of a strike school. Violet Potter, the pupils' strike leader, remembers the short speech she made when the school was opened in 1918.

I stood on the steps of this school in front of crowds of people at seventeen years of age, and opened this school. I remember what I said to this day. 'With joy and thankfulness I declare this school open to be for ever a school of freedom.'[68]

The strike school continued for two decades in opposition to the state system, bestowing upon the village children a political education that stressed the values of socialism, internationalism and trade unionism.[69]

To conclude, although strike schools were an extremely rare phenomenon, they possess a broader significance than their incidence suggests, for they encapsulated the demand for community control over education that, on a wider scale, was intrinsic to all the school strikes we have examined. These strikes can best be understood in terms of a fusion of residual and emergent cultural elements within working-class culture. The aims of many strikes echoed the traditional working-class view of the interrelated nature of education, work and family life. In fact, the principal demands of the strikers — schools located within, and controlled by, the local community; flexible attendance requirements and holidays geared to the needs of parents and pupils; and the promotion of non-authoritarian teaching methods — to some extent paralleled the form of education provided by private working-class schools prior to their suppression by the state in the late nineteenth century. Although the aims of the strikers were infused by residual cultural elements, their tactics, such as picketing, demonstrations and negotiations with the school authorities, were all imitative and expressive of the emergent labour movement. Indeed, the conception and deployment of the school strike as a weapon to assert control over provided education is comprehensible only within the context of a divided society and a broadly based trade union movement. The reversion to strike action both demonstrates the essential continuity between working-class youth and parent cultures and, more important, emphasizes the prevalence of mediated forms of class conflict within the education system. For, crucially, the school strike was an expression of the resistance of the local working-class community to the abuse of fundamental rights by the authoritarian and bureaucratic organization of state schooling.

CHAPTER 5

Larking About

Pranks and Parody

In they days we didn't have no gardens. You could 'ardly swing a cat between one front door and the one opposite. Well, what we did, wait till the evening come, then we ties one door knocker to the door knocker opposite with a long piece of cotton. Then we knocks one of the doors and hides, and as it opens inwards it raps the door over the other side of the road. Well, this goes on, with doors opening and closing, until they twigs it, then they'd shout, 'You stop that larking about, you bloody little nuisances!'[1]

This infuriating game of door-knocking, commonly known as 'Knock Out Ginger' was one of the huge repertoire of practical jokes known to working-class children, many of which aimed at the humbling and humiliation of adults. Other common pranks were the singeing of unsuspecting adult bottoms seated in outside lavatories by thrusting a stinging nettle or candle through the rear flap doors; the tempting of passers-by on dark evenings with coins attached to cotton, which would be pulled away by the hidden tormentors as soon as the victim grovelled towards his find; and the filling of sugar bags with horse dung, lures dropped tantalizingly in the streets in the hope that someone would pick them up and take them home. Some of the playful pranks conceived by local children were both ingenious and intimidating. Willie Robertson describes how he and his friends used to create arson panics among cottage dwellers near his Lerwick home in Shetland during the 1890s.

Get a cabbage, stalk of a cabbage, and we used to punch right through it, you see, fill it with straw, and then set a match to the straw and the straw'd just smoke. And get it up against somebody's keyhole and blow, and the smoke just filled the house, and then you fled and watched them coming out.[2]

121

The common-sense way of explaining practical jokes of this type is to dismiss them as trivial and timeless activities, indulged in equally by children of all classes, and as merely one aspect of the recurring conflict between children and adults. However, in listening to the childhood recollections of people all over Britain who grew up during the period 1889 to 1939 I was struck by two things that seemed to point to an alternative explanation: first, the frequency with which people from a working-class background used the phrase 'larking about' to describe devious techniques of resistance to authoritarian control and, second, the fact that people who came from a middle-class background tended to be unfamiliar both with the phrase 'larking about' and with the illicit activities it involved. This evidence suggests that not only was there a qualitative and quantitive difference between the larking about of working-class and middle-class youth, but there was also a clear distinction between the meaning and purpose attached to this activity by children of different classes. For middle-class youth, larking about was merely an occasional lapse or release in a highly regulated culture. For working-class youth, however, larking about was an important part of an informal, irreverent and independent street culture, which profoundly influenced the identity of the children and their attitude to authority during their growth to maturity. Also, the evidence from interviews suggests that during the period 1889-1939 there was a significant increase in larking about, produced by the clash between the independent traditions of working-class youth and the attempts to control and discipline it made by the complex web of educational, welfare and penal institutions that developed from the late nineteenth century onwards, one aim of which was to produce a more stable and efficient labour force. To understand larking about, it is necessary to look at it in the broader context of the parent culture from which it was derived, in particular the traditions of humour and leisure that were especially important in shaping this activity of working-class youth.

Larking about was rooted in the aggressive, insulting and coarse traditions of working-class humour that were widely condemned by middle-class cultural critics and social reformers as vulgar and a dangerous concession to the emotions.[3] Children like George Prince, for example, whose atheist father would often parody grace at meal times by saying, 'For what we are about to receive, may the Lord give us plenty of room,'[4] would often adopt this form of debunking humour for their own devices in order to ridicule figures of authority.

The other essential element in larking about derived from working-class leisure traditions. Although during the nineteenth century there were changes in the nature of leisure, which evolved from a spontaneous and sometimes violent release to organized and respectable recreation, working-class leisure remained to some extent resistant to outside control. For example, the street and the pub both remained major centres of leisure activity, and informal codes of conduct, particularly in manners and relations between the sexes, never conformed to middle-class standards of formal propriety.[5]

In the preceding chapters we have seen that the popular stereotype of submissive and regimented working-class children in schools is seriously misleading. In fact, a number of different forms of larking about flourished in schools because they provided an expressive and effective form of resistance to authoritarian control. The most innocuous form of larking about was mimicry, which was used to ridicule the comical self-importance, the formal manners and the authoritarian methods of some schoolteachers, as Alice Hemmings recalls.

I remember more than once a girl'd go out the front of the class and start mimicking the teacher, imitating her voice and her attitudes, while somebody kept 'kye' by the door. They used to do it in the playground too, when the teachers weren't around, little mincing walk, shoulders back, you know. And we'd all be killing ourselves laughing.[6]

Another form of larking about was the constant undercurrent of illicit note-passing, sweet-sucking and whispered gossiping and joking, usually undetected by teachers, which offered immediate relief from the day-to-day monotony of schooling. Sometimes, however, the children were indiscreet, and secret antics, such as the classroom carrot-chomping of the unfortunate Jessie Niblett, who attended St Phillip's school in Bristol during the early 1900s, came to the attention of the schoolmistress.

Yes, we used to eat carrots. Take 'em into the washroom and wash them, and have them in the desk. Sit and have it. I used to 'ave to write a hundred lines: 'I must not eat carrots in school.' And there used to be the kid next to me, she'd be writing out one lot and I'd be writing out another lot to help me get the hundred. Then I used to get the cane because the writing was different.[7]

A more subversive form of larking about was truancy. We have seen that regular and punctual school attendance was considered by the authorities to be essential in developing conformity and predictability in the working-class child. Many instances of truancy can be explained in terms of a deliberate and discriminating rejection of the rigid dictates of school. Although detection meant certain and severe punishment, many working-class children were determined and devious enough to abscond successfully from school, for a lark, at least several times a year, to play in the fields and on the beaches, to poach, to go to fairs, markets and processions and, later on, to swimming baths and picture palaces. The temptation of truancy, popularly known as 'mitching' or 'mooching' in many parts of Britain, was often irresistible to children attending village schools, as is vividly illustrated by Ernie Tucker's account of why he preferred to spend summer mornings exploring the countryside around his home in Brixham, South Devon, rather than at his school desk.

I used to mitch a lot, being a nature lover, go our bird-nesting, mornings specially. I liked the morning when the sun was out. I thought the country was better than school. . . . 'Course I got caught for mitching, and they used to put a dunce's hat on me, put me in the corner and, oh, my God, I've had the stick many a time. I kept pulling me hand back and he'd say, 'Right, on your knee.' Whack, whack, whack. . . . It was bad to cry, grin and bear it, cry when you got 'ome. . . . Yes, I never did like school. I don't like regimentation of any sort. I should've been born a blackbird or a whitebird [laughter]. Personally, I don't think you should go by the clock, for instance. I mean, animals and birds, they don't look at a clock, do they? If they wants to go, they goes. . . . That's the way I'm made. I used to walk miles out in the woods all on me own. I used to love that, picking primroses or something like that, watching insects. I like nature.[8]

In towns and cities throughout the country the highest truancy rates were recorded on market days, and in the following extract Jessie Niblett describes in gory detail why many Bristolian children preferred to spend a morning in the slaughterhouse rather than the schoolroom.

I hated school, especially scripture in the mornings, oh, it was murder. We used to mooch the whole morning, never go to school till after dinner. My brother and I, we always used to go together us two, always together, hand in hand. . . . If it was market day we used to go up a slaughterhouse in Dead Horse Lane when all the pigs was going in. It was fun . . . see them go and have their throats cut. Then they chuck 'em in great tubs of boiling water. You used to hear them squeal, the pigs. We'd go up next day with a big pillowcase and threepence, and the man would fill 'em up with bones from the pigs. Take them 'ome to my mother and granny and my aunty. They'd share it between them and make a stew. . . . Then we'd go round people's gardens pickin' flowers and take 'em to school in the afternoon so we wouldn't get the cane.[9]

Truancy for a lark cannot simply be dismissed as a childish rejection of work in favour of play, for in many cases the young truant was exploring interests and developing skills that were excluded from the elementary school curriculum, which for the most part was restricted to the three Rs. To avoid punishment on their return to school, children would attempt to dupe teachers, usually with faked notes and illnesses. Robbie Bairnson, who grew up in a Shetland fishing village in the early part of the century, remembers that on one occasion he was so determined to get permission to stay at home in order to pursue his own hobbies that he induced temporary nausea by smoking his father's pipe.

When I was going to school I had all sorts of hobbies at home, maybe making small boats. . . . And sometimes I was more interested in what I was doing at home than what I was learning at school. And I made excuses sometimes when I didn't want to go to school, played truant. But I remember one morning in particular I had something that I was doing. I didn't want to go to school, and I didn't have a very good excuse for staying home. Now, there was nobody in the kitchen and my father's pipe was lying on the mantelpiece, and I'd tried the pipe before and it made you feel a bit funny. So I took the pipe and it was full. It had tobacco in, and the pipe was fairly strong. And I lit it and I had a good smoke, and I didn't feel well and I couldn't eat my porridge. So I stayed home from school all day. But about ten o'clock I was alright.[10]

Despite this type of resistance, the vigilance of teachers and attendance officers, the threat of legal sanctions and the deterrent effect of truant schools and industrial schools had effectively established the practice of regular school attendance in the towns by the early 1900s. However, schools found it extremely difficult to eliminate the opportunistic and occasional truancy practised by many working-class children, which was one important reason why most education authorities were unable to make significant improvements on their attendance rates after the turn of the century.

In schools at which authoritarian control took a severely militaristic form, involving the imposition of rigid rules of silence, children frequently resorted to acts of sabotage as the only effective means of interrupting work or disrupting lessons. The two most common forms of school sabotage involved deliberate ink-spilling and stink bombs; as Ada Mudge, recalling her schooldays in Norwich in the early part of the century, put it:

we'd spill an inkwell accidentally on purpose over a girl's pinny, or perhaps let off a stink bomb. We did anything to disrupt a lesson.[11]

In fact, these tactics bear some resemblance to the plots of delinquent schoolboy gangs popularized in the comic paper *Larks* from the 1890s onwards. The most desperate and destructive of these comic inventions were the Ball's Pond Banditti, a ruthless teenage gang pledged to perpetual war against adult authority.[12] Whether this type of licensed hooliganism encouraged a disrespectful and devious attitude to schooling or merely provided a harmless safety valve for feelings of frustration or aggression is extremely difficult to establish. However, it is clear that many adults considered such comic characters to be a harmful and corrupting influence and subsequently confiscated subversive editions and controlled children's reading habits.

Our mother didn't let we girls read the *Larks* because it 'ad the Balls Pond Road Banditti in it. . . . They was very tough characters, always wrecking around, an' one of the gang, Piggy Waffles (we called 'im 'The Hog') 'ud say 'Damn it all.' And, of course, that was terrible language in them days. When we wanted to read 'un we had to sneak it from the boys an' go in the lavatory with it.[13]

The most ingenious forms of sabotage, though, were those that involved oaths of secrecy and allegiance. In the following extract Arthur Burley vividly evokes one such tradition of larking about, which was passed down through the generations at Perranwell village school in west Cornwall.

The masters in they days was very strict. And when you go in school there was no talking to another boy, because if you did, you'd have four cuts of the cane. . . . Well, at my school it was handed down for years and years, ever since the school was built, that the eldest boy in the school would learn the next eldest the trick we played, to take over when he left. Now, when I left school I got the other boy to swear to me on oath, 'I swear by

---

The first edition (published in May 1893) of the comic Larks! *which featured a desperate teenage gang, the Balls Pond Banditti, whose antisocial behaviour reflected and reinforced the larking about of the comic's young working-class readership.*

Larks!

FOUNDED AND CONDUCTED BY GILBERT DALZIEL.

Vol. I.— No. 1.]   MONDAY, MAY 1, 1893.   [HALFPE

½D   ½

THE BALL'S POND BANDITTI

(1.) THE INSPIRATION.

(2.) THE CONSTRUCTION OF THE BANDIT'S CAVE.

(5.) THE OATH OF ALLEGIANCE.

(4.) THE ELECTION OF THE CAPTAIN.

(3.) THE ENROLMENT OF RECRUITS.

(6.) THE COUNCIL OF WAR.

(1) "From 'enceforth I hemilate the doin's of the Robber Chiefs of hold!" observed Ticko pins, of the Ball's Pond Clothing Stores. "Sussiety shall tremble at the name of Bloodwing Brandon Ballyflathers de Bazan!" "Garn!" replied his admiring friends, Gorger Pain, the e's youth, and Figgy Waffles, from the grocery establishment, "yer don't mean it!"

(2) But he did, though ; and ere long the gloomy walls of the Bandit's Lair frowned upon a of waste land near by, frightening the stray cats from their recreation ground.

(3) Next, the reckless Bloodwing enrolled a desperate but chivalrous band of outlaws. Lurcher m, from the butcher's, and Sweppy Titmarsh, from the rag-shop, were the first to join.

(4) Having adopted the name of "The Ball's Pond Banditti," the desperate crew elected whom fear and pity alike were empty sounds. The name of Bloodwing headed the poll.

(5) Even the bold bloodhound Rocco seemed moved at the darkly impressive scene whil as each Bandit swore allegiance to his Captain and comrades. "I, Figgy Waffles, swears on gashly relicts of morality to execute horders and comrades, with promptitoode and despate me dyin' oath! S'elp me never!"

(6) The band thus organised, dark deliberations took place as to their first raid upon which, howeyer, must, we fear, wait in trembling suspense for the result till next week.

Almighty God that what I do with you up above the school I will never tell
another boy or anyone in the village,' see, because we didn't want the
schoolmaster to find out. Now, what I had to do, being the eldest boy, I
would stand by the main gate and as the schoolmaster come in, I would
say, 'Ring the bell, sir?' 'Oh, yes, Arthur, ring the bell.' Now, it wouldn't do
to happen too often, but I ring the bell for a little
while, then I start pulling him hard from side to side, then I leave the rope
go. Well, then the rope'd go up. So when the master come in I'd say, 'Oh,
excuse me, sir, the bell has gone round again.' 'Oh, yes, what a nuisance
that is. Well, you'd better get a boy and go up and put it right.' Well, that
used to be an afternoon's job, see, so we used to get a ladder, then walk
along the beams, right up inside the top of the school, and we used to have
a candle because 'twas dark up there, see. Then we used to go over to
where the bell was, fix 'ee, then we'd walk down through the school, and
up in the ceiling there was air vents. And we used to kneel down and spit
down through and it'd come right down on the side of a boy, see. Then this
boy'd think the boy behind spits, see, and he'd say, 'Wait till you get
outside the school,' like. We'd do that class, then we'd do the next one, and
do the next one, and do the same thing right down the school. Well, we've
done our business now, and there's a great beam running from the wall
right up to the roof, and every boy that held that job would carve his name
in that beam with a knife, and the date. Oh, they'd go back to 1870-
something, when the school was built. It was passed down from the eldest
boy to the eldest boy and 'twas funny, but it never got out, the secret.[14]

If a pupil was unlucky enough to be detected and punished for
acts of disobedience, then larking about would occasionally escalate
into violent resistance that verged on insurrection. Respondents
throughout Britain, especially in Lancashire, Scotland and the
West Country, recollected that older children would sometimes
resist or even break the cane when teachers attempted to administer
corporal punishment. Resistance of this type, however, frequently
resulted in brutal assaults on children by headteachers or, in the
case of church schools, the local vicar, as is illustrated by the
following incident, which occurred in Preston village, near Yeovil,
in 1926.

They [the teachers] were fairly strict, and I can remember one gorgeous
incident. We had one boy — he was a real terror — and we used to go out
doing PT, and we used to have to stand in four rows and the teacher would
do the exercises, and the leader of the children would follow the teacher
and then the rank would follow. Well, he was the leader of our rank and he
started going all haywire. When she went up, he went out and, of course,
we all followed him, and our line was all out with the rest, so she shouted
at him, what did he think he was doing? And he said, 'Oh, I got fed up with
doing that, like you're doing it.' So she said, 'Go in school. I'll deal with you

when I come in.' So he went into school. We finished our PT, and when we went in, he was standing beside her desk with a big smile on his face. And she went to the cupboard to get her cane out and she couldn't find it, so she got angry and she said to the monitor, 'See if you can find my cane. It's in there somewhere.' So he hunted, but he couldn't find it, so she went to the cupboard in a bit of a rage and she shook it and she said, 'It must be in here.' Well, the cupboard was always a bit rickety and the leg broke off and the thing toppled forward, and there were books all over the place, hell of a mess — I can always remember — and she was in a tearing rage . . . so she said to Lunn [the guilty boy], 'Go and get Mrs Parker's cane.' So he went in there and he came back out and he said, 'Mrs Parker says you've already had it once this morning.' 'I haven't,' she said. . . . Oh, she was mad at that, so she said — there were a Mrs Parker and a Miss Parker, no relatives — 'Go in and get Miss Parker's cane.' So, of course, he came back and said, 'You've already had it once this morning.' He'd been round and borrowed all the canes and made a fire out of them! And burnt them all up! There wasn't a cane in the school. So she got mad with him, like, and she sent him off home, and the next day the vicar came, and obviously she'd contacted him because he came there sort of prepared, like, because being a church school he had to come periodically and see how things were going. So he stepped out in front of the class and he said, 'Lunn, come out here.' So we all looked up, you see, but he didn't, he went on writing. So he shouted again, 'Can you hear me?' He didn't move. Everybody else did, but not him. So he went red in the face and he suddenly shouted again, called him by his surname, and he looked up and he said 'I've got a handle to my name' [common West Country slang for Christian name]. So he went, ooh, like a pillar box, and he said, 'Oh, you have, have you?' he said, and he reached out and got hold of him by the scruff of the neck and lifted him out of his desk, because he was a great big man, lifted him out like a jack-rabbit, and he turned to the teacher and said, 'Have you got a good strong cane there?' She said, 'Yes, I have.' She'd got another one, see, and he held him up off the ground and he just leathered him, and he didn't half leather him, right in front of the class. He hit him till he screamed. . . . Well, his parents took that vicar to court over that, for assault. . . . Well, he stood up in court when they started the proceedings and he said, 'I don't want to waste the time of this court. I am guilty of what I am brought here for. I did thrash the boy,' and he said, 'I am just telling this court here and now that if that boy speaks to me again tomorrow the same as he did, then I'll do the same again. I have no more to say,' and he sat down. So they went through the preliminaries and he was fined a nominal shilling — they had to you see, because he were guilty of assault . . . but they more or less upheld his actions.[15]

Although the combined forces of school, church and state effectively repressed subversive larking about in the long term, physically well-developed pupils occasionally enjoyed a momentary victory over authority by assaulting schoolteachers, as is illustrated by

Charlie Wichett's recollections of his expulsion from the Cornish village school of Manaccan, in 1889.

We didn't care for school much in they days, so we'd be larking about in lessons and the old schoolmaster couldn't do nothing with us. We was rough, mind, and we was proud of it, like. I was the biggest boy in that school and nobody could touch me, not even the schoolmaster. He only give me the cane once and that was because the other boys say that you take a hair from your head and put 'n on your 'and, 'e'd snap the cane. Well, 'e didn't work and, oh, my God, that cane did hurt. After that I always refused to hold me 'and out. . . . Anyway, this one day I'm sitting at my desk larking about a bit, and the schoolmaster come up behind me and hit me across the back with his stick. Well, it takes my breath away, but then I lose my temper, see. I pick up the book on my desk and start hitting 'n on the head with it. Now, the old schoolmaster, he trips backwards over a desk and do knock 'is 'ead on the floor. So I kick him everywhere now he's down, I hate 'n that much. Then I run out the class and go over the fields. . . . When I go home the policeman and the doctor are there, waiting for me, like. Now, what saved me was the weals across me back. When father saw they, he didn't have no more of their talk. He say, 'I learned the boy,' he say, 'to stick up for himself.' Now after that they said I weren't to go back to school and I never went for another year. I work with father instead. Now, you won't believe this, but they got a new schoolmaster and father took me up there to see 'n an' they had me back, and, do you know, I got on lovely with that man in my last year at school.[16]

Disruptive larking about was not confined to schools. It was also one of the main responses of working-class children and youth to the religious worship and instruction provided for them at church, at chapel, and at the numerous youth organizations indirectly attached to the church — Sunday schools, Band of Hope, Girls' Friendly Societies, Church Lads' Brigades and so on. These youth organizations were conceived as part of a middle-class civilizing mission bringing religion and moral standards to a brutalized working class in order to heal the severed bond between rich and poor caused by rapid industrialization and urbanization. They tended to stress authoritarian control, paternalism and the cultivation of deference as the most effective means of ensuring a stable and harmonious relationship between the classes in the next generation.

Larking about in these organizations was often expressed in the form of parody singing. The Opies, who have compiled the most comprehensive collection of such songs, argue that they were classless in their origin.[17] However, nationwide interviews have uncovered numerous parodies unrecorded by the Opies, and it is clear that these songs were to a large extent the property of working-class children. These parodies subjected every aspect of Christian belief and ritual to ridicule. Particularly popular were the comic travesties of hymns and carols, concocted by substituting for sacred and sentimental crude and commonplace images, such as 'Good King Wenslas' ass poked out, through the bedroom window.'[18] The following parody of 'Fight the Good Fight' has been used by generations of working-class children throughout Britain to sabotage religious services:

> Fight the good fight with all thy might,
> Sit on a box of dynamite.
> Light the fuse and you will see
> The quickest way to the cemetery.

The christening ceremony was another target for the ridicule of children, who sang, for example, the rhyme

> Wash me in the water
> That you washed your dirty daughter
> And I shall be whiter
> Than the whitewash on the wall.

Several respondents recalled that any unfortunate adult who was known to be a member of the Salvation Army was likely to be harassed by groups of children raucously singing:

> She's in the Sally Army,
> She's safe from sin,
> She'll go to heaven in a corned beef tin.
> Corned beef tin was too small
> So she had to go to hell
> And did never go at all.

Often the children's rhymes took the form of ridiculous chants, which were ideally suited for irritating or humiliating nuns and priests passing by in the streets, as Daisy Wintle remembers.

When we used to see the nuns come up Granby Hill we used to say:

> Catholic, Catholic, quack, quack, quack,
> Go to the devil and never come back.

We used to say that and they never used to take any notice of us. They just used to walk on. But one day they walked back and they saw where we lived; we lived in a square where there was a lot of cottages dotted round, and of course I runned in the house and she come and knocked at the door. I had the biggest hiding of my life. I never done it again.[19]

Some of the most derisive parodies of religion originated in the secularist sections of the socialist and labour movement, whose desire to profane the sacred followed from their rejection of the Church as an oppressive institution. They developed their own alternative organizations, such as socialist Sunday schools and Clarion Clubs, in order to encourage a political as opposed to a religious education for the young, and the sardonic attacks they unleashed on the Church from these independent bases reverberated through all sections of society. Jim Flowers, for example, remembers the uproar in the Bristol press in 1921 when his family christened their new baby at the socialist Sunday school with the initials REV, short for 'revolutionary' and also a parody of 'reverend'.

My father was an ILP [Independent Labour Party] man and he had a large collection of books, Robert Blatchford, Bernard Shaw, H.G. Wells. It was like a university. Well, I was only twelve years old and I read *The Rights of Man*, Tom Paine. And he said that the Bible was like a millstone round the world's neck, and he exposed all the inconsistencies and the inaccuracies in the Bible. He said there was no need for this bloodthirsty God they worshipped. His hands were covered in blood and all this. Well, he blew the gaff, as far as I was concerned, about religion. And I used to go down to the socialist Sunday school, and that put me off going to church and Sunday school and Band of Hope as well. I wasn't too fond of that at all. Well, when I was fourteen mother had another baby, and her and dad got us three boys round and said, 'Now we want you to pick a name for him.' One picked Ronald, the other picked Eric and I picked Victor. So dad got hold of the three names, and he said, 'R-E-V, Rev. He's a revolutionary. That'll do.' So that's how he got his name. From our point of view, it was a big joke. Well, we did the socialist christening ceremony. The baby was led out; someone said a few words: 'We now accept this new human into our ranks.' Then the youngest boys and girls came out and laid posies of primroses and violets on him. We sang a hymn out of the socialist song book, like the 'International' or the 'Red Flag' or something, and that was his name then. You should have seen the eruptions in the paper. Well, they used to call us all the names imaginable in those days. To call someone a socialist was the worst thing you could call anybody. Anyway, we didn't take any notice. We just laughed, thought it was funny, the stir they caused over Rev.[20]

Prayer, because it was the most sacred and solemn religious ritual in which working-class children participated, was also the most vulnerable to their profane and disruptive pranks, as is illustrated by Ernie Tucker's exploits in the Wesleyan chapel in Babbacombe, South Devon, in the 1920s.

We went to chapel regularly. Actually we went 'cos 'twas somewhere to go, a bit of a laugh, like. Prayers used to be automatic, they did, babble, babble, babble, and that was the end of that, like. . . . We was thinking more of whether we was going to get any tea when we got home, that's what we were thinking about. Anyway, I didn't used to get on too well with prayers because I used to put itching powder on the preacher's head; he 'ad a bald head and you used to lean over and just drop a bit on his head and make out you were reaching for a Bible or something and he'd be scratching away. And then my mates used to bring in these little glass stink bombs and put 'm on the floor and squeeze 'm, and sometimes they all used to have to go outside. It was terrible.[21]

The most pleasurable and prestigious forms of larking about, however, were those that involved not only opposition to authority, but also the promise of instrumental gain. Numerous respondents recalled turning the tedium of church attendance to personal advantage in two principal ways: first, by faking contributions during the collection and spending money meant for the collecting plate on sweets and, second, by forming illicit friendships with members of the opposite sex. Church services were among the few social functions open to youth in which sex segregation was not imposed, and many respondents recalled that as teenagers they were much more interested in ogling, whispering and scribbling notes to fancied ones than in any religious message. The recollections of Bristolian Alice Hemmings illustrate how this constant undercurrent of devious activity occasionally interrupted church services and punctured the atmosphere of sacred moments.

Often the boys'd put buttons on the plate, and at the end they'd announce it: 'The collection taken tonight was so much and so much and so many buttons.' That was supposed to shame 'em. When the boys got outside they went nuts about it. . . . But the funniest thing was, I used to wear hats with streamers on, and one night the boys tied 'em to one of the chairs, and when I got up to say the prayers the bloomin' chair an' all came up with me, and the Reverend Swann said, 'Will the person who is causing the disturbance at the back of the church please go out.' [Laughter][22]

Similarly, at Band of Hope or Sunday school meetings many older children and youths would view the proceedings with humorous detachment, and would sometimes gain comic relief by inverting the oaths and pledges that many voluntary organizations required them to take. Bert Mullen, for example, recalled that when all the children at Band of Hope meetings were required to chant the pledge, he and his friends would change it to 'I promise not' to abstain from alcoholic liquor.'[23] Interviews indicate that this type of playful resistance was an important contributing factor in the dramatic decline in church, Band of Hope and Sunday school attendance when members reached the age at which they were no longer compelled by parents to attend. In England and Scotland during our period the vast majority of the working-class members of these organizations were lost between the ages of fourteen and seventeen.[24] This growing detachment and disaffection from religious organizations was, to some extent, the fruit of many years' larking about, which effectively distanced working-class youth from religious dogma and loosened bonds of duty and deference.

Larking about also acted as the major obstacle that frustrated the endeavours of uniformed youth movements such as the Boys' Brigades, Boy Scouts, Boy's Club cadets and so on to instil order, regularity and patriotic duty into the working-class younger generation. The recruiting officers of these quasi-military movements were impressive and their propaganda celebrated the power of uniforms and drilling in order to dupe unruly youths into submission.[25] However, interviews suggest that sport, the band and the annual camp were the activities that most attracted members and that drilling and military manoeuvres were usually regarded as tiresome concessions to authority, to be avoided wherever possible. It is also clear that the grand pretensions of group leaders and the public school ethos of manliness that permeated these movements were often viewed with cynical detachment. This disrespectful attitude has found its most lasting expression in a long tradition of parodies, an example of which is the following obscene version of the 'Eton Boating Song', known to many working-class youths at the turn of the century.

> The sexual urge of a camel
> Is stronger than anyone thinks,
> And when the urge is upon him,
> He climbs on the back of the sphinx.
> But the sphinx's exterior orifice
> Is blocked by the sands of the Nile,
> Which accounts for the hump on the camel,
> And the sphinx's inscrutable smile.

Interviews also indicate that Boys' Brigade marches commonly met with ribald jeers, derisive songs and occasionally stone-throwing by youths, not just in slum neighbourhoods, but also in respectable working-class districts. It is significant that large sections of the socialist and labour movement were bitterly opposed to militarism and imperialism both before and after World War I and that many parents refused to let their children participate in Empire Day celebrations or to join uniformed youth movements. It was this breadth of opposition within the working class that accounted for the diffusion of the following parody to most parts of Britain.

'Ere comes the Boys' Brigade,
All smovered in marmalade,
A tuppenny 'a'penny pill box,
An' 'alf a yard of braid.

Scurrilous songs such as this, often expressing sardonic insight and detachment, formed part of a continuous tradition stretching from Boys' Brigade to army barracks.[26] They are a reminder that many working-class army recruits were forced to join up either by economic necessity or by legal compulsion, and their primary aim was personal survival, not the patriotic self-sacrifice encouraged by youth movements.[27]

Another aim shared by many youth organizations and schools was the elimination of uncontrolled contact between the sexes through the imposition of a rigid policy of sex segregation, and again in this context the practice of larking about generated powerful resistance to control. The sexual behaviour of youth was a perennial cause for concern, especially during the late Victorian and Edwardian periods. This anxiety was rooted in the fear that casual and informal relationships between the sexes would damage or destroy the fruits of formal conduct — regularity and obedience — that had been carefully cultivated by various character-forming agencies.[28] Increasingly, the independent courting traditions of working-class youth were subjected to the restrictions imposed by middle-class theories of adolescence, which prescribed a prolonged, regulated and institutionalized dependency on adults as essential to normal and healthy sexual development. Much psychological theorizing and evangelical moralizing pronounced that adolescence was an impressionable and traumatic stage of life, in which individuals were particularly vulnerable to the seductive power of the sexual instincts, which, unless controlled and channelled in a wholesome direction, would result in an orgy of depravity, idleness and crime. Fears such as these were heightened by a widespread anxiety that the kaleidoscopic nature of city life encouraged a restless search for stimulation and excitement and by the eugenic reformers' warnings against the dangers of the 'racial poison' of venereal disease, illegitimacy and unplanned and imprudent marriages.[29] The policies of sex segregation generated by these theories were often interpreted and administered in a harsh and punitive manner by lower middle-class officials, especially school-teachers, who were involved in daily contact with, and control of, working-class youth. For the social purity movement, with its crusades for sexual restraint and moral propriety, found its strongest support among the lower middle class, members of which were anxious to reassert conventional Victorian values, which they feared were flaunted not just by unskilled and uncivilized workers and their families, but also by hedonistic followers of fashion in the highest social circles.[30] In their earnest endeavour to maintain these rigid moral standards, some schoolteachers felt no compunction at using violent methods, and children found guilty of such innocent and innocuous activities as exchanging love letters, ogling or kissing in sex-segregated playgrounds were often severely punished. Reg Summerhayes, for example, recalling his schooldays in Bath in the early part of the century, remembers: 'the girls' school was next door to ours, like, an' they caught I kissin' a girl through the railings. I 'ad four cuts of the cane for that.'[31]

However, authoritarian measures failed to eliminate a strong undercurrent of resistance to segregation and illicit contact between the sexes, widely referred to as larking about. But, since it was generally acknowledged that boys were naturally more devious and more determined than girls — to quote the contemporary maxim, boys will be boys — their lapses were generally treated with greater leniency than those of girls, who rapidly became the major target for middle-class moralizing. By the early 1900s the phrases 'skylarking' and 'larking with the lads' became watchwords for worried officials, denoting the informal and illicit friendships that working-class girls persisted in forming with the boys. 'The noisy laugh and reckless romping ways'[32] of young girls, together with their unashamed enjoyment of mixed groups and gang activities, such as those described by Ada Iles, were often considered improper and injurious for members of the fairer sex.

I was in this gang of six boys and three girls. . . . We used to go up the quarry an' we 'ad this old bath that we flattened out, an' we used to take it in turns, with a boy on the front an' a girl on the back, to slide down the quarry. I did come 'ome most nights with me drawers broke. [Laughter][33]

'Larking with the lads' was viewed even more anxiously when physical attraction replaced robust play. It was sometimes alleged by conservative critics that one of the chief uses to which working-class girls put their newly acquired literacy skills was the composition of insidious love-letters to boys. Certainly, in many schools there was a busy exchange of scribbled humorous notes between older girls and boys, and as Jane Taverner, recalling her Exeter schooldays in the 1920s remembers, some girls had devious ways of ensuring that their letters were not detected.

I remember love letters which used to come and we hid them in our knickers. And then we went down to the toilets and had a good laugh and read. . . . If you got caught, you'd get the ruler, and it'd be tore up.[34]

Insolent humour was one of the principal skills involved in larking about between the sexes. Whereas most middle-class youth might meet suitable partners only through formal introductions, normally planned by parents when their children were in their late teens,[35] horseplay and humorous exchanges provided working-class youngsters with a ritual introduction to anyone they fancied 'getting off' with. Boys would often begin the repartee with a question like 'Does your mother know you're out?' to which one common reply was, 'Yes, she gave me a farthing to buy a monkey with — are you for sale?'[36] Girls sometimes took the initiative, playfully knocking off boys' caps, bumping into those they fancied or 'plucking from the lads' button holes the flowers which many of them wear'.[37] Many middle-class reformers were repelled by girls' involvement in this type of larking about, for it implied a worldliness that was incompatible with the purity and innocence that they believed was the basis of female virtue. For example, Walter Besant, a prominent figure in the *Contemporary Review*'s campaign to publicize the degeneracy of working-class youth in the late nineteenth century, was so shocked by the coarse repartee of a few young girls he listened to in Hampstead Heath that he was inspired to write the following invective:

Their conversation grows continually viler, until Zola himself would be ashamed to reproduce the talk of these young people. . . . And . . . although not all can become so bad as those foul-mouthed young Bacchantes and raging Maenads of Hampstead Heath, it would seem as if nothing could be left to them after the education of the gutter — nothing at all — of the things which we associate with holy and gracious womanhood. . . . poverty has many stings; but there can be none sharper than the necessity of marrying one of these poor, neglected creatures.[38]

Moral crusades such as this sensitized agencies of socialization to the behaviour of working-class girls, encouraging a more vigilant control of conduct that had once been viewed as irritating and insolent but not dangerous or deserving of punishment. Many schools and youth organizations not only penalized girls for disregarding the formal manners and behaviour thought appropriate for respectable young ladies but also reprimanded them for any attempt at beautification or self-adornment.[39] However, efforts to impose such rigid standards were often counter-productive in their effects, reinforcing resistance and disassociation from institutions. May Loveridge, for example, who attended a Catholic school in Bristol during World War I was alienated from the church for life by such regulations, particularly the callous punishment of a teacher who confiscated her treasured bracelet.

There seemed to be a cruelness or something, too strict; they weren't human, like you couldn't go and speak to them or tell them anything or confide in them or anything. They were too stern. . . . Well, as soon as I was fourteen I turned right from the religion, never gone in a Roman Catholic church since I was fourteen, soon as I left school. . . . If [you] were found playing with the boys, even outside school — 'I must not play with the boys, I must not play with the boys', used to have to write it out. . . . I had the cane once and that was off that Sister Lucy, that nun. My father sent me a bracelet from Germany. Anyway, I was doing me sums and she came round and she said, 'What's that you've got on your wrist?' 'Oh,' I said, 'It's my dad's birthday present that he sent me over from Germany.' 'Take it off,' she said. Now, we were three storeys up, and our classroom overlooked the boys' playground. She took it off, opened the window, and threw it out. You could tell how I felt. Anyway, I ran out the class crying, and I clambered right over the railings, over to the boys' playground, and got it, and she was down there waiting for me at the gate. And she belted me; she took it away again. Anyway, my mother went up as well about it, but I never had it back.[40]

'Larking with the lads' was closely associated in the minds of both working girls and reformers with 'having a fling' or 'having a good time' before beauty faded and the routine drudgery of work and marriage took its toll.[41] High-spirited larking in the little leisure time available to working girls can, of course, be seen to some extent as a dramatic compensation for boredom at school and at work. The main occupations open to working-class girls were domestic service and factory or shop work, which often demanded between forty and a hundred hours a week of tiresome, unskilled and lowly paid labour and offered little opportunity for promotion or personal satisfaction.[42] However, contemporary fears, from the 1890s onwards, that the craving of working girls for escapism and excitement as a relief from meaningless toil was tempting some to indulge in 'a non-moral, aimless round of seeking momentary excitement'[43] were grossly exaggerated. In fact, working-class autobiographies and interviews indicate that parental control, lack of privacy, lack of sexual knowledge and fear of pregnancy were such powerful restraining factors that larking with the lads rarely involved sexual intercourse. The fear and shame attached to menstruation, sex and childbirth is vividly illustrated by Iris Bradford's memories of her teenage years in Bristol in the 1930s.

I used to think babies came from Palmolive soap. You see, mum only had perfumed soap in the house when the midwife was coming round to deliver the baby. She used to go all posh then and buy the soap and we were so innocent, not knowing how babies were conceived, we thought you made them from Palmolive soap. I was about thirteen at the time, and I used to go round saying to me friends, 'If you want a baby, get some Palmolive soap.' Anyway, when I was about sixteen dad used to do his nut about staying out late. If you arrived in late after the dance, he'd be waiting at the bottom of the road, take my dance shoes from me and flip me all the way back home with them. About this time I was having a lot of trouble with my periods and mum took me to the doctor's. Well, after examining me, he asked me what I thought was a very stupid question. Had I been naughty? I was flabbergasted. What on earth was that to do with the pain I'd been having? Well, I looked at mum, found she was blushing to the collar and I thought I'd better own up. Yes, I had been, actually. I'd broken a cup the previous day. That doctor nearly went into hysterics. He eventually took my mother aside and whispered a few words. And when we got outside I exploded to mum about the silly doctor, to ask such a stupid question. She didn't answer, just told me to hurry up as we had to get dad's tea. She didn't tell us anything about sex, and what we heard in the factory we didn't believe anyway. It was talked and laughed about in a very crude way and I just couldn't believe it, because for the life of me I couldn't imagine our vicar doing those sort of things. Why he kept coming to mind then I don't know — probably because he was the most respected person I knew.[44]

Although some courting couples might occasionally indulge in pre-marital sexual intercourse, interviews suggest that for even the most flirtatious working-class girls, like Ada Iles, 'larking with the lads' usually involved little more than petting in picture palaces, promenading in smart, colourful clothes and conning boys for as many treats as possible.

All day at work we'd be looking forward to going out at night. We girls'd be talking about what clothes we was going to wear. . . . We'd a go after the boys in real earnest after we'd left school, out nearly every night of the week. I went out with literally 'undreds of boys before I started walking out seriously with one of 'em. I was a real she-cat. Mother'd say, 'No skylarking, mind, or it'll be the workhouse for you,' 'cos there'd be a different one every night waiting by the back gate. We'd either go promenading or get them to take us to the pictures an' get 'em to pay as well. . . . We'd give 'em a kiss an' let 'em do a bit of smooching but we wouldn't let 'em get far. There was never any sex. . . . We didn't know anythin' about it, an' in any case we'd be scared of getting caught. There wasn't much chance for that 'cos most of us 'ad to be in by ten o'clock every night till we was married.[45]

Just as larking about in school, in youth organizations and in free leisure time generated excitement and created freedom from authoritarian demands and restrictions, so at work it helped to reduce tension and frustration and to assert informal control over repetitive and depersonalized production processes. Larking and 'kidding' formed a basic part of the male manual labourer's culture, especially among the young. Its most characteristic features were aggressive repartee, practical jokes, illicit smoking and drinking and raucous singing and horseplay.[46] John Challis, reflecting on his experience of the tedium of factory labour as a young man in the Essex town of Halstead in the early 1920s, remembers:

that was all you had almost to live for, you know, the fun that you could make. We had to make fun of almost everything you see. It was the companionship between your pals of your own age; it seemed to be about the only thing that kept you going.[47]

Tom Vaisey, who worked in the silk mills in Halstead a decade earlier, remembers that where strict supervision was not possible the factory-floor antics of young lads would escalate into a marauding misbehaviour that often resulted in dismissal.

As far as the young lads were concerned, there usually used to be three or four sacked every week, you know. They used to be up to their antics — it was such a large building . . . if one wanted to play tricks and get away from your job and that, you could do it there, and I mean you could probably do it for some time. But they used to get so bad that the exasperated foremen would get hold of them and take them into the manager, and without much thought he just used to sack them, you see.[48]

Young workers active in the labour movement tended to favour forms of larking about that undermined respect for those in authority or that playfully provoked dormant middle-class fears of subversive activity. Alf Drury staged this sort of seditious trick when, as a member of the Black Watch, he was posted to Edinburgh in 1921 to assist in guarding key installations in the city from the rumoured threat of the Triple Alliance and potential revolution.

They put me on guard outside the wireless station in Edinburgh. One night I was on duty and there was a crowd round us. A woman was selling a paper called the *Communist*. For a lark I bought six copies and put them in the library at the Castle. In came the sergeant and when his eye lit on them, his moustache literally curled. Bolsheviks on the station![49]

Larking about also formed a key element in the shop-floor culture of girls and young women — indeed, factory work was one of the few female occupations that offered scope for this type of playful activity. Independent and lively girls tended to shun domestic service for factory work because the former involved an intolerable regulation of personal conduct that precluded larking about.[50] The common boasts of working girls that factory work was 'just a lark' was an expression of the victory of humour and devious tactics over the alienating effects of routine drudgery, as is clearly illustrated by the recollections of a chocolate-factory worker in the early part of the century.

The forewomen there were just bloody-minded. You weren't supposed to talk, even though you sat in a row. 'Course, we didn't take much notice of that. There was a lot of chatting and larking about went on behind her back; there was a lot of good feeling between us girls in they days. It stopped us getting bored. And sometimes we'd talk about the people with all the money grinding the noses of the poor like us, making marvellous chocolates for them to eat. Still, we 'ad a lark. We'd eat 'em whenever we wanted. If we were doing walnuts, we'd pick out all the best ones and pop 'em in. We were too fly to ever get caught.[51]

However, in the more closely controlled small cottage industries girls who risked larking about were far more likely to be detected, reprimanded and punished by their employers, as is illustrated by Bessie Angwin's recollections of her dressmaking apprenticeship at Newquay, Cornwall, in the early 1900s.

The missus said she was going off for the day . . . but she didn't go at all. She went down the passage and shut the door with a click, and we thought she was gone. Quiet as a mouse she was, and after it was time for her to have gone, off we was, gamin'. . . . May said, 'Come on, let's have a little sing-song,' and May started off. She said, 'I'm going to play the piano.' Now, the next morning I was the first one in. 'Good mornin', mistress,' and she said, 'Good morning,' a bit snotty, and I thought, oh, my God, and I said, 'There's somin' we didn't do yesterday, didn't do right, miss?' The next one came in and the next one, and I said, 'What can I get on with, Mrs Pegler?' and she said, 'Unpick the job you done yesterday.' I was flabbergasted. We had pyjamas that we'd made, fine stitch, and we had to rip that and put it all together again, and it was perfectly alright, and she made us rip it and do it all again. She said, 'You was gaming and laughing and singing yesterday. I was told it.'[52]

Interviews clearly indicate that working girls were not as deferential and conformist as has often been assumed. The most daring risked dismissal from work and disgrace at home rather than sacrifice the social life of the shop floor. But to maintain such a rebellious stance was a hazardous affair, for even if a disobedient working girl managed to avoid the sack, her employer would often force her along a perilous path of suspensions and transfers from one factory to another. She would then have to lie to her parents in order to conceal the evidence of her unsatisfactory conduct and to prevent conflict at home, as Winnie Ettle remembers.

We used to 'ave a bit of fun. They'd say, 'Go on, Win, start singing,' an' we'd start singing all the old songs. We 'ad to work this night till seven an' we'd been workin' since a quarter past seven [in the morning]. The fellas on the machines were whistlin' away an', of course, I gets up in the middle of the room an' starts doing the Highland Fling. All of a sudden they stops singing. So I said, 'Go on, girls, don't stop.' 'Course, they all went on doing their work an' I went on doing the Highland Fling. Then somebody tapped me on the shoulder. I looked round an' it was the manageress. She said, 'And what do you reckon you're doing, Ettle?' Never called you miss or Winnie, always called you by your surname, like you're below them. 'Course, I being simple, I said, 'The Highland Fling, Miss Coombes.' She said, 'Well, Highland Fling outside. You're suspended for three days. Before you start work, come into me.' 'Course, I 'ad to go home. I 'ad to pretend I was bad. I told my mother I was ill, that I 'ad an awful headache an' I couldn't go to work. Finally I went back. I 'ad to report to Miss Coombe's office. 'You again — you're always carrying on. I've had complaints about you, always singing.' Because the foreman came up to me one day an' said, 'You know, that would sound better out at mid-ocean.' And if there was anybody to be moved, it would be me. Glad to get rid of me.[53]

Although employers had the power to impose trivial rules and regulations, larking about was frequently used to ridicule such petty authoritarianism. For example, in the following account a teenage working girl gains comic revenge on an interfering official who, suspecting the factory workers of pilfering, meticulously searches them.

When you did go out past the time-keeper he'd say to you, 'What have you got in that parcel?' Old Killersley, the time-keeper, he put me in mind of some old witch. If he did see anybody with a parcel, he was on 'em right away. 'What 'ave you got in that parcel?' So one of the girls one night, she said, 'He's always ruddy stopping us. He gets on me nerves. I'll 'ave 'ee.' So what do you think she done? She saved up all the bloomin' sanitary towels, wrapped 'em up in a parcel, tied 'em up and she carried 'em out under her arm. So he said, 'What have you got in that parcel?' She said, 'Only me overalls.' He said, 'Let me see. That's more than a pair of overalls.' She said, 'Well, 'ere you are, then, 'ave a look.' 'Course, he opened it up and there was all these sanitary towels. [Laughter][54]

Another type of larking about frequently practised by young workers to overcome the grinding monotony of work was absenteeism. Although during the nineteenth century the middle class achieved some measure of success in imposing a time-oriented factory discipline and regular habits on a working class accustomed to working discontinuously on a task-oriented basis,[55] widespread absenteeism has remained an insoluble problem for industrial management. A number of traditional practices associated with task-oriented work have proved resistant to the pressures of scientific management techniques and have persisted in a modified form throughout the twentieth century. Thus the tendency for one-day absences to occur on Mondays as opposed to other weekdays can be seen to some extent as the persistence of the pre-industrial tradition of Saint Monday, and the high rates of short-term absenteeism in physically arduous occupations — notably mining, in which between 3 and 10 per cent of the labour force were regularly absent once a week throughout the period under study — can be regarded as the continuation of time-honoured practices. Of course, a vast proportion of absenteeism has little or no connection with larking about and can more accurately be explained in terms of accidents, genuine illness, fatigue, poverty and harsh working conditions. However, both oral and documentary evidence clearly reveal that in some instances absenteeism was a consequence of a discriminating rejection of tedious discipline at work, and illness was faked in order to enjoy alternative leisure pursuits. Indeed, one of the principal aims of the glut of investigations into morbidity and malingering that have been sponsored by industry and the state from the 1900s onwards has been to establish the numbers of 'loafers' and 'scroungers' whose irregular work habits and illegitimate claims for welfare benefits undermine economic efficiency, and to suggest ways in which they might be detected and disciplined. It is beyond the scope of the present study to analyse complex data in order to gauge variations in patterns of absenteeism according to different age groups, occupations, standards of living and so on;[56] for our purposes it can simply be stated that young workers in many occupations absented themselves several times each year for a lark, usually to attend picture palaces, dances and sporting events or to go courting in the countryside. Autobiographies and oral interviews vividly illustrate the resentment, desire for revenge and resistance that provoked this short-term absenteeism. Iris Bradford, for example, recalling her youth in Bedminster, Bristol, during the 1930s, describes the cunning way in which she occasionally duped her employers, workmates and parents so that she might escape from tedious factory labour and enjoy Wednesday afternoon tea dances in the city.

I hated practically every minute in the factory. It was so tedious. All sitting at a long table surrounded by mounds of tobacco, stripping the leaf from the stem in rhythmic movements which seemed to me like galley slaves. We weren't allowed to take sweets in, which might have helped to relieve the boredom. I was caught chewing away once, and when I felt the dreaded tap on my shoulder I very nearly choked. 'Come with me Iris.' I was frog-marched to the manager's office. After a good old dressing-down and being informed how very lucky I was to be working there, I was finally allowed to leave his room, after being told I should now work twice as hard to make up for my terrible behaviour. But I used to have a lark sometimes. On Wednesdays the Berkeley at the top of Park Street had tea dances, which were very popular. So now and again, when I was fed up to the teeth in the factory, I'd fake a stomach ache in the morning and tell the girls at work that if I didn't feel any better after dinner I might go to bed. I'd cycle home, have my dinner, then sneak upstairs to get a dress and dance shoes, smuggle them downstairs and pack them into my saddle bag. A 'Cheerio' to mum, and off I rode to the tea dance. Then my bike was propped up outside the toilet on the Centre while I dashed inside to step out of my overalls and change into the dress. Then I pushed the bike up Park Street and left it in a back street while I danced my way round the floor. What lovely afternoons! A quick change, back into the toilet, and home again.[57]

Another form of larking about closely related to absenteeism, which aimed at relieving pressures experienced at work, was industrial sabotage. Sabotage was, of course, primarily a syndicalist strategy designed to disrupt the production process; it included not only the violent destruction and disablement of machinery, but also the deliberate limitation and disorganization of output, the ultimate goal of which was the overthrow of capitalism. The significance of sabotage and its adoption by members of the trade union movement, especially during the pre-World War I period, has been accorded scant attention by historians.[58] Equally neglected has been the widespread occurrence of casual acts of sabotage committed by young workers, for a lark, in order to enjoy the satisfaction of unscheduled stoppages and to take revenge against those in authority. Bob Stewart, for example, who worked as a 'half-timer' in the Dundee jute mills during the 1890s, recalls that he and his friends resorted to minor acts of arson to gain momentary relief from long hours of exploitation.

We were 'shifters', employed by the bobbin setters to shift the bobbins. You didn't have a name; all you were called was 'lazy young bugger', and the shifting wifie had a leather strap to keep you moving. . . . We shifters had our own little ways of getting out of work, a little bit of sabotage. Put a match in the right place, get a wee fire going among the waste, then all run about for water to put it out.[59]

The frequency of this type of sabotage was determined to a large extent by the opportunities for disruption available to workers in various occupations, the degree of control that employers were able to exert and the availability of alternative employment for the saboteur, should he or she be unfortunate enough to be detected and dismissed. Because of the hidden nature of secret disruptive activities, it is extremely difficult to estimate its precise extent, but it is likely that sabotage for a lark was most common in the innumerable casual and unskilled jobs associated with the retail and distributive trades, in which there tended to be little supervision and a huge demand for, and turnover of, labour.[60] John Bellringer, for example, recalling his youth in Bristol during the 1930s, remembers how he turned this situation to his advantage in order to gain revenge on his employer.

As a lad I worked for several shops, doing odd jobs, running errands and the like. You were made to work very long hours for very low wages, and if you asked for a bit more money, they'd just laugh in your face. The only way to get your own back was to sabotage the stuff in the back of the shop when the boss was out the front, serving. You know, you'd be lifting big bags and boxes and accidentally on purpose, like, you'd drop one or split the sides, and the sugar, flour or whatever it was would go everywhere. And delivering groceries, you'd get so fed up. Well, once I had a box to deliver to a posh house. I thought, I've had enough of this, and I took it to where this poor old lady lived and dumped it on her doorstep, and I never went back again. Well, you could get away with it in those days because there was a lot of jobs going in that line. You could just walk into another one, no questions asked.[61]

So far we have seen how larking about acted as a multi-faceted means of resistance to the institutions of control and manipulation in which working-class children and youth were incorporated. Finally, I wish to explore briefly the significance of larking about on the streets. Essentially, it was motivated by a desire to make things happen, to create some form of immediate excitement that would breathe life and spontaneity into the drab daily routine. This desire for action and for a release of aggression often found expression in sudden, unpremeditated scuffles and minor acts of vandalism, as Bill Harding remembers.

I was caught by the police once for larking about. We were all walkin' about, five or six young fellows, all in the road. An' I was the lightest in weight of the lot, an' I was on the inside. Then all of a sudden, without a word of warnin', everyone started charging one another, hittin' an' pushin' an' using their weight up against one another. I was the last to get clouted an' I went through a shop window, knocked a quarter of an inch of plate glass straight through. An' I picked meself up an' I ran like the devil, an' we all ran.[62]

Many similar incidents ended in prosecutions, especially between the 1890s and the 1920s, a period when the police tended rigorously to enforce petty rules and regulations in an attempt to eliminate traditional street activities such as gambling, loitering and 'dangerous' play.[63] This harassment aroused fierce resentment within street gangs, which sometimes exploded into violent acts of resistance and revenge against the police. Since conflict between older youths and the police was often characterized by calculated viciousness, as opposed to the humour and customary constraint associated with larking about, it has no place in the present discussion and will be explored in chapter 7. However, there was an important element of larking about in the relationship between the police and younger children, who viewed the uniformed officer as a symbol of authority to be taunted from a safe distance with nicknames and insults such as 'beetlecrusher', 'narker' or 'copper-copper wax-ass'.[64] More defiant children, like Joe Flower, who grew up in Sneiton, Nottinghamshire, during the 1900s, would try to win a symbolic victory by knocking the policeman's helmet off.

Used to climb up the lamp post, you know, and turn out the gas mantle, stretch the string across the causeway and then wait for him coming, you see. And then we should probably say something to start him running, and he'd run after us and his helmet would catch on the string and off it'd pull his helmet, you see. . . . But generally speaking he would take it all as a boys' lark. If he caught us, well, we knew what we'd get. He'd give us one with his stick, but he wouldn't be vindictive.[65]

On most occasions children were able to escape from the clutches of the law by running away; nevertheless, if they were unlucky enough to be collared while larking or merely loitering in the street, they would normally be summarily punished with a 'backhander' or a painful flick of the policeman's gloves or cape — as Stan Gibson, reflecting on his childhood in the East End of London at the turn of the century, bitterly recalls.

I remember one Christmas time we was looking in the Post Office at the top of the road, and it had Christmas goods in it. And we was looking in there, both of us, my friend and I was looking in most intently and all of a sudden, oh, we had a clip round the ear 'ole. It was a cold night, and the lobes of your ear was frozen and this copper had a knack of — most coppers did in those days — had a knack of flicking their gloves onto the lobe of your ear. I very nearly cried of pain.[66]

Children developed elaborate strategies so that they could enjoy the pleasures of larking about without having to suffer this type of punishment. For example, Eric Walsh remembers how he and his friends in Manchester during the 1890s regularly enjoyed the combined pleasures of naked bathing, breaking local by-laws and plaguing the police in such a devious way that the officer on his beat was powerless to intervene.

We were always getting into trouble — playing football and kicking balls about, breaking a few windows, you know. Now, one time, if you stood at the corner of the street, you'd get locked up for it. They'd call it 'obstruction'. If you played football in the street, you got summonsed for it, and if you went selling papers on a Sunday morning, you'd get locked up for it. Wasn't to sell papers, you see. Wasn't allowed to shout on the roads at night on account of people objected to it, you know. . . . We used to go in the Cut, oh, aye, we went in the Cut. It was clean because, you see, all the works, such as Elkaha's, Walker's and Carver's, all the hot water used to come from the boilers and it was thrown into the Cut. So we was always in there, with it being warm. We'd stop in nearly all day then. And we had to take us clothes off, was always stripped, no shorts to put on, nothing like that, you know. We used to wrap us clothes up on the canal bank and just leave it there, you know. Well, the other side was Pendleton Forge. And

many a time we used to get hold of us clothes, put 'em on us head, you know, the bundles, walk across — it wasn't very deep, you know, in some places — and put them over the other side, and the policeman couldn't come over there. He couldn't get over the water, so we was plaguing, you see.[67]

In conclusion, it may be useful to clarify some of the more obvious limitations and difficulties involved in the attempt of this chapter to conceptualize and document such a subterranean cultural tradition as larking about. Most important, different people held different views about what constituted larking about; while some respondents recollected regarding occasional truancy, fighting or pilfering as forms of larking about, others claimed that in their youth they defined these same activities as delinquency, criminality and so on. The problem of contrary definitions makes the construction of a broad theory of larking about difficult. Also, different individuals seem to have attached different meanings to similar larking activities. Thus, for example, some respondents recollected mimicry as a means of unmasking social pretensions and deriding authority figures, while others viewed it as merely a sadistic diversion. However, despite these qualifications, the concept of larking about is considerably more useful than the value-laden concepts used by middle-class investigators — irregularity, immorality, apathy, vulgarity and so on — because it gives direct expression to the thoughts and feelings that motivated working-class youth's rule-breaking activities. And although no detailed statistical or quantitive analysis has been attempted, it is clear that there was a significant escalation and elaboration of larking about during our period, which can be attributed to the resistance of working-class youth to efforts to regulate and restrict its activities. Not only did larking about loosen bonds of deference and obedience, which many institutions sought to inculcate, but it can also, in some circumstances, be seen as a nascent form of class-consciousness. Admittedly, its rewards and victories were usually only symbolic and short-lived, but in the final analysis larking about was one of the most effective means of opposition available to working-class children and youth to resist, individually or collectively, authoritarian and bureaucratic control.

Nude bathing in lakes and rivers was a popular form of larking about among working-class children. The pastime provoked an angry response from police and park attendants, as is illustrated by this picture of a chase along the bank of the Serpentine in the 1920s.

CHAPTER 6

Social Crime
and Family Survival

Most repeated offenders are far from robust; they are frail, sickly and infirm. Indeed, so regularly is chronic moral disorder associated with chronic physical disorder, that many have contended that crime is a disease.... The frequency among juvenile delinquents of bodily weakness and ill health has been remarked by almost every recent writer.... Poor health means poor control; and even a temporary physical weakness may be the occasion of a passing criminal lapse.... When health deserts us courage is diminished; laziness increased; and the heated temper simmers over in perpetual peevishness or bursts out in some sharp blast of violence. The youth whose work needs energy and application, whose business entails long hours and irksome drudgery, finds it harder than ever, on these days of transient weakness, to rise promptly from bed in the morning, to toil punctiliously from eight till six, to withstand the onset of fatigue, and to do all that's incumbent to gain a hard-earned living in an honest way.... parallel histories of ailments and of crimes will often make it clear that the child's offences were chiefly carried out when, owing to temporary ill health or transient weakness and fatigue, his moral control was at an ebb.[1]

This explanation of juvenile crime in terms of a fundamental weakness of character, and the portrayal of the young delinquent as a person whose moral deficiency is aggravated by ill-health, fatigue and long hours of work is in many ways a typical example of the form of analysis that dominated criminological thought from the 1890s to the 1930s. Written in 1925, this passage clearly calls on some of the derogatory labels of delinquency and psychopathology that have long been favoured by criminologists who, with few exceptions, have uncritically accepted a bourgeois perspective in condemning all juvenile working-class crime as evidence of ignorance and immorality.[2] In this chapter I will offer an alternative

150

class-based interpretation of delinquency and will argue that many offences can more accurately be viewed as expressions of social crime.[3] I intend to use the concept of social crime to encompass the innumerable minor crimes against property committed by working-class children and youth that were condoned by large sections of both the youth and parent cultures as legitimate, despite their illegality. For oral interviews reveal that many property crimes were necessitated and justified by extreme poverty and the working-class family's struggle for survival. It is significant that many people described their illegal activities as traditional customs, such as 'chowding' or 'scrumping' apples and 'picking' or 'scrounging' coal, all of which conveyed a belief in time-honoured rights in opposition to property law.

The most common form of property theft, which was regarded by both parents and children as the customary right of the working-class community, was that which involved the reappropriation of nature's bounty and supplemented the family's food and fuel supply. This type of offence formed the single most important category of juvenile crime during the period under study, that of 'simple and minor larceny', which comprised taking coal from pit heads, chumps of wood from timber yards and vegetables from farmers' fields, poaching rabbits and so on.[4] Although judicial proceedings were only instituted against a very small percentage of working-class children, which rarely exceeded a rate of 0.5 per cent per annum in any one district, most criminologists and penal experts were of the opinion that these delinquency rates grossly underestimated the extent of child crime. If the multitude of hidden and undetected juvenile crime, the dismissed prosecutions, the cautions for first offenders and the immediate physical retribution administered by policemen in the city streets for petty larceny were all taken into account, then, as Cyril Burt put it, 'one could expand the percentage to almost any degree. . . . Delinquency shadows the life of the city child with far more persistance and frequency than either bodily illness or economic want.'[5] This growing awareness, especially from the 1920s onwards, that juvenile delinquency was not restricted to a subnormal criminal species but was an integral part of working-class youth culture stimulated a series of government-sponsored statistical investigations and psychological case studies. Three principal findings of these inquiries, which recurred with some consistency, were that petty crime was most common among unskilled, unemployed and one-parent families,[6] that considerably more property crimes were committed by thirteen-year-olds than any other age group[7] and that the older members of the family, especially the first- and second-born, were more likely to become delinquent than the younger members.[8]

These patterns of delinquency were explained in the dominant medico-psychological tradition of criminological thought by reference to a cluster of converging theories rooted in a Freudian view of the fundamentally egotistic and individualistic nature of man. The excessive number of crimes committed by twelve- and thirteen-year-olds was interpreted as a symptom of adolescence, which came to be viewed, as we have noted, as a stage in the life characterized by inner turmoil and uncertainty, commonly expressed in cruel or criminal behaviour. As Stanley Hall, in one of the most influential works on the subject, put it, 'adolescence is pre-eminently the criminal age.'[9] The concentration of juvenile crime among the working class, and especially among large families and those disrupted by unemployment or the premature death of either parent, was attributed to defective discipline. The parents of such families, it was claimed, exerted inadequate moral control over the savage instincts of their offspring, notably those of acquisitiveness, hunting and herd behaviour, which emerged with great intensity during the early teens. This 'general laxity of morals'[10] meant that the working-class family was failing to perform what was commonly referred to in the literature as its 'civilizing', 'socializing' or 'sublimating' function, thereby producing children who were impulsive and irrational, characterized by their 'striking failure to inhibit instinctive action'.[11] In the words of Cyril Burt,

the commoner delinquencies committed by the young are the direct expression of a few primitive impulses. Accordingly the delinquent . . . is to be approached more as an animal than as a hedonist. . . . We must consider that he is liable always to be spurred fatally onward by some natural force — a force which closely resembles those vital springs which animate the humbler brutes.[12]

This jigsaw of psychopathology, which created a disturbing image of the working-class family as the mainspring of delinquency, was completed by the insertion of elaborate theories of genetic inferiority and imbalance to explain the greater incidence of crime among older siblings. In this dominant tradition biological and psychological interpretations of delinquency maintained a hegemony that ignored or underplayed the significance of poverty, inequality and class conflict as important factors in the production of crime.[13] As a consequence, a mere handful of sociological inquiries into adolescent crime were undertaken, and of these only Bagot's study of Liverpool in the 1930s regarded poverty as a 'vital factor among the causes of juvenile delinquency', reporting that 'more than 50 per cent of the delinquent families were below the Merseyside poverty line.'[14]

However, while middle-class penal experts confidently condemned juvenile crime as rooted in the antisocial and selfish impulses of adolescence, old people's recollections of family life between the 1890s and the 1930s suggest an alternative set of motives, which were eminently social and were rooted in the domestic economy of the working-class household. A number of interviews in both the Essex and Bristol collections indicate that within working-class families, especially those whose survival was threatened by chronically low wages, prolonged unemployment or the death of one of the parents, the elder children were forced by economic necessity and grinding poverty to commit minor property crimes in order to obtain free food and fuel. The eldest children, who by virtue of their superior strength, skill and self-reliance committed these offences, often seem to have taken an enormous pride in their unearned contribution to the family budget, despite the fact that such tasks were often arduous or dangerous. The proud recollections of respondents who claim that their devious activities before and after school were essential to the family's survival should not be dismissed as mere exaggeration or romanticism. In fact, such memories find overwhelming documentary support in the evidence of social investigators into the cycle of poverty, which discovered that the working-class family experienced the most extreme hardship and deprivation just before the eldest child reached the school-leaving age and could begin to contribute to the family income as a wage-earner.[15] The family cycle of poverty is, it seems to me, a powerful but until now unconsidered alternative explanation for the prevalence of crime among older siblings, the peak in crime at the age of thirteen and its decline a year later and the concentration of delinquency among large and single-parent families. To illustrate this point, I wish to quote at length from Charlie Portingale's recollections of the property offences he regularly committed while a schoolboy in Bristol during the early 1930s, for they vividly illuminate social crime as a rational, discriminating activity in the context of class inequality and the day-to-day demands of the family economy.

Being the eldest boy, I was the one that kept the family going. I did a bit of pilfering when I was small, never thinking that it was wrong — I mean, in them days you used to. My mother was crying one day an' I said, 'How much money 'ave you got in your purse?' She had four pennies, the old pennies. Well, I took that fourpence out an' then it was up to me what I could do about it. I go out early to Witts — that was a very small bakery then, an' they used to have their vans come in over the weekend, where they'd take fresh cakes to their shops an' take the ones that were a day old back and if you were first there, you had the best pick, so I used to be there very early in the morning and wish everybody 'Good morning' as they come in, so you know they seen you an' they know that you were the first there. Well, then, for threepence I used to 'ave a great big bag of Burton cream cornets, broken cream slices, Chelsea buns. Then I got my bag of cake waste, as they called it, an' then I used to go down to a Mr Punky — he used to keep the grocery shop. Now, on the counter in them days you used to 'ave packets of sample tea on the counter, but you couldn't have the samples unless you bought somethin' in the shop, so I used to stand just round the side of the doorway an' wait for any woman. I'd walk by the side of 'er into the counter, so he didn't know whether I belonged to the woman or what, see. Anyway, I always made sure that the woman was ahead of me so she can get served before me. Well, as soon as he turns his back for the first item she've asked for, I would take a handful of tea bags an' put 'em in my pocket. Then I'd wander outside and I used to run across the road to a mate called Kenny Adlam. I used to go and knock on his door, and I had a penny left. I used to say to him, 'Now, if I give you a ha'penny, I want you to go an' get some sugar in a bag for me mum, and I want a drop of milk in a bottle.'

I got the tea, got me cakes, got me sugar, got me milk, an' I got this ha'penny, so the next place is the railway bank, and I put the ha'penny on the line. I used to judge where the train slowed down, because if you put it on where the train did go fast, he would flatten it too flat an' you'd 'ave a job to find your penny. But if you could judge where he used to 'ave to stop — always had to stop at the signal because there was a tunnel ahead at Montpelier; we used to mark the sleeper, because I wasn't the only one who used to do it — where he was just slowing down, so it was just enough to run over the ha'penny to flatten it big enough for the penny for the gas, an' I used to take that home and we'd got our meal. . . . Well, I don't agree with people stealing things, but in them days you didn't think of it as stealing. I mean, to knock the man's biscuits over outside of his shop, just because you've been in the shop an' said, 'I want some broken biscuits' — 'I haven't got any.' So you made your own broken biscuits; you go out and hit his stand over, then you'd run off an' half an hour after you get one of your brothers to go in and say, 'Half a pound of broken biscuits.' Then we know he's got broken biscuits because you've just broken them, see. You're being criminal in a way. . . .

I used to go down Sevier Street near the park, especially in the summer when all the chrysanths and all the flowers were out. I'd take two flowers from each garden, steal them, till I had an armful of flowers, an' I used to go up on the tip, hide them away, go back home, find anythin' — old bootlaces — go back on the tip and bunch them up and go down York

Street, Minton Road, an' sell them in the doors and come back with an armful of money. And that was stealing, but to me it wasn't stealing. I mean, because even today if you 'ad a family of kiddies and you were desperate, they were starving, I'd sooner go out and steal a load of groceries and do six months in prison as long as them children's fed. That's how it was then. I'd never get caught, I'd make sure of it. I mean, there's many a time we used to sit and have army blankets round us where we was so cold. Grate was empty. That's the time when I used to go down the railway bank an' wait for the train to stop at the usual place and throw abuse at the driver. The only way the driver can get back at you is by throwin' lumps of coal at you, so the more you abused him, the more coal you took home. Over Fox Road, used to be a coal yard, an' then we used to have Grade 1, Grade 2 things for coal, anthracite an' all this. They used to start separating it. I used to take a sack over on a nighttime, and there used to be one part there with the bars bent where somebody had bent it purposely to get in there, an' I got in there. Been over in the afternoon an' had a look to see which was the grades and memorized it, then take a bag an' get through the hole, fill me bag up. And I went over one day, I went about ten o'clock at nighttime, an' filled the bag up and I was just going to come out. Now, this was the only place because the spike railings was nine or ten feet high; just comin' out with the bag when there was a courting couple stood right by the hole, kissin' and cuddlin', and they was cuddlin' till about half-past twelve from ten o'clock. So my mother, she knows where I've gone, she starts getting hysterical because she thinks I've been caught. I couldn't go till they went. But at least we had a fire.[16]

Charlie Portingale's testimony, like those of many others of the older working-class generation, reveals a determined and explicitly moral resolution to provide for his family whatever the legal consequences. Such oral evidence offers a direct challenge to the views of the criminologists, magistrates and youth workers who have controlled all official records relating to this type of crime and who have invariably, from the late nineteenth century onwards, represented it in terms of a culture of poverty that degrades and brutalizes the working-class child. This documentary evidence can be reinterpreted in the light of such verbal testimonies to reveal a rich seam of deeply-embedded class resistance. For example, the following social worker's indictment of a seventeen-year-old girl who persisted in stealing small amounts of coal for her family and who was in 1924 sentenced to three years in borstal to reform her character vividly illustrates how images of immorality were imposed on those who most tenaciously refused to acknowledge the property rights of the privileged.

Coal lifting in X is commonplace; everyone more or less does it. Girl is very simple and weak, but morally innocent. Feels justified in stealing if family is in need.[17]

I will not labour this point here, as I shall be examining critically this type of class-prejudiced criminological literature elsewhere;[18] for the present I want to focus on the motives and meanings attached to social crime and to let those who were themselves involved in it describe their activities.

The nature of social crime between the 1890s and the 1930s was extremely complex and diverse, varying widely between country and city, between different neighbourhoods and even between different streets in the same neighbourhood. The precise form it took was shaped by such factors as the opportunities for property theft offered by the local economy, the vigilance with which the authorities were willing or able to enforce property law, and the prevalence of community traditions that sanctioned this type of illegal activity. Most important, however, was the experience of class relations in everyday life as an aspect of the unequal distribution of advantage and control mediated through work, the school and the family. It is significant here that social crime was likely to be most intense in neighbourhoods or families which experienced the most severe economic hardship and often increased dramatically during strikes in which the local community was involved.[19] To understand fully the dynamics of this process would require a series of detailed local studies, a task that is necessarily beyond the limited scope of this chapter, which aims instead to sketch the broad outlines of social crime. To do this, I will distinguish four types of social and geographical location — the coal-mining community, the countryside, the coastal area and the city — which, despite their interrelated and overlapping natures, are useful for the purposes of analysis.

During the inter-war period it was acknowledged by a number of social commentators and criminologists, among them Hermann Mannheim, that

stealing coal occupies an important place in adolescent delinquency of the coal-mining districts and it becomes clear from the records that activities of this kind, according to the verdict of large sections of the local population, are not regarded as comparable to ordinary thefts. The children sometimes seem to concentrate exclusively on this type of offence, which strongly confirms the view that they do not regard it as morally wrong.[20]

The illegal 'picking' of coal from pit heads and slag heaps was common in mining communities, especially during strikes. This photograph of girls collecting coal in their aprons was taken in South Wales during the miners' strike of 1912.

The 'picking' of coal from pit heads and slag heaps was a habit so deeply ingrained in mining communities that it formed part of the daily domestic routine for many children, who were expected to salvage coal both before and after school. Pit owners and the police, in order to encourage a harmonious relationship with the local working-class community, chose to prosecute only a small minority of miners' children for 'picking' coal, and as a result children were more likely to be punished at school for their late arrival in the morning and their dirty, dishevelled appearance than for their persistent property offences. For, as Bill Bees, a miner's son in the south Gloucestershire village of Hanham in the 1930s, recalls, collecting coal was a dirty and time-consuming chore, for which most teachers had little sympathy or understanding.

And I used to 'ave to get up every mornin' to go to this slag heap 'cos we couldn't afford to buy coal, an' on this slag heap you could 'ave it for nothin'. I've been many a time with no shoes or socks on, an' going to there you 'ad to go through a mucky yard, an' if it'd been raining, the water'd hang in there, but my feet was 'ardened to it — my feet was as hard as nails. Used to walk through this water, didn't bother to wipe 'em or anythin', and when you finished gettin' out of the water, you just shake yer feet an' they'd dry. But when it'd been snowing I used to walk behind me father in his footsteps, because where he did work he did 'ave to pass the colliery. I did step in his boot marks. But where he walked out, he did take such big steps that I did sometimes miss an' go in the snow. An' he did say, 'You follow me, son, you'll be alright.' And that's what they call followin' in yer father's footsteps. [Laughter] But those mornings it didn't make no difference if I came 'ome wet through; I still 'ad to go to school after. It was like a quick lick and a promise. 'Where's the towel, mother?' an' no grub, then run to school. No breakfast, never 'eard of that in my day. When you got to school you knew what you was going to get. You was going to get the cane for being late. If I wasn't in when the handbell went at nine o'clock, the doors would be bolted so you couldn't sneak in after roll call. You was left then to explain why you were so late. I had to tell 'im what I 'ad to do for my mother but he didn't believe me and he would get the cane out and give me three good smashings across my hand. I used to say to myself, I wish I could get there early and miss that cane. I used to tell my mother 'bout it an' she used to say, 'He'll get tired, he'll get tired, son.' But 'twas me taking the punishment. And he used to glory in it, an' my fingers used to swell up, an' they'd be like sausages, all swollen up. Sometimes I didn't wash before going to school. Well, then I was sent straight to the lobby. I 'ad to wash an' they made me strip right off, and my mother an' father didn't like that. They did lead you round the classroom by your ear an' show the people how much dust or dirt you 'ad up in yer ears. And box you one in the ears an' make you go to the sink an' wash, a proper show-up.[21]

Traditions of resistance to property law were also prevalent in the countryside. The misleading stereotypes of the political conservatism and social deference of the rural working class have tended to blur the contours of class conflict between labourers and farmers, which has historically found one of its most powerful expressions in social crime. The capitalist redefinition of customary

---

Woodchopper's Court, Bedminster, Bristol, in 1902. Here parents and children could frequently be seen chopping up wood, some of it stolen, which they then hawked around the city.

rights of use as exclusive private property rights, which occurred principally in the eighteenth and nineteenth centuries, and the consequent criminalization of traditional activities such as poaching and the collecting of wood, fruit, peat, acorns and so on, has been documented elsewhere.[22] But oral interviews reveal that the struggles of the underprivileged to maintain customary rights of use persisted into the twentieth century and that this tradition was most fiercely upheld by working-class youth in rural areas. For those who felt morally justified in abiding by customary rights and resisting the private property rights enshrined in criminal law the countryside, by virtue of its vast and usually unprotected nature, offered innumerable opportunities for the plunder of its rich bounty, as Jimmy McNeil remembers.

There was so many things you could do. Well, the thing is that you would call them stealing, but we didn't look at them as stealing. . . . Well, the likes of gurdling a few fish, we didna think that was stealing. But it was stealing, you know; it was theft. And any apples falling off a tree, picking them off the ground and eating them, that was stealing. We didn't think it was stealing because it had fallen. Anything that fell down — that was the law — as long as it had fallen you could eat it.[23]

Although the annual rates of minor theft were proportionately lower in the countryside than the city, they do not reflect the large amount of hidden crime committed by teenagers who were sufficiently devious generally to prevent detection. And even when discovered they were often quick-witted and fleet-footed enough to avoid arrest and a possible summons by escaping across the fields, as Derwyn Jones, who grew up in the South Wales village of Tongwynlais in the 1890s, remembers.

Go in the field and pinch the blessed mushrooms in the morning, three o'clock in the morning. Yes, get up early in the morning, and go up, pick about six or seven pounds of mushrooms. And that used to help us to live. . . . I was caught many times going out to pick blackberries. The farmer, around his barns he'd have an hedge, you know, with tons of blackberries on, but you're not allowed on there. So I used to be in the fields close by and waiting now for him to take his cattle in to milk 'em. And as soon as he'd go in there I'd be in this field. Have, oh, seven or eight pounds of blackberries while he was milking the cows. Many times he came out and caught us but he never caught me. I could go and he'd be after me, but he never caught me.[24]

The peak time at which most juvenile crime was committed was the hour between four and five o'clock in the afternoon,[25] and oral interviews suggest that a considerable number of thefts in the countryside were the work of older children, who pilfered fruit and vegetables on their way home from school in order to provide a more varied and substantial tea for the family. As Elsie Pegler, recalling her childhood in the south Gloucestershire village of Almondsbury in the early 1900s, put it:

if nobody was around we'd often nip in fields and grab a turnip or a cabbage or something, and mother'd always be glad of that for tea.[26]

While such petty thefts tended to be committed by children in a very casual manner, poaching, because it involved much more serious consequences for those who were caught and convicted, required much more careful planning and secret codes of conduct and was often organized by older gangs of young men in their late teens and twenties. Bill Breakspear remembers how his political conversion to socialism as a young teenager in the 1900s influenced his decision to act as an informer for a gang of poachers in the Oxfordshire village of Northleigh. His testimony is of value partly because it illuminates the submerged conflict between the working-class village community and the local landowners but, more important, because it clearly expresses the deeply felt but often inarticulate feelings of resentment and hostility that formed the moral justification for poaching.

I suppose I would be about eleven, and I believed in torture for wickedness and all that. Suddenly I came into contact with this man . . . he was a socialist, a shoemaker from Oxford . . . and he was telling me different things and he said, 'Whatever you do, boy, when you leave school never sell your labour cheaply because that's the only thing you have. And always learn to be kind and good.' And this man persuaded me to see life in a different way, and from then onwards I began to query and puzzle what had happened to life in a Christian way. And as I read newspapers and things, I began to see things in a different light. Before I left school I would not sing

> The rich man in his castle, the poor man at his gate,
> God made him high and mighty, and all of their estate.

I would not sing that at an early age. . . . The fruits of the earth were there but not for you to pick. But that was accepted because the other people had control of it and you couldn't visualize that that was part and parcel of your heritage. . . . Now, I worked on Eynsham Hall Estate, and I worked with keepers very often, and the conversation was where they were likely to catch poachers. And I used to listen very attentively. Now, the people in the village would trust me, although I was a youngster; they would absolutely trust me with everything. I would give them information. Well,

Many country children pilfered fruit and vegetables on their way home from school. In this photograph, taken at the turn of the century, a Scottish policeman interrogates children who have taken turnips from the fields.

Stolen food often found its way on to the dinner table of poor and unemployed families like this one, photographed in the 1930s.

they'd go up at night when rabbits were out at feed. They knew where the hedges were and where the rabbits were likely to run. They'd set the nets along. They had a well-trained dog, and this dog would round like a sheep dog would round sheep; he would round the field and, of course, the rabbits dashed and they'd catch them in their nets.[27]

Just as the deep-rooted tradition of poaching persisted into the twentieth century, so did the time-honoured custom that sanctioned the right of coastal communities to plunder all wreckage washed in by the sea.[28] Many young working-class boys and girls defied the elaborate regulations of coastguards and harbour masters that controlled or prohibited such activities. For, as Billy Spargo, recalling his childhood in the Cornish fishing village of Newquay in the 1900s, explains, beachcombing for driftwood and wreckage provided essential fuel to keep the family fire burning.

We was a bit of a hefty crowd, robust, like, living down the harbour and on the beaches, beachcombing, as we used to call it — pickin' up wood to carry 'ome. We used to burn a huge amount of wreckage, pieces of driftwood, wood washed in from wrecks or cargoes been washed over board, any driftwood. And, of course, the rules and regulations of the coastguards was that anythin' over six feet had to be turned in back in those days . . . but we never took no notice; the bigger the better, as far as we were concerned.[29]

Oral evidence, such as that of Allan Rees of Birkenhead, illustrates that although official regulations were disregarded by children, coastal plunder was governed by an equally elaborate set of customary practices, which protected the right of the smallest child to valuable flotsam, should he be skilful enough to lay claim to it with a toggle bar and lead weight.

Very often we spent quite a lot of time gathering flotsam and jetsam, firewood to take home. Well, flotsam, as you know, is the tideline debris that is floating and the jetsam is the tideline debris that's been deposited on the shore. And we used to just gather firewood and people would be there before you very often for the jetsam, so that you had to develop a skill in getting in flotsam and you'd have to get a line over. Although a very young boy, I was skilled at getting the lines over because my father taught me to fish on the sandbanks with leaded throw-out lines. You had a good long twine with a lead weight at the end and a toggle bar — that's a little piece of wood at arm's length from the lead weight. You unwound the line and loops on the shore, gripped the toggle bar in the two main fingers with the line between and swung the lead weight round your head as fast as possible, gathering momentum, and then let go to let it fly over the waves, taking the line out over the target piece of flotsam you were aiming for. If your line was the first over that piece of flotsam, then it was yours. That rule was almost religiously observed, no matter how little you were. And many boys, youths and even men went after firewood. I waded into my chest sometimes to get distance, almost losing sight of the target.[30]

Another popular target for juvenile theft was the timber yards that proliferated in many dockside areas and held the promise of free firewood for needy families. For Dick Cook, who was caught attempting such a theft in Bristol during World War I, the experience offered him political education and taught him that some property owners had little compunction at fabricating evidence in the hope of securing a conviction.

We was playing and we got alongside this timber yard an' the padlock was broken on the gate. So we went in and I picked hold of a chunk 'cos they did have these felled trees, great big things, and they used to saw them up. I pinched one and another kiddy got one. We thought it would be for firewood, as we were a bit on the poor side then. Anyway, we just started off and this man chased us. Well, he caught the pair of us and he summonsed us — yes, he summonsed us. I remember my mother sayin',

'Trust you to get caught. If there had been a dozen, it would have been thee.' When we got to court (our mother had to go) he said, 'Why did you steal it?' I just naturally said, 'Well, we wanted some firewood.' He said, 'If you come here again, you're headed for the reformatory.' We got let off, but coming out I said to our mother, I said, 'Eh, ma, that in't the chump I pinched. I couldn't carry that one they had up there.' She said, 'Are you sure?' I said 'Yes, I could never carry that.' He'd put another chump up, see.[31]

It was in the city that juvenile crime assumed its most dangerous proportions, and the disturbing image of an amoral and antisocial working-class youth culture inspired three generations of middle-class social reformers to campaign for prohibitive and preventive legislation aimed at solving this urgent social problem. One of their most compelling fears was that family and community relationships were being undermined by urbanization, and that while middle-class parents could protect their own children from the evil and degenerative forces of city life, working-class children, because of defective discipline at home, were extremely vulnerable to its sinister power.[32] The temptations and enormous opportunities for crime offered by markets, shops and department stores, the depersonalization of relationships in the anonymous city crowd and the independent street culture of young people, which resisted adult interference and control, were all powerful influences that encouraged juvenile delinquency. However, contrary to the middle-class fears that these social forces destroyed family relationships and dissipated the finer instincts of working-class children in a brutalized and desocialized mass, interviews suggest that a proportion of juvenile delinquency in the city was inspired by family duty. The reason why so many middle-class commentators and reformers were blind to this bond between children and parents was because they could not or would not conceive of an affectionate family relationship that led to the defiance and transcendence of property law. A common target for this type of urban social crime, which supplemented the budget of the poorest families, was the corner shop, as Willie McGee remembers from his Edinburgh childhood in the 1900s:

My mother used to send Jimmy or me for a bottle of Tizer or a couple of half-loaves, a tin of milk, something like that, you know. Well, Jimmy and me would work out a plan of action and go into a shop to see if we could skim something off it, you know. And my mother, she'd said, 'Get two apples' — I've seen me coming back with four; 'A pound of tatties' — coming back with a peck (that's half a stone, I think). Things like that, see, we used to nab it, steal 'em in the shop, you know. Pretty cheap but then people must have thought they was nae stealing.[33]

I have discovered no oral evidence to suggest that working-class parents actually instructed their children to pilfer food or steal money from shops, and it is likely that parentally instigated crimes were restricted to an extremely small minority of families on the verge of destitution. Instead, the attitude of struggling parents whose teenage children committed such crime was gratefully to accept the bounty and to avoid asking too many questions about where it came from, as John Bellringer, who worked a number of fiddles while employed as a Saturday boy by a Bristol greengrocer in the 1920s, remembers.

We'd go out in the country buyin' eggs, and he taught me, 'Don't forget, there's not twelve eggs in a dozen; there's fifteen.' An' I weighed it all up in a week, an' he'd say, 'You go in the farm. A pair of kippers, sixpence.' An' I used to think, well, a pair of kippers isn't sixpence, they're eightpence, so I would make twopence for myself. It wasn't being dishonest, in my mind; I don't think it was dishonest because the people you delivered to could afford to do without it. Well, all those twopences in a day'd be, say, three shillings. An' I'd give my mother two and six out of that. I don't think she ever queried me about it. I just used to say, 'Well, that's me wages,' but when I reached the age of fourteen or fifteen she knew bloody well what I was doing an' my father also knew, but I don't think my father ever really reproached me in any way.[34]

There were some occasions, however, when poor parents had little choice but to conspire with their children in deceiving the authorities; for example, in the infamous 'moonlight flit' to avoid the payment of rent. And to enjoy an annual treat at the seaside, the poorest families practised a devious strategy that took full advantage of the crowds on the station platforms, as Marie Smith recalls:

Our mum used to be determined that we should 'ave a day at Weston once a year. 'Course, we didn't 'ave any money, so what she did, she'd get us to wait until there was a big crowd of people moving on to the platform, then one at a time she'd get us to sneak behind 'em past the ticket inspector. We'd do that on the way there and we'd do the same on the way back again.[35]

The form of city delinquency that aroused the most bitter condemnation of middle-class reformers was the devious and dishonest practice associated with street trading by young people[36]

— some of this too, I believe, can properly be seen as social crime. The growth of cities as commercial and industrial centres created a wide range of part-time or full-time opportunities for working-class children in street employment as newspaper sellers, hawkers, costermongers and so on.[37] And although these 'young barbarians of the slums'[38] were often portrayed as aimless and amoral beings, oral interviews suggest that, on the contrary, they formed part of a complex street culture whose members infinitely preferred the independence and freedom of street life to the rigid discipline they experienced at school and in factories. Despite the fact that they prided themselves on their ability to outsmart customers, mainly through a variety of ingenious short-change techniques, interviews clearly reveal that they were discriminating in their choice of victims, who were normally middle- or upper-class. The main beneficiaries of their dishonest earnings tended to be their mothers, as is illustrated by James Bushnell's memories of his exploits on the streets of London in the 1900s:

I could impersonate a taxi call, like a commissionaire outside an hotel — he'd blow a whistle. And if while I'm walking around the City of London, if I noticed that commissionaire wasn't on the door and I could see somebody waiting for a taxi who couldn't whistle and who couldn't call out or anything, I used to say, 'Taxi, sir?' or 'Taxi, madam?' 'Yes, please, son.' Right. And bring the taxi over. I used to get a couple of bob. And then I was doing that one day outside the hotel, a lady pulled up in a taxi, so I rushed and opened the door for her and, 'Oh,' she said, 'very kind of you. Here you are, take this.' And she give me a shilling. At the same time she pulled the shilling out, she dropped a half-sovereign on the ground. Well, I didn't know what was dropped, might have been anything, but when she went into the hotel I looked on the ground. Holy smoke! Cor! I picked it up, whipped it in me pocket quick and run. That lady must have a lot of money, carrying half-sovereigns about with her. I thought of me mother. That'll do my mother a wonderful good turn that will. . . . Oh, she kissed me all over. She soon went and spent most of it anyway, food for the children and meself and dad.[39]

From the 1900s onwards the imposition of successive prohibitive measures that regulated street trading, together with the extension of compulsory state education to the age of fourteen, led to the virtual extinction of this street children's culture by the mid-1930s. However, there was a direct relationship between the criminalization of these practices and the upward trend in petty crime among city children during the 1920s and 1930s, for they were forced to turn to other illegal activities to compensate for their dispossessed earnings, the loss of which placed an intolerable financial burden on the poorest families.

So far we have focused mainly on the social crime committed by working-class children and young people in what was nominally their leisure time: the young street trader struggling to make a precarious living in the city streets provides a natural link with the world of work. The workplace itself generated a powerful tradition of social crime, that of pilfering, which was rooted in the feeling that it was the inalienable right of the worker to appropriate a small proportion of the goods that he or she produced. In many occupations pilfering was referred to in the trade by customary names, some of them dating from the pre-capitalist era, such as 'cabbage' for the leather taken home by shoemakers, 'sweepings' for the food and drink appropriated by dockers and 'waxers' for the samples of wines and spirits consumed by journeymen coopers. Employers sometimes seem to have treated minor pilfering as a legitimate perk, though their response was unpredictable, and the extent to which they chose to institute criminal proceedings against those found guilty of pilfering varied widely between different trades and different individuals.[40] Most working-class boys and girls experienced an early initiation into this form of social crime, and in this context James Bushnell's memory of dockside pilfering in London during World War I is particularly interesting, partly because it reveals the collective bonds of trust and solidarity that concealed such activities from the eyes of the authorities and, most important, because it illustrates graphically a young worker's awareness of the rules of the pilfering game — that pinching a few bananas would be viewed benevolently by the dock police as a perk, while drinking rum would be treated as a criminal offence.

When I worked on the docks I used to find a banana barge and stuff me pockets up with 'em, fetch 'em home. Of course, if I had a nice big bag on the back of me bike, I'd fill the bag up. Although it wasn't allowed to take 'em, police never used to say nothing. Copper on the gate, as you went to go out, he'd say, 'What have you got in your bag, son?' 'That's the old torch, guv'nor, and a couple of bananas.' 'Alright, away you go.' . . .

One day the ship come in, and the dockies started work on her, uncovered the hatch, and I noticed there was great big barrels of wine, some sort of wine, don't know what it was. I found out afterwards what it was. And, of course, the first thing they do, the dockies, they have a drink. They got their hooks what they pull the cargo about with, and they give it a tap where the bung is and out flows the wine. Well, I was a crane driver at the time, and I'm looking down the hold, and one of the dockies hollers up to me — they used to call me Darkie — 'Darkie, get us a bottle of water, or a bucketful if you can.' So I go down the galley and say to the cook (I knew 'em all well), 'Have you got a bucket I can get some clean water in? Lend me, I'll fetch it back.' 'Yes.' So I go to the fresh-water tap, fill the bucket up, get a bit of string and lower it down the hole for the dockie. 'All right, chum?' 'Yes, thanks.' Well, of course, I hadn't a clue what was in the barrels, so I had to go up in the crane to do my work, and I went back down the hole during the afternoon. I just went to have a look-see how they were getting on. So this same dockie I spoke to first, he said, 'Got any bottles, Darkie?' I said, 'Bottles? No, I'm afraid I ain't.' He said, 'You'll find some on the quay.'

On the quay they used to stack all the empties up. So I went on the quay and got a couple of bottles, put 'em in me pocket, empty ones. Poured a little drop of water in and give 'em a shake, washed them bottles out, and he filled one of these bottles up with this wine, and he caught it up with a bit of wood and 'Catch!' 'Right.' He threw it up to me. Of course, it leaked a bit and splashed down me shirt. 'Cor, 'struth!' I said. 'It's rough.' I knew I'd get court-martialled if the policeman smelt rum on me. So I nipped down to the engine room with it quick, and I give it to the chargehand fitter. He said, 'What have you got there?' I said, 'Well, I don't know what it is,' I said. 'It smells like rum. You can have it if you want it.' 'Where did you get it?' I said, 'A dockie just give it to me out of the hold,' I said. 'He wanted a bucket of water and so he give me a drop of rum in the place, kindness, like.' 'Blimey.' Anyway, he said, 'Did the dockie say what country it came from?' I said, 'No, ain't got a clue.' He said, 'Well, if you get a chance, you ask the dockie what country it comes from and what proof it has.' So on the quiet I see this dockie. I said, 'I had to give that bottle away. I couldn't drink that.' So he said, 'Oh, who did you give it to?' I said, 'Chargehand fitter.' 'Oh, that's all right,' he said. 'He'll know what to do with it.' So, of course, the old chargehand fitter, he had what they called some distilled water in a big glass container, down the engine room, and he mixed some of that with this rum, so when he see me again he said, 'Want a drop of your drink, Jim?' I said, 'I don't mind.' So he give me a cup, half a cupful. 'Cor,' I said, 'a lot too strong.' I said, 'I see the dockie and he said it's 75 per cent over proof.' 'Did he? Have a drop more water in it, then.'[41]

Because he enjoyed regular full-time employment, James Bushnell could exercise some choice over whether to pilfer or not, but for the young casual labourer who in times of trade depression and high unemployment could only find a few days' work each week 'fiddling' was necessary in order to survive, as Ernie Tucker of Torquay remembers.

We did it because of necessity, the mother of invention. I mean to say, if you didn't fiddle, you didn't live. You just had to, were forced to. They all fiddled. They'd go up and pinch a cabbage in a field or a cauliflower or something. You had to; you wouldn't live otherwise. It was the survival of the fittest. You had to for the necessities of life, really, and if there was enough for a pint of cider, well, that was better still.[42]

In this struggle for survival those whose wits had been sharpened by the rigours of street trading were quick to seize any opportunity for appropriating valuable materials at work, and for the most ingenious the money obtained from selling these pilfered materials was considerably more than their weekly wage. Fred Gotts, who served an apprenticeship as a shoemaker in Stepney during the 1900s, remembers that this additional money was of great assistance to his mother, helping her to feed a large family.

I become what I call a helpmate. I used to go out and right from a kid bring her [his mother] in money, in the City, go selling papers and things. And when I was fifteen I was a lord because I found a little goldmine in that old factory where I was apprenticed. I saw in the dustbin old bits of brass, see. And we was always learnt to be what you call jackdaws, find things, you see. And soon as I saw that brass I knew we could sell it. So I says to this boy — he asked me one day what I was doing down there — I said, 'Do you want to come partners with me? We tip the dustbin right over, we'll sort it out and we'll put all the dirt back and we'll keep the metal ourselves and we'll sell it.' And, of course, he was an East End boy and he knew the tricks as well, so we did that, and then we did that every day. We had a little brush and shovel there what we hid away from the dustmen; they wouldn't see it. Down this courtway we used to take the brass or copper pieces, screws and bolts or whatever they were, and at the end of the week the man used to pay us. We used to take in as much as fourteen, fifteen pounds of a night in that rag shop there in Shoreditch. Then the Friday night came when we went in, he paid us, that man. I've nearly a hundredweight in there, hundred pounds-odd, you know, in weight. Well, if you had, say, fourpence a pound — hundred pound, fourpence a pound, you see, you had four hundred pence, didn't you? It was a week's work and we was quite happy, and it cost us nothing. All we had to do was to carry it.[43]

Although some shrewd employers tolerated minor pilfering as a fairly harmless means of supplementing meagre wages, others viewed it as a serious infringement of private property rights and sought to eliminate such deplorable conduct. There were innumerable opportunities for petty theft open to working-class girls entering domestic service, and their honesty was frequently tested by suspicious employers, who would deliberately place a coin in a half-protruding position where the servant was expected to clean, normally beneath a carpet. This practice, and the angry response it provoked, vividly illustrates two key dimensions of social crime:

first, the moral test clearly expresses the deep-seated middle-class fear of property theft and the bourgeois assumption that all crimes committed by working-class youth were a symptom of moral deficiency and debasement; second, it illustrates that attempts to apprehend and discipline young offenders were often counter-productive in their effects, further aggravating class conflict, for most working-class children and young people were extremely discriminating in their pilfering and considered such treatment to be a gross insult to their dignity and sense of loyalty and trust. Only the most desperate would consider stealing personal possessions from the family for whom they worked. Since there was an unsatisfied demand for domestics, especially from the 1900s onwards, working-class girls were no longer intimidated by the threat of dismissal and unemployment and increasingly felt free to give full vent to their feelings of contempt for this insulting practice. For example, Violet Dicks, who as a child felt morally justified in participating in minor pilfering activities in the streets and fields around her home in Bath during the early part of the century, was so incensed by the moral tests set by her employer that she resolved to take revenge.

My employer planted a half-crown piece on the stairs to try to see if I was honest, not once, but two or three times. So I just got a hammer and a nail and I told her where it was. I'd hammered it right through the stairs. I was only fourteen and a half, but I told her she could keep her job.[44]

And Kate Gillies, whose family was involved in the collecting of driftwood and wreckage along the shores of her village home in Balla, Shetland Islands, at the turn of the century, was so disgusted by her mainland employer's suspicious attitude towards her that she felt compelled to hand in her notice immediately.

I was only a few weeks there, och, when this happened. This afternoon she said to me, 'Kate, will you now go up to the spare room and collect my things and put them back in the wardrobe?' She'd left them on the bed in the spare room. I went up to the spare room, and when I walked into the door a beautiful fawn mat had lovely roses in the centre and roses in the corners, and a new Scottish pound note laid on the mat, not crumpled nor crushed, but flat laid there. Oh, gracious, my blood boiled when I saw this. I took it in my hand and went over to the dressing table and took four pins out of the cushion. And I stretched the braw new pound on the pillowsham and put a pin in each corner. 'Mrs Haig,' I said, 'will you please come up with me to the spare room?' I said. 'I've something there that I would like to show you.' Oh, she came up, her fur coat on and hat. 'Now, then,' I said, 'that's a pound that was dropped or left on the mat intentionally' (it was done intentionally). 'Now,' I said 'Mrs Haig, you take my notice from today because,' I said, 'very, very little I think of furs and of your money. Now, supposing I would get the whole of the gold that's in Britain, my own character,' I said, 'is worth to me more than that. That's all I have in this world,' I said, 'to take me from this world, my character.'[45]

It is very difficult to estimate the precise significance of pilfering and of the other forms of social crime that we have examined. Interviews clearly reveal that this assertion of customary rights was experienced as a victory of profound expressive and instrumental importance, won by the propertyless over the propertied. Yet although social crime released deep-rooted feelings of hostility, there was in fact little correlation between participation in social crime and the development of militant class-consciousness. For some, like Bill Breakspear, who acted as an informer for the Northleigh poachers, social crime was indeed a political act. But despite the fact that many young people justified their thefts in terms of the injustices of social inequality, social crime was for the majority a short-term family solution rather than part of a long-term political solution to their problems. Understandably, for families confronted by desperate problems of economic hardship and day-to-day survival social crime was a much more immediate and relevant means of alleviating their situation than involvement in political activities. However, disappointment at the fact that these minor property thefts were rarely motivated by a clear political purpose has soured the classical Marxist tradition of criminology, which has viewed such crimes as an expression of a war of all against all generated by the avarice, exploitation and economic misery intrinsic to the capitalist system. This type of interpretation must be rejected, for it tends to conflate and over-simplify the complexities of criminal behaviour. More seriously, despite differences of ideological emphasis, it has led many left commentators to rub shoulders with the theorists from the pathological school who condemn juvenile delinquency as a symptom of amoral and antisocial behaviour. I have no wish to romanticize working-class crime; elsewhere I discuss how minor property crimes committed by street gangs met with the general disapproval of the parent culture and led to considerable intra-class conflict between different generations. However, while only a small minority of the property offences we have discussed can be seen as an expression of an open class-consciousness, it seems to me that there is much oral and documentary evidence that suggests the presence of a distinct tradition of social crime that was rooted in class feeling and class solidarity. This tradition was prevented from deteriorating into a war of all against all by customary codes of honour and by the complex set of loyalties and obligations that developed within families, streets and the local working-class community. And, as I have insisted throughout, the primary source of this flood of working-class crime, especially among children in their early teenage years, can be traced to social inequality and the family cycle of poverty as opposed to the uncontrolled instincts of desocialized adolescents. I have deliberately steered clear of an attempt to quantify the extent of social crime with any degree of precision, for the vast majority of offences passed unnoticed or unrecorded in the official archives. Although oral evidence makes possible a more graphic study of this submerged tradition, it too presents difficulties, one of which is that some old people are reluctant to discuss their memories of social crime, sometimes in order to project a respectable image, occasionally because of their fear that the revelation of crimes committed in childhood might lead to some form of delayed prosecution. However, despite these problems, the social crime of working-class youth deserves to be recognized and explored in greater depth by historians, for in many ways it constituted a noble tradition of resistance to the property laws of the privileged.

CHAPTER 7

Street Gangs

Revolt, Rivalry and Racism

No one can have read the London, Liverpool, Birmingham, Manchester and Leeds papers and not know that the young street ruffian and prowler with his heavy belt, treacherous knife and dangerous pistol is amongst us. He is in full evidence in London — east, north and south. The question for every man who cares for streets that are safe after dark, decent when dark, not disgraced by filthy shouts and brutal deeds, is what is to be done with this new development of the city boy and the slum denizen? Not one tenth of the doings of these young rascals gets into the press, not one half is known to the police.[1]

Doom-laden reports of gang violence in the inner city were, as this extract from the *London Echo* of February 1898 suggests, a ubiquitous feature of the emergent popular press. The law-and-order campaigns they kindled parallel those of the post-World War II period in their urgent demand for the punishment and rehabilitation of rebellious working-class youth.[2] For although these early youth subcultures remained locally based — the distinctive style of dress and behaviour of such groups as the Bengal Tigers of Manchester, the Peaky Blinders of Birmingham and the Redskins of Glasgow never spread across the country, as did those of the contemporary Teddy Boy, skinhead or mod — they nevertheless achieved local notoriety and were seen by local authorities to pose a serious threat to public order. In fact, hooliganism was a constant cause for concern throughout our period, and this undercurrent of anxiety occasionally escalated into widespread moral panic as a result of the crusades mounted by the press, the police and educational and welfare organizations.[3] It is significant that the two most prolonged and powerful campaigns to control hooliganism and to rehabilitate working-class youth originated during the Boer

War and then World War I, when reported increases in delinquent behaviour coincided with economic and military threats to national stability.[4] This recurrent pattern suggests that the key factor in the formation of law-and-order campaigns to control working-class youth during our period was not so much a rapid increase in delinquency *per se* as the increased public sensitivity to law-breaking that followed from internal and external threats to the power and stability of the state. It is also significant that during these moments of crisis there was a rapid reversion from the rhetoric of rehabilitation to coercive methods of control, which found expression in a dramatic increase in the number of young offenders who were subjected to the 'short, sharp shock' of a birching.[5] The emergence of the young working-class gang member as the symbolic folk devil of capitalist society is a complex process. However, although the moral panics of press and public were generally disproportionate to the actual delinquency involved, and despite the undoubted class prejudice that infused these hostile reactions — the violent activities indulged in by middle-class youth at rags, rugger matches and town-and-gown fights were condoned as a healthy expression of a spirit of adventure and manliness[6] — I do not wish to underestimate the crucial importance within working-class youth culture of the street gang and its aggressive stance against society. My main concern is to penetrate the stock images of brutality that were associated with gang members and to look beyond the epithets ('savage hooligan', 'slum monkey' and 'street blackguard') that were commonly used to condemn them. Equally, I wish to expose the in-built class bias in the pseudo-scientific theories of psychologists and criminologists such as Grace Paithorpe, who, in an influential study of delinquents in the 1930s, concluded that they manifested 'a very remarkable lack of sentiment development', which she suggested was due to 'a far greater variation of this quality between social classes than has been allowed for'.[7] For while delinquency experts like Paithorpe dismissed the illegal and antisocial acts of working-class youth as evidence of a simple lack of feeling and moral sensibility, oral interviews with old people indicate that such acts grew out of resentment and hostility rooted in a shared experience of inequality and subordination. These feelings found one of their most potent expressions in rebellious gang activities, which, although often divisive, self-destructive and futile in the long term, did offer working-class youths momentary reprieve from their inferior social identity. In this chapter I will explore the internal structure, the focal concerns and the illegal activities characteristic of the street gang and will seek to outline the ways in which it provided an inarticulate and immediate solution to the problems of disadvantage that confronted working-class youth in all spheres of life.

The terms 'gang' and 'subculture' tend to imply a commitment to a delinquent way of life involving not merely a rejection of conformist middle-class values, such as respect for property, but also an inversion of these values, so that, for example, vandalism itself becomes a virtue. The image of structured delinquent gangs with a clearly defined leadership, hierarchy and membership, whose aim was to plunder and avenge themselves on respectable society was one that was cultivated assiduously by sensational stories in the popular press. Lurid reports of vicious hooliganism, especially during times of moral panic, aroused a middle-class nightmare of lawlessness, mob rule and the violent dispossession of the propertied. For example, in May 1916 a special correspondent of the *Sunday Chronicle* warned, in an article headlined 'The Terrorists of Glasgow — Savagery of Hooligan Gangs':

each gang out vies the other in savagery and frightfulness. Ladies are held up and robbed; policemen are clubbed or cut with bottles when trying to take some of the ruffians to prison; and old men are beaten and left lying after their pockets have been gone through. . . . With many districts at night so infested with these brutal ruffians that ladies are afraid to venture out and even men have often to run for their lives, the citizens are demanding that this state of matters must end.[8]

Violence and brute physical force were also widely believed to be the basic principles upon which the hooligan gang was organized internally. Social investigator Charles Booth was of the opinion that the gangs of Hoxton, east London, were ruled by a reign of

terror exercised by the leaders of these boys over their followers. Sitting safe at home the follower hears the whistle and turns pale but obeys the summons.[9]

I have examined a number of court cases relating to hooliganism in London, Manchester and Glasgow from the 1890s to the 1930s, and while it is clear that the press and social investigators distorted and exaggerated their reports of juvenile delinquency, I am certain that they did not simply fabricate the existence of organized gangs of teenagers in inner-city areas. One of the few authentic accounts of this delinquent lifestyle was that written in 1899 by Clarence Rook, who opposed contemporary myths of brutalization when he asserted:

the average hooligan is not an ignorant, hulking ruffian, beetle-browed and bullet-headed . . . he is nervous, highly strung, almost neurotic.[10]

He traced the origins of hooliganism to a lack of opportunity for personal advancement or self-expression, which encouraged the more resourceful working-class youths to develop a delinquent subculture geared to exploiting conventional society, with its own alternative argot, skills and hierarchy of status that reversed respectable values. Rook characterized hooligans as

sturdy young villains who start with a grievance against society and are determined to get their own back. That is their own phrase, their own view. Life has little to give them but what they take. The leader gains his place by sheer force of personality. The boy who has kicked in a door can crow over the boy who has merely smashed a window. If it becomes known — and it speedily becomes known to all but the police — that you have dragged a toff and run through his pockets or better still have cracked a crib on your own and planted the stuff, then you are at once surrounded by sycophants.[11]

This type of delinquent lifestyle, however, was representative of only a small minority of gangs, which normally comprised older youths who could find no regular employment or who rejected regular employment in favour of the relative freedom offered by itinerant street trading and petty crime. This delinquent subculture formed a link with the underworld of professional gangsters and criminals, whose network of protection rackets at race courses, drinking clubs and restaurants provided an alternative career structure for juvenile gang leaders.[12] My own interviews with lifelong criminals suggest that their careers were chosen deliberately as an escape from the life of monotonous and low-paid labour that confronted them as youths. For Bert Cox, who graduated from minor gang thefts to cat burglary, it was the experience of gruelling labour in the pits that led him to embrace a criminal lifestyle.

I got a job working down the mines . . . and I worked down there until I was eighteen, in the clay pit and coal pit. Pretty grim. I mean, down the clay pit you'm only got a candle light, you see, and then down the coal pit it used to be all done by hand. I mean, you had no conveyor belts or anything like that; you had to load with the shovel and you got to be on your back and pick away at the roof. I think that's what started me working like this. There was not many days when I wasn't angry with all the hard work I had to do. Well, I started getting mixed up with other known crooks and one thing and another, and I didn't bother, you know, like what came or went. Well, I've nothing to lose, that was it. Well, you've either got to work or you've got to go thieving for money, as you know. So that's the way I used to live.[13]

Interviews indicate that most street gangs were loosely and informally structured, usually comprising 'cliques' or groups of friends, with no clearly defined status hierarchy or leadership, and no connections with the criminal underworld. The majority of working-class boys were involved in street gangs at some stage in their lives, usually drifting into them between the ages of ten and thirteen. The formation of informal gangs, which were defined more in opposition to rival streets than in terms of any distinctive internal structure and identity, originated essentially in the overcrowding of families in densely packed neighbourhoods, in which the street was the only available play and leisure space for the young, as Henry Grimshaw, recalling his Manchester childhood in the early part of the century, remembers.

You were born in a gang if you lived in that area. There were so many children in the streets, they looked like one of Lowry's paintings, you see. So wherever you were born, in that area you automatically had ten, twenty children to play with all the time, and that was the gang. You didn't realize you were in a gang; you were just playing with children, see. There was the Cogan Gang, the Kendall Street Gang. I was in the Willesden Street Gang. We did used to fight each other.[14]

Just as individuals drifted into street gangs, so the street gangs themselves drifted into delinquency in a fairly casual and spontaneous way, not necessarily with deliberate purpose, but rather because delinquency was an extension of their concern with satisfying basic material needs and with creating action and excitement out of the monotonous daily routine. Vandalism, fights and conflicts with the police, for example, all emerged from attempts to transcend the boredom of hanging about on street corners, as Bristolian Fred Harris remembers:

The gang wanted to bring 'ome trophies, an' what we'd do, three together — it was very risky doing it — knock a copper's helmet off and then whip 'is helmet, and we got away with it. . . . We'd fight and throw stones at each other and bricks at each other. It was an outlet, just to let steam off. You've got to do things; you're prevented by rules and regulations to do what you want to do, so you got to. There wasn't no vicious harm in it. You didn't use to plan nothing.[15]

Young people tended to drift out of these street gangs between the ages of sixteen and nineteen, usually as a consequence of the alternative commitments of courtship and marriage; girls who were marginal to gangs were often the prime instigators of this change. In fact, many respondents recalled that girls were often suspicious and disapproving of boyfriends who continued to indulge in street-gang activities and would exert pressure to loosen the bonds of these male-dominated groups.

It didn't go on and on. 'Course, we 'ad other things to think about. Most fellows started going out with girls and that was the finish of 'em. If you was in the Black Hand Gang, the girls didn't approve of it, and out you 'ad to come, and strange how it was, there was only three of us left, and we was all bachelors, three of us.[16]

I have attempted to draw a broad distinction between the internal structure of two types of street gang — the delinquent gang, which inverted many of the values of respectable society, and the semi-delinquent gang, whose members drifted in and out of delinquency in a casual manner. This distinction is a useful one, though clearly these different types of gang were to some extent interrelated and overlapping. Individuals sometimes changed allegiance from one type of gang to another, and several innocuous street gangs developed a delinquent purpose and a violent image as their members grew older. Of course, the precise nature of these gangs varied widely and was shaped by specific structural and historical circumstances, such as the degree of material deprivation experienced, the level of local unemployment, the vigilance with which parental and police control was exerted and the age, sex, and race of the participants. Thus delinquent gangs tended to be concentrated in inner-city areas of deprivation and high unemployment among white working-class boys in their mid- to late teens, and they proliferated at times when parental and police control was relaxed, notably as a consequence of wartime recruitment.[17]

The street-gang culture derived to some extent from the parent culture, which valued physical strength and was tolerant of aggression, but essentially it offered working-class youth the opportunity to conquer its feelings of hunger, failure and insignificance and to assert a proud and rebellious identity through which its members could feel masters of their own destiny. Despite the clear differences between delinquent and semi-delinquent gangs, they shared three focal concerns: the assertion of masculinity; a desire to create immediate excitement; and the exploitation of any opportunity to supplement a meagre diet and income. The characteristics that formed the basis for these focal concerns were the development of a tough independence, the celebration of the individual's or the group's ability to outsmart and defeat any opposition and ritual displays of physical prowess, which among older boys were designed to impress girls. Invariably, the most rewarding and challenging activities in which the gangs engaged were those that involved law-breaking and violent behaviour. One of the principal distinctions between the delinquent and the semi-delinquent gang was the degree of commitment, the intensity and the frequency with which they were involved in these activities, which took several interrelated forms — petty crime, territorial battles, vandalism and conflicts with the police. The remainder of this chapter will deal with each of these in turn.

Gang thefts can be distinguished from the social crime we have discussed above in the sense that the illicit gains were shared and enjoyed exclusively among gang members and were not passed on

The start of a pilfering expedition in Bethnal Green, London, in 1904.

A gang of unemployed working-class youths loitering on a street corner in the 1930s. The tough individualism and rebellious attitude towards authority that characterized such street gangs made them a constant cause for official concern.

to parents, who usually strongly disapproved of this type of illegal activity. Criminologists discovered with some consistency that the majority of juvenile property thefts were committed by gang members, usually in groups of two or three, who tended to be either brothers, sisters or close friends. And, contrary to the theories of psychopathology that were dominant during the 1920s and the 1930s and claimed that delinquency was motivated by severe psychological disorder, the most thorough investigations into juvenile crime revealed that it was grounded in the aims and attitudes of the street gangs themselves. (For example, in 1930 the School Medical Officer of the London County Council reported after his inquiry into the causes of delinquent behaviour among 803 boys and girls that 'in less than 2 per cent of these cases did there appear to be a deeper psychological reaction calling for investigation.')[18] And although the existence of these gangs was generally attributed to inadequate parental control and discipline, which allowed an amoral children's culture to flourish on the streets, oral interviews suggest that gang members did possess their own alternative code of morality, which opposed property laws and which governed the commital of crimes. The most fundamental principle shared by juvenile street gangs, which justified their crimes, was the belief that it was legitimate to steal from the propertied in order to satisfy basic needs such as hunger and thirst. It is important to remember the meagre diet, the inadequate clothing and the poor health experienced by many working-class children, especially those from large families whose parents were unskilled or unemployed, all of which made material and physical deprivation a powerful motive for juvenile theft.[19] Because many children did not accept that it was morally wrong to steal from shops and markets occasionally, one of the main factors determining the nature and extent of juvenile crime was the opportunity for theft that was available to them, as Charlie Miller, recalling his childhood in Barton Hill, Bristol, during the early part of the century, remembers:

I think most of the kids were opportunists in those days. I think if they could sneak in smartly and pick up something, they would. I did it myself. We thought it was just legitimate, stealing, you know what I mean? I think our consciences worked to the point that we knew there were going to be consequences if we were caught, but we didn't think about it too much, because most of the things were done on the spur of the moment. If it was something you wanted because you were hungry and there was a bar of chocolate on the counter and that sort of thing, we got up to all manner of peculiar dodges in those days, because lots of the time you were hungry and we needed an extra bit of sustenance, you know. That was the only reason we did it, not because we do it for its own sake, just to be difficult. We just felt we needed these things.[20]

Street gangs developed a variety of pilfering techniques, which depended upon the mutual co-operation and trust of other gang members to minimize risks and maximize the chances of success. The most common form of gang theft was that from sweet shops, which usually involved one member distracting the attention of the assistant while the other committed the crime. Cliff Hills, recalling his Edwardian childhood in the Essex village of Great Bentley, remembers an ingenious variation on this strategy that he used occasionally.

Boys then were full of tricks. I remember going to the shop sometimes for a penn'orth of lemonade crystals or pink sweets, and he put the ounce or two-ounce weight on the little brass scales, and then the other boy would say, 'How much are those sweets up there, mister? What are they? Are they aniseed balls or so-and-so?' And the other boy would quickly put another weight on the scales, which the shopkeeper didn't notice very often, so sometimes we got an ounce and a half or two ounces of sweets. You could call it stealing, but I think more or less it was a little joke, getting a little more for your money.[21]

Youths who possessed the nerve and skill to pilfer successfully in the most difficult and dangerous situations won enormous prestige among their peers, and boys with this form of casual contempt for property law tended to be accepted as leaders by delinquent gangs of older boys, as Joseph Maddison of South Shields remembers.

Jack Lyle, he was the terror of the gang. He came from a right rough family, and he was never out of trouble. . . . We'd all got to market on a Saturday, 'cos Shields had a lovely market on a Saturday. And if you were with Jack, when you got out of the market you had stuff in your pocket which you hadn't when you went in. You didn't know it was there. He used to pinch that much stuff, man, he couldn't put it all in his own. There was one Sunday night, went into Joe Merciani's ice-cream shop — we all used to go in there every Sunday night. We didn't spend a lot of time in, and this night Jack comes out and he had a great big basin, must have been a foot in diameter, full of pineapple cubes he'd stole off the counter. Nobody had seen him take it. He was a wonderful leader of men. He was sent to Borstal, a lad that didn't like discipline at all.[22]

Although older boys, by virtue of their superior ability to 'knock off' sweets and cigarettes, enjoyed a dominant position in street gangs, there was a common code of honour that all the members of the gang should share in the illegal proceeds, however marginal the role that they had played in the actual theft. Billy Spargo's memories of gang thefts in Newquay, Cornwall, during World War I clearly illustrate this communal tradition.

The old grocer's shop on top of the hill 'ere had underground kitchens. Well, if you tiptoed into the shop, time the old lady got into the shop, up over a flight of stairs from the underground kitchens, well, you'd have filled your pockets with a few sweets or packets of cigarettes or anything else. The lads that actually did it were a bit older than us. We used to be outside and they'd do the necessary, and then we used to come down on the beaches 'ere. And if they had cigarettes, then we had a packet of cigarettes. Well, that was a grand job![23]

In order to avoid detection and retribution while enjoying the profits of their theft, gang members would usually be careful to hide from the suspicious eyes not only of the authorities but also of their parents, who would often reproach their children severely for participation in such activities. Parental disapproval and punishment of gang thefts was motivated by a number of interrelated concerns, the most important of which were loss of control over their children and of respectability, the threat of damaging legal consequences and the struggle to maintain some standards of honesty. Children whose pilfering was detected by their parents usually received a reprimand and a ritual threat of prosecution, as Bristolian Daisy Wintle remembers, though more perceptive children like Daisy realized that, at least for the first offence, there was little chance that the threat would actually be carried out.

When we were hungry, my sister an' I, I'll tell you what we done. Outside the vegetable shops they always used to keep the sacks of potatoes outside. Well, as we went by we stole a potato. I nicked one an' my sister nicked one. And we runned 'ome an' we put it in the fire an' let it bake, an' then we'd take it out, peel the skin off an' eat it, and only too glad to eat it too. We used to do that pretty regular, then one day we done it, father 'appened to come in, looked at mother. He said, 'Sarah, they've bin takin' your potatoes.' So our mother said, 'I haven't got any.' 'Come here, where did you get they potatoes from?' My sister an' me, we knew we mustn't tell a lie, he'd murder us, we said, 'Well, we went over to Mrs Langley's an' took a potato off the sack.' 'Oh, right,' caught hold of us by the shoulders, 'Over to Mrs Langleys,' he said. 'Mrs Langley, would you mind getting a policeman, please?' She said, 'What for?' I can see 'er now. 'These two girls of mine have been stealin' your potatoes.' And, of course, he was looking up at the woman an' I could see 'er grinning, an' I thought to meself, oh, she won't get a policeman, our dad's just doing that. I could tell by the way they were looking at one another. So, anyhow, she said, 'Well, I won't get a policeman for 'em this time, but if they does it again, I will send the policeman over.'[24]

While food and cigarettes formed the principal targets for the thefts of street gangs, they also possessed numerous devious strategies for gaining illegal free entry to cinemas, music halls and sporting events. Stan Clowes, for example, remembers that his inability to pay at the turnstiles never prevented him from regularly supporting Stoke City at the turn of the century.

I'd be down the football ground and we used to jump over the top of the corrugated sheets, seven or eight foot high. Used to dodge over the top. That went on. I think I've followed Stoke City since I was about six or eight, and for years and years we've never paid.[25]

In the cases of the crimes we have examined so far the people concerned have stressed the instrumental motive of material gain. However, another motive that recurs in interview accounts of illegal activities is the expressive significance of street-gang crime, which offered action and excitement, a challenge to adult authority and an opportunity for the individual to assert a rebellious and independent identity. Occasionally, thefts were committed purely for the element of risk and excitement involved, as illustrated by David Smith's memories of raiding wagons loaded with oranges in east London.

We took a chance on everything. Old Morocco Wharf, down over the Wapping Bridge, used to be in the season, used to come with orange ships, with fruit ships. And, of course, it was all horse-drawn wagons in those days, and we'd wait for the vans to go along, and sometimes they might have a look-out sitting on top. We'd always break a case of oranges open at the back, pinch a few oranges and dive down the side turning. Well, you couldn't get caught 'cos you had a couple of the boys policing the copper, occupying his time wherever he might be, while the rest of the gang was doing the raid. But, of course, it was only petty, when you come to think of it. If we'd have gone down the wharf our own relatives would have filled our hats and our pockets with loose oranges. Yes, part of the excitement was getting an orange out of the case.[26]

This expressive role of juvenile theft was particularly important for teenagers, who experienced most frustration and disillusionment at work. Several investigations established a correlation between job dissatisfaction, persistent job-changing and minor crimes against property. Of those delinquents who were clearly motivated by disgust with monotonous labour, the most interesting group were those officially classified as being of 'super-normal intelligence' — those who possessed particular talents that were denied any expression at work and for whom crime acted as a symbolic revenge against oppressive authority.[27] One common form of theft favoured by this group was joy-riding on motorbikes and in motor cars, which offered not only excitement and an outlet for aggression, but also the opportunity for a parting gesture of personal dignity, as Fred Harris, a former member of Bristol's Black Hand Gang, remembers:

One fellow, he got caught for theft, stealing a car, 'cause there weren't many about and this car 'e stole was the vicar of St Mary, Redcliffe, church and 'e returned the car back again. It was just entertainment and 'e put down on the car 'ow much 'e'd spent [on petrol]. We were what you call gallants, gallants we were.[28]

Another means of expressing hostility to exploitation by employers and of supplementing inadequate wages was through systematic gang thefts at work. Such activities, however, tended to be restricted to a small minority of delinquent subcultures, and I have discovered no interviewees who recollected thefts such as those committed by the all-female Check Skirt Gang of Paddington, which were reported in *The Times* of July 1914.

At Marylebone yesterday Nellie Sheehan, 17, pattern matcher, was charged on remand for stealing a pair of shoes. She belonged to a gang of about twenty girls who went about the West End obtaining situations as pattern matchers and then taking advantage of the first opportunity to steal anything they could get hold of. One feature of the gang was that they dressed alike in check skirts and blue coats and all came from the neighbourhood of Harrow Road.[29]

While dissatisfaction at work provided a powerful motive for gang crime, equally important was unemployment and the material deprivation and deep feelings of personal humiliation and resentment against society that followed from the inability to find work. The close casual link between unemployment and juvenile crime was a constant theme of Prison Commissioners' Reports, criminological investigations and statistical surveys — although, of course, blame tended to be attributed to individual moral failure rather than the structural inequality built into the capitalist economy.[30] The memories of men and women who committed street-gang crimes while unemployed reveal a complex and interrelated set of motives, among which economic necessity and retaliation against the petty bureaucratic apparatus of the Means Test were particularly important. However, the most fundamental principle that legitimized their thefts was the feeling that it was the inalienable right of the individual to work in order to procure food and to enjoy simple pleasures like cigarettes and alcohol, and that if this right was not upheld by society, then the individual was morally justified in transgressing property laws and appropriating these basic necessities illegally.[31] A sense of injustice, though rarely articulated in a clearly class-conscious form, was intensified by the sacrifices made during World War I, which for many led only to grinding poverty, unemployment and broken political promises. The following interview extract illustrates why the anger and bitterness felt by many young men and women, because of a deep suspicion of the state, was much more likely to find a delinquent than a political expression:

I thought I ought to do my bit for me country when the war was on. Joined up when I was sixteen. I went up the Colston Hall, an' the man behind the desk said, 'How old are you?' I said, 'Sixteen.' 'Too young,' he said, an' I went to walk away, but the recruiting sergeant called over to me and said, 'Go over to the other desk and tell him you're eighteen.' And that's what I done. Ended up in the trenches in France. Wounded three times. I was back an' forward in an' out of hospital. I got a bullet in me leg, a bullet in me thigh an' shrapnel in the back of the leg. Not serious wounds, flesh wounds. But after all that trouble, when we got discharged they give us six months' money at twenty-nine shilling a week, an' when that six months was up — finished, nothing. An' that was how they treated the First War soldiers. They'd said we were fighting for a better country, we'd be well looked after, but it was all propaganda. They soon forgot you. When we come out they give us an' old army shirt, army pair of boots, army pair of grey socks, army overcoat an' a Martin Henry suit of clothes, which was the same as what they used to bloody wear in the Union. The only thing pawnable was our medal, silver medal, used to pawn that for half-a-crown. An' Earl Haig, they've got a statue of him up in Clifton College, the man who sent thousands to their deaths, he never heard a gun shot in the whole war, an' he had ten thousand pounds an' a mansion. And the poor devils such as me got nothing. I was unemployed, no job to do an' no money coming in. Bitter? I should say I was. But what could you do? All you could do was look after number one; you felt you 'ad a right to things, you didn't want to have to pay for it all, so a lot of young blokes got it whatever way they could. You was feeling revolutionary. I know I did nearly go off the deep end. Only those who went through it knows. That's when we nearly had a revolution in Bristol, smashed the tram cars up. But I didn't bother with it, didn't bother with politics. I joined no party, not many did. All politicians is poison, in my eyes.[32]

As youth unemployment was concentrated to a large extent among the unskilled and the semi-skilled in their late teens and early twenties,[33] the street gangs with unemployed members tended to be most common among this age group. And while gangs that comprised younger children rarely resorted to any form of physical violence in their crimes, older youths did occasionally use the violent techniques of assault, mugging and extortion.[34] However, even in the most notorious criminal neighbourhoods in which delinquent subcultures proliferated, such as the Greengate area of Manchester, social relations were not reduced to lawless violence, for a complex network of street obligations and loyalties developed that ensured a degree of protection and safety for the local inhabitants, as Billy Alty remembers:

There were drunkards that wouldn't work. They became criminals that couldn't get work. Their wives drank. Where they got the money from was always a mystery to me — they must have stole it somehow. The criminals used to attack the police. There was one they called Navvy Jack; he was a big hulking fella, but one of the toughs of Greengate told him to shut up and knocked his helmet fast down over his face. Gangs used to meet and fire at one another, and belts with buckles on, and they called them 'scuttlers'. There was the Adelphi Gang and Red Shelley was the leader of them, and Jerry Hoddy was the leader of the Greengate Mob. . . . Now, the decent people in Greengate was safe from the roughs, the criminals. My mother used to go and help nurse her friend at the pub when she was ill, and I used to come home early and go and stand at the corner of Gravel Lane, and I could see my mother come out of the Bull's Head and I was watching for her safety coming home. No local would interfere with her but a stranger might. Well, a chap comes out of the pub and he offers me a handkerchief. I didn't know him so I knew he was a stranger. He said, 'Give me five bob for this.' And he started edging towards me. Well, the only way for me to stop him was to hit him or something. I'd no intention of giving him five shillings. And a woman came along. I'd never spoken to her in my life, but she was known as a few things — the thieves used to deal with her — a receiver. . . . Anyway, this woman, I was afraid of her, like she had such a reputation. I used to pass her cellar shop going to work, on the other side. And she said, 'What's to do?' and I said, 'He wants five shillings for this.' And another criminal, a schoolboy at the same time as me, comes out of the pub. He'd had penal servitude, Teddy Brown. And she said to Teddy Brown, 'Give him a good hiding. He's trying to get five shillings off Billy Alty.' Well, I was astonished she knew my name. But everybody knew my mother, like, as she was such a good person. So I said, 'Thank you.' Teddy Brown, he wiped the floor with this fella. And she said to him, 'If you are in Greengate tomorrow morning, you'll know about it. Get out tonight.' And he had to get out.[35]

Another common feature of street-gang activity, touched upon in Billy Alty's recollections, was the territorial conflict between rival neighbourhoods, traditionally known in Lancashire as 'scuttling'.[36] This conflict was rooted in fervent street pride and in the fierce rivalries between local neighbourhood gangs. Their concern with the aggressive assertion of territorial identity was reflected in the names they adopted, which were often based on the street or neighbourhood where the members lived. In many towns and cities older gangs of teenagers attempted to create an awe-inspiring image by borrowing names with violent associations from comics

and films, like Redskins, Cowboys, Hell Hounds, Black Hand
League or Belt and Pistol Club.[37] They combined these with names
derived from their own neighbourhood to produce arrogant and
rebellious gang names such as the Anderston Redskins of Glasgow,
renowned locally during World War I as the Skins.[38] Some gangs,
however, preferred unique and obscure names whose significance
was known only to gang members. For example, in the following
interview extract Morris Brock recalls the origins of the name of
Manchester's most notorious gang of Jewish boys during the early
part of the century, the Shaun Spidah.

We had a customer, I think he was a tic-tacker, and he knew a bit about
racing. And it was just prior to the Grand National, and I says, 'Have you
got a tip for the Grand National, Mr Moody?' 'Well,' he says, 'I've heard of
one horse, an Irish horse this is. It's supposed to be a good one,' he says,
'I'm having a pound on it myself.' I says, 'What's the name?' He said,
'Shaun Spidah.' So when I came back at night, when I met a few friends, I
told them about this. They says, 'Oh, well, we'll have a few bob on it.
There's nothing much to lose.' And word gradually spread, and the whole
lot backed Shaun Spidah — which won. I think it was about 100-8. And
the following night, like, somebody says, 'Hurrah for Shaun Spidah!' And
all me friends says, 'Right.' And somebody amongst the crowd suddenly
starts singing, 'We are the Shaun Spidah boys,' and all that kind of thing.
And that's how the name came into being, the Shaun Spidah.[39]

Although territorial conflicts between rival street gangs were
frequently condemned by middle-class observers as evidence of
animal brutality, oral interviews show that in fact they were to a
large extent ritualized and involved customary constraints that
prevented serious injury. A number of people recalled that children
in opposing streets and neighbourhoods 'declared war' on each
other, but stressed that these violent feuds were strictly annual
affairs and that after these ritual conflicts relations between children
in rival areas would be relatively harmonious for another year.

Once a year we'd declare war on the kids in the next street. That was a
regular thing, happened near enough before Christmas. It came round like
playing marbles came along in the summer. It was near enough a game.
There'd be about forty youngsters in each street and we'd throw stones
and chase each other with sticks. Nobody got hurt really. . . . We weren't
enemies the rest of the time because we'd go to the same school.[40]

These violent conflicts were usually extensions of traditional
festivals of misrule or religious celebrations such as St Patrick's

Day, when districts in which territorial rivalries were reinforced by differences of nationality and religion often experienced pitched battles, as Ralph Pemberton, recalling his childhood in Jarrow-on-Tyne at the turn of the century, remembers:

The only trouble we ever had was on St Patrick's Day. The Catholics used to come round our school, EILS, and of course they used to have paper balls with string round them, and EILS, it started you know, English, Irish or Scots. And of course we were English . . . and they would try to get stuck into you with these paper balls and hit you and this, that and other. . . . That was once a year, yes.[41]

Of course, sporadic fights between rival gangs were a recurrent feature of street life, but victims were rarely chosen in a random or malicious way, as was often suggested in the popular literature on hooliganism. Conflicts were governed by elaborate conventions and constraints, which required the selection of a rival group of roughly equal age, strength and numbers and involved preliminary rituals of eye contact, verbal abuse, weapon brandishing and pushing and shoving before the actual encounter. Many conflicts did not progress beyond this ritualistic expression of aggression and masculinity, but even when actual fighting developed weapons such as sticks and belts tended to be discarded in favour of fists and boots, for despite their vicious displays, few boys wished to risk serious injury to themselves or others. Some of these customary constraints are illustrated in Morris Brock's recollections of gang fights in Manchester in the early part of this century.

Sometimes we used to have 'scuttles' — we used to call it 'scuttling'. They'd come down and we'd have little 'does' with them, little fights, Jewish against non-Jewish. They used to come down, say about twenty of them, come down looking for a row. We'd sort of glare at one another at first and wait for the first one to start. . . . Now, if one started, to show what a hero he was, he'd walk forward and one of our boys would step forward to meet him. . . . We could tell that they were looking for trouble; you could sense it. They used to come in a menacing mood and shout names. . . . They used to shout 'Sheeny' and all that, 'Smug', to like insult us. They used to have sticks and all that, not big hefty sticks, small sticks. 'Course, if they came, we'd sort out something ourselves. It was more or less brandishing them to frighten one another, more or less it was fists. . . . We rarely used the belts. It wasn't too serious; every party was more or less satisfied with a black eye or a nose bleed. And when I came back I can remember me mother says, 'What again, eh? I'll murder you if you start any fights,' which we didn't really. But they got so used to it that the women more or less took no notice of it. We just went and washed our faces and we were ready for the next round, kind of thing.[42]

Occasionally, however, some gangs directed their hostility not only towards opponents of a similar age and disposition, but also towards innocent victims. The Napoo, for example, a teenage gang that originated in the Ancoats district of Manchester during the early years of World War I, established a reputation for hacking off young women's plaits and claiming them as trophies, as Larry Goldstone remembers:

They'd creep up behind girls and women in the street, grab the long plaited hair which hung down the back (that was the style of the day) and with a sharp pair of scissors cut off the plaited hair and run off with it as a souvenir. They got bolder and bolder hunting the women with plaited hair. Some used to go upstairs on the trams late at night, and if a woman was sitting on her own, they'd cut off her hair, then, like lightning, dash off without being caught. The idea was probably hatched from the films of Red Indians scalping the whites. The tough would take the plaits to the public house to show how clever he was at hunting.[43]

The Napoo, who were recognized by the distinctive pink neckerchief they wore and the razor blades that they displayed in waistcoat pockets or in slits in their cloth caps, would also create panic by charging through the streets or by instigating mass brawls at public events and dances.[44] In the following interview extract Henry Grimshaw reflects on the gossip, the exaggerated rumours and the genuine fear that the Napoo inspired, and on the feeling of power and excitement that the gang members must have enjoyed as a result of their frightening image and violent activities.

They became notorious and everyone was talking about them, see. The children you played with, elder brothers, mothers, fathers — if you went to the corner shop, they were all talking about them. So it became a very important thing. The women were afraid because they did tackle women quite a lot, women with long hair. They did all sorts of things, smashing windows, fighting everybody they could fight, and they had razors stuck out of their waistcoat pockets, cut-throat razors, that sort of business. But you never got to the truth of it. It was always second-hand; it was what people said. . . . At Belle Vue they used to have a firework display. Opposite the lake there was stands where you could sit to watch this display. And I was sat up here with a couple of my aunts one night, and below us there was an old danceboard. And all these fellows were fighting. They were kicking one another and they were on the floor, like football match crowds now. And, of course, everybody was shouting, 'Napoo! Napoo! Get out, it's the Napoo!' Must really have been enjoyable to be a Napoo because everybody run away, you know. . . . And the second time, at Heaton Park, I looked round and saw this gang, must have been about fifty or sixty strong, and they were coming running like mad, you see. And there was trams then. They used to run in the park. Well, we made for these trams, and fortunately one was just on its way and I got on. I don't know what happened to those that didn't get on, but everybody started to run. They were nasty, mind, but I should imagine as young men they had a little bit of fun out of it to see people run away like they used to.[45]

When the violent activities of street gangs like the Napoo escalated to such a level that they threatened to disrupt the daily life of the working-class neighbourhood, then serious efforts were sometimes made by older youths and men to reassert community control by dispersing the delinquent gang. For example, the Napoo was finally suppressed after a series of attacks on Jewish girls and shops led to the formation of a local Jewish vigilante group, which armed itself with makeshift weapons removed from workshops and factories. Henry Hoffmann remembers that the youths used

heavy rollers . . . what the waterproofers used to stick down the garment, and the shears as well, and they went to Oldham Road in Ancoats and battled with 'em. And that ended it, that was in war time, 1916.[46]

Although concerted action such as this might re-establish community control, it is clear that this type of gang violence acted as a destructive force that divided the local working-class community. For the desperate desire for personal dignity, self-assertion and escape experienced by many working-class youths when confronted by problems of poverty, monotonous labour and wartime conscription was diverted from potentially subversive inter-class conflict into socially divisive intra-class conflict. This divisiveness tended to affect most seriously inner-city areas of extreme poverty and social deprivation, where on some occasions all the customary constraints that we have noted were discarded and weapons were used by gangs, resulting in the serious injury or death of combatants. Some delinquent gangs possessed a wide range of dangerous weapons, such as spiked knuckle-dusters, sharpened bicycle chains, knives, razors, coshes and pistols.[47] And gangs in some localities improvised their own unique weapons, such as the 'blood knot', which was particularly favoured in the St Jude's area of Bristol for many years, as Charlie Dallimore remembers:

We used to get a piece of iron, a bolt, an iron bolt, and get a piece of rope, wrap that all the way round and he did hang and we used to swing 'ee. 'Course, windows did get broken. And that was called a blood knot.[48]

It must be stressed that dangerous weapons were possessed by only a small minority of city gangs, and even then they were rarely used and were carried largely as symbols of defiance and resistance.[49] For example, the government inquiries that preceded the passage of legislation in the 1900s to control the circulation of firearms and to restrict their sale to those over eighteen indicated that, contrary to public opinion, the vast majority of deaths and injuries that resulted from pistol shots were accidental or suicidal in nature and had no connection with gang conflict. Similarly, many of the middle-class youth workers who from the 1880s onwards established a network of boys' clubs in the cities, primarily in response to the threat of urban disorder and degeneracy posed by hooliganism,[50] often acknowledged the pluck, the courage and the loyalty of delinquent street gangs — values that matched their own ideal of Christian manliness. As Manchester youth worker Charles Russell put it:

the 'scuttler' was not wholly bad; he would rather be a blackguard than a dullard. His real desires were natural and healthy. . . . The rougher and more unscrupulous gangs, when nothing better was on, would make an unknown passer-by the subject of their sport, though in justice to the Manchester lads who gloried in the name of 'scuttler' . . . it must be recorded that they were wont to declare that no real 'scuttler' would ever commit such an act.[51]

However, court records do reveal some utterly brutal cases of gang violence throughout the period under study, such as the incident in which three sixteen-year-olds in the Lime Street Gang planned and executed the murder of a rival Manchester gang member by 'dosing' him with a knife in the back — as a result of which bare-footed William Willan, who committed the deed, was sentenced to death and was, according to press reports, led away from court screaming, 'Oh, master, don't, have mercy on me, I'm only sixteen, I'm dying.'[52]

Gang fighting was most likely to escalate into serious violence when it involved immigrant groups, particularly newly arrived immigrant groups, for in these circumstances territorial divisions were deepened and reinforced by racial divisions. Working-class racism was most deeply felt in inner-city communities and tended to be concentrated in dockland areas in, for example, south-east

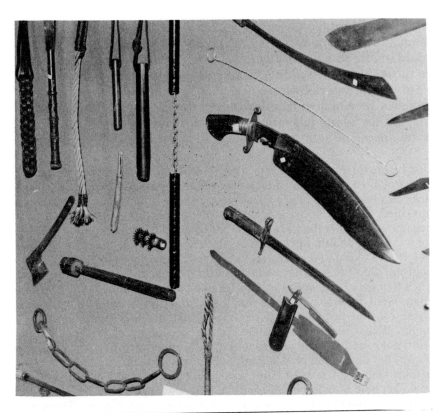

Some delinquent gangs possessed a wide range of dangerous weapons, such as spiked knuckle-dusters, knives, razors and pistols. This photograph shows a selection of weapons used by Glasgow street gangs in the late nineteenth century.

London, Liverpool and Cardiff, where prolonged periods of socio-economic decline coincided with the arrival and growth of immigrant groups. In such a situation racist views developed to provide an immediate explanation for the deterioration of the local neighbourhood, and there was an increasing tendency, especially among the unskilled and unemployed, to associate the experience of poverty with the severe competition from immigrants for scarce resources such as jobs and housing and with the formation of a reserve army of immigrant labour that was frequently mobilized by

Gangs of youths often played a prominent part in racist attacks on immigrant groups. This anti-German riot in High Street, Poplar, in the East End of London, was photographed in May 1915.

employers to undercut wages paid to the white working class.[53] In moments of economic crisis minor provocations by immigrants could inflate this resentment into violent, localized race riots, such as those that occurred in a number of provincial cities in 1919 and 1936.[54] Oral interviews suggest that sporadic outbreaks of racial violence in which unemployed white youths were the principal instigators were not uncommon occurrences — Stan Gibson remembers one such incident, which took place in Tottenham:

Just before the First World War, there was a load of Jewish refugees came from Poland and Russia, and it was rumoured that there was about thirty-three in a house. And Levi's absorbed quite a lot of them because they was unskilled workers and there was a lot of unskilled work. But then it became so bad that there was really a conflict. Two blokes went into Levi's for a job, and couldn't get taken on and they saw these immigrants. They fled from Poland and all round there. They were the Jewish. They had a pogrom, didn't they? They come from the ghettos of Russia and Warsaw. They fled over here, and the factories used to take 'em in. When that two chaps went down to Levi's and they found that they couldn't get a job, they wrote on the vacancy board outside the factory 'No Englishmen need apply.' Well, of course, the Labour Exchange had just started up, and the word got round to them. There was quite a lot of unemployment in those days. They all congregated at High Tottenham and marched to Ferry Lane to meet Levi's, you see. And they was taking hammers and everything they could get hold of to have a go, you see. The Jew boys down there, they got their saws and chisels, you see, and they were going to meet. There was going to be a rare old flare-up. So Levi's had to shut their gates and stop them from coming out, and phoned for the police. The police come down on horseback, but what did happen? All the unemployed lined on the other side of Ferry Lane, throwing bricks over into Levi's factory, and they were going through the blooming windows and everything. They was getting bombarded. But it was only because somebody wrote up 'No Englishmen need apply.' It really created a panic.[55]

A parallel form of provocation was directed at most immigrant groups — principally Negroes, Jews and Irish — the intensity and frequency of which tended to vary according to the numbers and visibility of the immigrants. Negroes, many of them impoverished sailors who had settled in British ports, were one of the most visible immigrant groups by virtue of their black skin, and their everyday experience of colour prejudice and discrimination in childhood and youth generated potentially explosive feelings of resentment, as Tom Kingston, recalling life in Cardiff, remembers:

Every coloured child that was born in this district learned of colour prejudice growing up. You felt it. Well, it grew up in you. You could see it; you could sense it. Jobs we had a tough time at. It was mostly through prejudice that we couldn't get jobs and that kind of thing. The prejudices were shown years ago. A coloured man, if he went into town, never knew when he was going to get insulted. . . . the prejudice was so bad that if I happened to be going to the pictures with my wife and a white fellow stared too hard at me, I'd want to punch him right away. That's how bitter I felt.[56]

To give an overall view of racial conflict between street gangs is extremely difficult because its nature and extent varied in different cities and according to the different immigrant groups involved. To illustrate the complexity of the issue, I wish to look at one form of racism, anti-Semitism, and contrast briefly the interaction between young Jews and young working-class whites in two cities, Manchester and London.

Although Manchester possessed a huge Jewish population, it had been gradually assimilated and integrated over a long period spanning the nineteenth century.[57] This community cohesion was reflected in street-gang conflicts between Jews and non-Jews that were usually ritualized into relatively innocuous stone-throwing battles, as Ben Malevsky remembers:

There was quite an annual thing to see dozens and dozens of non-Jewish boys come into the locality and the Jewish boys meet them, and each would be on both sides of this great ditch, throwing stones at each other. And it was really large battles, battles . . . involving dozens and dozens on each side. And the stones used to fly like hail.[58]

By the inter-war period integration had progressed to such an extent that it became common for Jews and non-Jews to become members of the same street gangs. For example, Henry Schatz recalls that territorial allegiances were much more important than religious or racial loyalties in the formation of a street gang to fight the annual battle with the invading Hightown Jewish gang.

There was one or two Jews with us. See, the Jewish lads in our street and round about, like I was with them. We was all brought up together, so they didn't know any different. They just fought the Hightown lot.[59]

However, in east and south-east London between 1890 and 1914 there was considerably less integration of the massive influx of Jews, who tended to cluster in ghettos and in distinct ethnocentric communities.[60] This situation was exacerbated by severe competition for jobs and housing, and it is in this context that the frequent verbal and physical attacks that characterized the relationship between young Jews and non-Jews in London must be placed.[61] Gangs of non-Jewish youths would seek to provoke young immigrants and would use the slightest excuse, such as a brush on the shoulder, as a pretext for a brutal assault. This is clearly illustrated in the report on the manslaughter of Nighogosa Krikorian in March 1897:

The deceased was one of the Armenian refugees. On the afternoon of Sunday, December 27th, he and another Armenian went for a walk and when they were in Bermondsey a number of lads among whom was the prisoner followed them. One of the lads struck the hat off one of the Armenians who however thought it was a joke and took no notice of it. The lads passed them and went on in front and the prisoner stood on the kerb so that it was impossible for them to pass without touching him. The deceased touched him as he went by. The prisoner struck the deceased a blow which knocked him down, and while he was lying on the ground he was kicked by some of the lads.[62]

Although most commentators have explained such incidents by reference to pathological disturbance, brutalization or jingoism, when viewed within the local context of unemployment and urban decay it becomes clear that they can instead most usefully be seen as misdirected expressions of class feeling and class hostility.[63] The persecuted immigrant becomes the symbol of and scapegoat for the processes of economic decline and inequality that white working-class youngsters failed to comprehend in terms of the complex contradictions of capitalism. The fragmented and personalized nature of this resentment is exemplified in Martha Goodhew's explanation of the unpopularity of the Jews in Stepney during the World War I period:

They didn't treat 'em very well over the neighbourhood where I lived, the Jewish people. They used to pelt 'em with tomatoes or specked oranges, all sorts of things. That's how they were then. In fact, the turning I lived in, a Jewish person couldn't walk down there. No, they didn't like the Jews. Well, my opinion was, you see, the Jewish people, they're very thrifty. Now, the best trade that they used to get into was tailoring, dressmaking, and cigar-making, and all those sort of trades that they knew they could earn the most money on. You would never find any of them people going cleaning for people, like our people used to. They didn't like a lot of Jewish people for that reason, and they always seemed to get on better than anybody else. Now, they'd take a stall in the market with two boxes of matches. They wouldn't have that long before they'd work and strive and get on, then suddenly you'd see 'em with a big shop. But our people never seemed to be able to do it.[64]

This racial antagonism and violence rarely sought political expression; on the few occasions that it did it was attracted to the violent and anti-Semitic solutions offered by the radical right, as is illustrated by the support among sections of white working-class youth, especially in east London, for Mosley's National Union of Fascists in the 1930s.

A discussion of territorial and racial conflict provides a natural link with the next gang activity that must be examined — vandalism. For the deliberate destruction of property was in many cases another violent expression of the territorial or racial tensions within the working-class community. There is, of course, a radical working-class tradition in which the destruction of property has been a last resort to achieve social and political goals, clearly evident historically in food riots, machine-smashing, election violence and so on.[65] In some circumstances, notably in school strikes and industrial sabotage, the vandalism of working-class youth can be seen as a direct expression of this tradition. However, the target of deliberate vandalism in the city streets was more often the working class itself and was rooted in racism and street-gang rivalry. Delinquent gangs of older youths played a prominent role in vandalizing the property of immigrants during race riots and also often led reprisals against expatriates whose nations opposed Britain during World War I.[66] Henry Spencer remembers that in the Broughton (Manchester) riots of 1916 that followed the sinking of the *Lusitania* street gangs searching for revenge were not particularly accurate or careful in their choice of foreign victims.

The youths . . . they were looking for Germans when they sunk the *Lusitania*; they was looking to get their own back. They came to Lower Broughton Road, but there was only one German. There was a poor butcher's shop there . . . and they smashed that shop to pieces. . . . And right opposite Brown, a Jewish fellow, had a second-hand furniture shop . . . and just for devilment they smashed it. The furniture, they were throwing it about. Then they went down the road to [another] shop and threw a piano through the bedroom window. Then they went on, and there was a Jewish shop called Boltiansky's. It was a draper's shop . . . and with it being a foreign name, they thought he was a German as well, so they smashed his shop up, and I can remember to this day he came running out and trying to save the stuff, and the man next door, who was a Christian tobacconist, he was stood there giggling with his pals, watching. And Henry, that's me, I picked up half a brick and threw it through his window. And after that they smashed his shop in, and in ten minutes he had no stock. It was all gone. That's the truth. I had the needle. He was the nextdoor neighbour, stood there laughing and joking, and there was about fifty people and I was at the back, and there was half a brick and I picked it up and threw it right through the centre of his window. And that started it.[67]

Although it is possible to detect in wartime vandalism an inarticulate and misdirected element of social protest — the unfortunate German shopkeeper becomes the scapegoat for conscription and the personal losses experienced by working-class families — the vandalism that resulted from gang rivalry was motivated purely by revenge. Of course, acts of revenge did offer the opportunity for self-assertion, action and excitement, but the type of vandalism described by Julius Goodman in the following extract was a divisive force within the working-class community.

The Shaun Spidah . . . they set upon one particular gang [of] Jimmy O'Neil. He had a milk float and he used to come down Southall Street to distribute the milk. That time, Sunday morning, Shaun Spidah gang was waiting. Got hold of the horse, got hold of three of the O'Neil gang on top. Dragged them off. Tipped the cart up, tipped the milk up and they made a mess of it.[68]

Benny Cohen, reflecting on his own involvement in this gang conflict in Manchester, describes and explains the social oppression that led working-class Jews to participate in this self-destructive rivalry.

It was frustration, solely frustration. These young boys, they were the first generation of these immigrants. They went to work first thing in the morning, eight o'clock in the morning, under candlelight, till eight o'clock at night. Came home. They had very good parents, and they would have their tea, whatever it was, according to their means. And they would go out of the house, because they had nothing to do in the house. There was no conversation with their parents, see. The young man might have known a bit of Jewish, but he spoke English and the parents didn't know a word of English. They went to a street corner and they assembled. The gathering

---

Harsh sentences were often imposed on children and youths who were guilty of minor acts of vandalism. These two children were arrested for vandalism and sentenced to hard labour in the 1890s.

there was twenty, twenty-five at the street corner. There was no objective. It was sheer frustration, which is a terrible, terrible thing when you learn to understand it.[69]

However, the most ubiquitous form of vandalism, window-smashing, was in most cases accidental and resulted from enthusiastic participation in ball games, especially football, which young people were often forced to play in the closely confined space of the street, as parks and fields were usually situated long distances from their homes. Football provided a creative physical outlet for tension and aggression, and it is clear from interviews that watching, discussing and playing football were very important street-gang activities. Football also made a direct appeal to the focal concerns of the street gang in the opportunity it offered for group participation, the assertion of masculinity, the creation of excitement and, for the exceptionally skilful, escape from a dead-end job into a more pleasurable and profitable professional career representing the local town.[70] But high-spirited participation in street football led gangs into bitter conflicts with the police who, throughout the period under study, enforced elaborate rules and regulations designed to prevent 'dangerous play' in the streets. Although these regulations were a necessary precaution for the protection of life, property and the smooth flow of traffic, there is much oral and documentary evidence to suggest that the police, in response to the moral crusades of middle-class reformers for the elimination of street activities, were often petty and brutal in their treatment of those who resisted the law and continued to play street football.[71] In the following interview extract David Smith recounts a typical incident from the Edwardian era, in which unnecessary police interference led to an act of revenge by his Stepney street gang.

We used to have a policeman who used to stop us playing football round the back wall. Well, I don't know why, 'cos we wasn't hurting anything 'cos there was the dock wall and there was only one or two houses and then a factory, but he insisted upon us stopping playing football round there. And the football was a sack made up of sawdust and rags, see. Perhaps might have an inner leather doings. And I remember that some dockers

---

The street remained the most popular venue for impromptu football matches among working-class children long after World War II, despite victimization by the police and numerous arrests for dangerous play and for disturbance of the peace. This photograph shows a match in progress in north London in April 1950.

gave us a football and, oh, we was tops then. And when old Bloodnut come on, he started his beat, he pinched our ball, and he knifed it, pierced it. So what we did in vengeance was, coppers then in those days used to always have to go on duty in the winter with their very heavy tarpaulin cape, so we pinched his tarpaulin cape. We know where they used to leave it. They used to put it over a little gateway round the back of the Scotch Arms, the pub. And we chucked it over Hermitage Bridge. He done our football, we done his cape.[72]

Even when street gangs travelled — sometimes long distances — to play their football in local parks they were liable to be cautioned or arrested for any form of exuberant activity en route, such as singing, shouting and swearing, which the police might regard as a 'disturbance of the peace'.

We used to go over in the park and play football. 'Course, coming back — the old trams was on the road then — coming back the tram stopped and we was singing 'Nellie Dean'. And a copper got on the tram and I finished up in Bridewell, 'disturbing the peace'. . . . He catched hold of me, took me down to Bedminster police station and I was breaking me heart. I had to appear up Bridewell, and they fined me a shilling for disturbing the peace and I was singing 'Nellie Dean'. I shall never forget it.[73]

The victimization of youths playing street football often provoked fierce resentment, violent resistance and community solidarity in support of those unfairly arrested — all of which are illustrated in Bristolian Bert Teague's bitter recollections of police harassment in the pre-1914 period.

I remember one Bank Holiday Monday I was kicking a ball about in the street, went in to have a wash and brush up an' some breakfast. I got dressed and put me suit on to go up town. I stood on the corner waiting for me mate when a copper came up to me and said, 'What's your name?' 'What?' What did he want to know my bloody name for? 'You've been round here footballing.' 'What d'you mean? I've only just come out.' Anyway, somethin' was said an' he hit me across the head with the bloody truncheon. I went for him and he went for me, and out came the people. Anyway, I got sent down Stapleton Road police station and put inside. I didn't give a bugger 'bout anyone. They asked me my name but I wouldn't give it them. Anyway, someone must of give it to them 'cos I got a summons. I got told off and fined about two bob an' people had a collection for me. I was done for breach of the peace, footballing in the street.[74]

Although street football was one of the principal targets for police prosecutions, other innocuous gang activities traditionally tolerated by the working-class community, such as gambling and loitering, were also redefined as criminal offences. But this legal assault, which was particularly vigorous during the period 1890 to 1914, only served to intensify the solidarity and resistance of street gangs against the police, for older teenagers would often pool their money to pay court fines, thereby saving victimized gang members from prison sentences. Indeed, the notorious Penny Mob of east Glasgow, which originated in the latter part of the nineteenth century, derived their name from the custom of each member contributing a penny a week to a communal fund for the payment of fines.[75] Some delinquent gangs honoured members who attacked the police and were subsequently imprisoned by electing them to a position of leadership on their release. Although this inversion of conventional values was restricted to a small minority of gangs, many teenagers felt a deep respect for friends with sufficient physical strength and courage to resist or attack policemen who attempted to disperse gangs by forcing them to 'move on' from street corners that youths considered their own territory. This admiration is clearly apparent in Julius Goodman's recollections of the conflict between street gangs and the police in Manchester in the early part of the century:

When I say tough, he was tough as nails. He got hold of one copper. He was standing on his own street corner. Told him to move. Said, 'I'm not moving for you or King Dick.' He said, 'I want to go on the whistle.' So he gets hold the whistle . . . and did he give it him! Two hits and he hit the floor. That was it.[76]

Gang attacks upon the police must be seen to a large extent as a form of resistance of working-class youth to the criminalization of traditional street activities. However, they should also be considered in the broader context of the profound suspicion and hostility felt by the parent culture towards the insertion of this bureaucratic arm of the state into the heart of the working-class community. Hostility flared into sporadic acts of violent resistance in response to the suppression of disorderly popular recreations and customs, the prohibition of political activities and the containment of, and victimization in, strikes.[77] In fact, the police came to be viewed by many as a symbol of class oppression, and hostility found its most potent expression in strikes, when even young children, aware that the police were the enemy of their parents, would often seek revenge on the unfortunate sons and daughters of policemen, as

Grace Eddy, recalling the Cornish clay strikes of 1911, remembers:

Back when the clay strike was on we had an awful life. A policeman's
daughter or a policeman's son, they was all against you. When we did go to
school, the other children'd chase you and pelt you with stones. Well,
'twasn't our fault that there was a strike on. We had the policemen come
from Wales. I've never had so many uncles in me life. My brother, the boys
used to fight him awful. After we come out from school you'd see a crowd
of 'em, and I used to say 'Oh, they've got my brother again,' and I'd go up,
take 'n by the arm, pull 'n out through the crowd and take him home to
Charlestown. I used to say 'twas a wonder I wasn't killed. They used to
bully me — 'tisn't all fun being a policeman's child. They used to have a
fun time chasing us; we was just 'Bobby's child'. You were outsiders,
really, being policemen's children.[78]

For street-gang members one of the few escapes from authoritarian control, rigid regimentation and the grim city environment
was roaming and rambling in the surrounding countryside. But
even there they were confronted by repressive authority in the form
of gamekeepers and police, who ruthlessly defended the exclusive
rights of the rich to enjoy hunting, shooting and fishing on much of
Britain's moorland, which had been enclosed for this purpose in the
previous century.[79] The struggle of working-class youth against
landowners for access to the countryside continued for many
decades — for example, in Scotland, the Home Counties and
especially the Peak District, which was surrounded by the
conurbations of the industrial north. This conflict became most
intense during the depression years of the 1930s, when five youths
were imprisoned after a mass trespass by over five hundred youths
on the grouse-shooting moors of Kinderscout in April 1932.[80] In the
following extract one of three Jewish boys victimized by the police
on this occasion describes the motives for what the contemporary
press condemned as an unprovoked act of hooliganism.

There used to be very, very many boys and girls used to go hiking. For
years if you went on a Sunday morning towards London Road (used to be
called London Road) Station, Piccadilly Station, you'd see 'em going up
Market Street, all with their shorts, or maybe not shorts, but certainly with
their rucksack and their hiking boots. Be crowds and crowds there, and
the train would be full. It would take you to Hayfield or Glossop or
Mottram, but wherever you wanted to go, used to have to go over
Kinderscout. If a gamekeeper caught yer, they wouldn't charge you with
trespassing but they'd go for you, you know, throw you off, especially the
time they shoot grouse, August 12th. You wouldn't risk it, because it
would be full of gamekeepers. And then there was the Ramblers

Association. They were asking for access to the moors, and that meant going over Kinderscout. Eventually, members of the Young Communist League and other people outside the Young Communist League, young lads, formed the British Workers Sports Federation. A branch of that was a rambling section, and they decided that we'll force our way through over Kinder whether they liked it or not. So there was a great deal of publicity. The *Evening News* and the *Chronicle*, they splashed it, and of course there was handbills out to the hikers on Sunday. Had to meet at Hayfield — it was early May 1932. The meeting [decided to give] signals: if you blow once it means stop; if you blow twice it means spread out 'cos we're expecting opposition from the gamekeepers. And as soon as we went over the moors there was all the police and the gamekeepers, and it was a set-to. We went to the top of Kinder. We had a meeting and it was decided to march back in a body. And as we got into Hayfield, there was a row of police, stopped everybody, and they were picking out who they wanted, who they thought were foreign-looking; if they were Jewish, it would set prejudice against them when the trial took place. I was certain of that; I could see it going on. My brother Max was with me. I says, 'To hell with this. You're getting picked up like idiots,' so I broke away. I says, 'Come on, let's go.' So we went. Max was very fair; he didn't pick him up but he picked me up. I broke away. I wanted the whole bloody lot to disperse, but they didn't take the hint, like, and they picked me up. In the meanwhile they picked five up besides me. They just took us in. Then they started all sorts of tricks, which was bloody stupid, actually. They had detectives there quizzing us. They wanted to know all about it. Well, they didn't get any change — we just didn't tell them anything. And then there was the trial. We went on trial in Derby, and I got two months. Benny Rothman got four months, so they knew he was the leadership, like, Dave Nussbaum got two months, and the other blokes — I don't know why the hell they picked them up because one bloke, Anderson, he got charged with assaulting a gamekeeper. Most stupid. You'll never believe this, but he was one of those that were against the blasted thing. He said so at the trial, but the police have got to have their victims. Somebody had to suffer, for there was an assault on a gamekeeper. I did me two months in Leicester. And then when I came out there's a bloke waiting outside with a raincoat on, typical detective, you could smell him a mile away. He's just come out of jail as well, so he says; what did I do while I was in? All that sort of business. So I went along with him, like. I was pretending I didn't know who he was, bloody idiot. They think you're stupid.[81]

The resistance of working-class youth to control over its leisure time only occasionally found direct expression in class conflict over fundamental rights, such as the mass trespass for freedom to roam in the countryside; this type of overt political struggle rarely played an important part in the lives of gang members. Indeed, it must be stressed, in conclusion, that it has not been my intention to celebrate or romanticize the street gang. As an antidote to theories of brutalization and psychopathology, I have emphasized throughout the rationality of the gang's focal concern with tough individualism, immediate excitement and material gain. Similarly, I have argued that the crime, territorial conflict, vandalism and resistance to the police were of enormous instrumental and expressive importance to gang members, and that these activities originated in, and developed as a solution to, the experience of inequality and subordination in all spheres of life. However, although the street gang provided a space, free from authoritarian control, in which young people could attempt to create excitement and enjoyment and could adopt an aggressive and rebellious stance against respectable society, this resistance was itself riddled with contradictions. For anger and bitterness were often misdirected into divisive intra-class conflict, notably territorial gang rivalry and racism. And even when gang resentment assumed a more class-conscious form, hostility was frequently aimed at local and personal targets, such as a policeman, a shopkeeper or an individual employer. The narrow and contradictory nature of this resistance arose from the street gangs' failure to question, or consider any alternative to, the all-encompassing institutions of marriage, the family, the state and work in an industrial-capitalist society. Such powerful and firmly established institutions appeared immovable and inevitable to the street gang — and understandably so. But their resignation meant that gang life could offer only momentary solutions to the problems of gang members, because street gangs were operating principally in the sphere of leisure and not on the terrain where class contradictions could be confronted. Thus the enormous energy, solidarity and hostility generated by street gangs was directed away from class conflict into activities that could have little impact on the organization and control of wider power structures. The rewards of street-gang rebellion were likely to be transitory and the consequences ultimately self-defeating.

CHAPTER 8

Reformatories
Resistance to Repression

I went to the orphanage in 1910, November 1910, I'll always remember. It was on a Monday morning, and a lady took the three of us there, me, my brother and sister. We arrived at this huge building, number 3. There were two thousand children in the five big homes altogether, and my brother was taken from us and taken to number 4. My sister was supposed to go to number 5 because she was quite young, but she wouldn't leave me — they could not part us. They were very strict, but it was no good — she was such a strong-willed child — so in the end, for the time being, they gave in. We were numbered. I was 381 and she was 382. We were taken to a changing-room and all our nice clothes that we had on were taken from us, and we put on calico chemises and calico knickers and a flannel petticoat and long black stockings. I found out eventually that we knitted them. We had to do it ourselves, and we had black in the winter and white in the summer.... We had to knit our own stockings and there hadn't to be a flaw in anything, and I think I'd made a little mistake in the heel, nothing much, but she made me unpick it all, and it had to be reknitted in a certain time. I was so fearful, I used to sit up in bed and knit in the dark to try and get it done in the time she allotted me to reknit it. I remember one or two girls coming in. I expect they were very nervous; they did wet the bed. And the poor dears, they were humiliated. They were just held up to ridicule. They would be put right down the end in the other dormitory, on a straw bed, and that was their punishment. Really, it was inhuman.[1]

Ivy Petherick, together with her brother and sister, were removed from their home in Barnstaple and deposited at Muller's Orphanage, Bristol, after the premature death of their mother and father. Her recollections of the rigid classification of inmates, the formalized and regimented daily routine and the harsh discipline and brutal punishments inflicted upon working-class children are very similar

209

to the memories of others committed to orphanages. They closely resemble the experiences of delinquent and destitute young people who were incarcerated in the complex web of reformatory institutions, such as truant schools, industrial schools, approved schools and Borstal, that developed from the late nineteenth and early twentieth century onwards. For whether a working-class child was an orphan, a vagrant, a truant, a rebel at home or school or a thief, the assumption was often made by magistrates and officials that he or she was the offspring of a degenerate and deprived class, requiring intensive disciplinary treatment in a reformatory. Indeed, it is the argument of this chapter that all reformatories must be seen as institutions of class control, designed to inculcate discipline and obedience in working-class children and youth who either resisted authority or whose family life was disrupted by poverty and destitution. Before looking in detail at the resistance of young people within these institutions, it is first necessary to examine briefly the origins and nature of reformatories, in order to understand their key role as agencies of class control.

Reformatories experienced a steady growth from the mid-nineteenth century onwards, and by the turn of the century over 30,000 young people were incarcerated in industrial and truant schools, training ships and other reformatory institutions. In addition, more than 70,000 children were placed in Poor Law institutions, such as barrack schools, scattered homes or work-houses, and a similar number were contained in homes and orphanages operated by religious organizations. Despite a growing official preference for family- and community-based treatment for respectable working-class children, which led to a slight decline in reformatories from the 1920s onwards, these institutions remained influential, accommodating over 100,000 young people during the period under study.

Reformatories were established in the early nineteenth century by philanthropic and religious organizations, and their main aim was to combat the irregular, itinerant and delinquent lifestyle of the 'perishing and dangerous classes'.[2] As one supporter of reformatory institutions put it in 1841, their role was to convert 'turbulent unruly urchins . . . into tolerably quiet orderly schoolboys'.[3] This preoccupation with repression was eclipsed in the late nineteenth

---

Infants at Muller's Orphanage, Bristol, in 1919 pose for a photograph that illustrates the uniformity, discipline and regimentation demanded by reformatories and other institutions.

century by the rhetoric of moral rehabilitation, emphasized by social reformers and child savers who claimed that proper corrective treatment could modify or even transform a child's personality. For it was increasingly the view of psychologists, criminologists and educationists that childhood and youth were crucial stages in the life cycle, characterized by immaturity and susceptibility to outside influences; if a child could be rescued from its corrupt environment and placed in a morally regulated situation such as a reformatory before its delinquent habits had become ingrained, then it was believed that rehabilitation was possible.[4] Thus the reformatory was an attractive proposition to the middle class, not only because it protected the propertied and the respectable from delinquent and antisocial elements, but also because it promised to stabilize class relationships through character reformation. Although it has often been assumed that penal reform was motivated by a humanitarian concern for the rights and protection of deprived children, in fact the issue that dominated public debates and government reports was that of the control and reformation of rebellious working-class youth. Indeed, the ideal of rehabilitation, together with increasing state control of reformatory institutions from this period onwards, were themselves expressions of a broader movement, that of social imperialism, the principal aim of which was to regenerate national strength through state intervention to improve the moral and physical fitness of the working-class younger generation. From the turn of the century onwards reformatories were controlled by a professional body of penal administrators who attempted to infuse the system with the public school ethos of Christian manliness and patriotic duty. Alexander Paterson, for example, one of the most influential figures in the reshaping of reformatory institutions during the pre-1939 period, wrote that Borstal training methods were based on the assumption that there was 'among nearly all an innate corporate spirit which will respond to the appeal made to the British of every sort to play the game, to follow the flag, to stand by the old ship'.[5]

The establishment of Borstal institutions for offenders in their late teens and early twenties during the inter-war years clearly illustrates the broadening definition of adolescence and youth as a period of immaturity and responsiveness to corrective treatment that underlay the development of reformatories. Prior to this delinquents aged between sixteen and twenty-one had normally been committed to prison and treated in the same way as adults. However, it was increasingly thought profitable to segregate them in order to prevent contamination from incorrigible adults and to break the cycle of crime among the urban poor.[6] Indeed, segregation both between and within institutions according to age, sex and criminal record was an important organizational principle of reformatories, insisted upon so that the danger of the corruption of innocent inmates by older, more experienced offenders might be reduced to a minimum. From the 1920s onwards officials increasingly kept case histories and conducted personality and intelligence tests to assist them in classifying delinquents and determining the most suitable treatment for them, whether it be probation for a first-time offender, approved school for a vagrant child, Borstal for a hardened teenage criminal and so on.[7] The key factor that influenced the decisions of magistrates and welfare workers with regard to commital to reformatory institutions was their opinion of the moral responsibility and respectability of the offenders' parents. For the main thrust of the reformatory and child-saving movement was directed at the offspring of 'rough' and 'dissolute' families living in extreme poverty and deprivation. There was a growing awareness among the authorities that the incarceration of children from respectable families was often counter-productive, and legislation during the inter-war period sought to protect children of respectable parents, who were guilty of only minor and occasional lapses, from commital to reformatories by promoting the development of a probationary system.[8] The critical element in the entire process of classification and segregation was the removal of children from families considered to be morally and physically degenerate. This discrimination against the poorest classes was clearly reflected in the similar corrective treatment prescribed for both criminal and non-criminal children in institutional care. For example, in 1927 'industrial' schools, which accommodated destitute children, and 'reformatory' schools, which contained criminal children, were merged under the title of 'approved schools', for, in the words of the government Report that recommended this assimilation, 'there is little or no difference in character and needs between the neglected and the delinquent child.'[9] This process of discrimination, whereby a child who had committed no offence other than being an orphan or a member of a destitute or one-parent family received harsh corrective treatment that closely resembled that inflicted upon a young criminal, began in the nineteenth century. As an official inquiry into 'industrial' and 'reformatory' schools in 1896 stated, 'the children in the two institutions are, in the main, of the same class; and as a fact there is no substantial difference in the discipline and regime beyond what can be accounted for by difference of age.'[10]

The fundamental purpose of the reformatory was to incarcerate the children of the dissolute poor and inculcate in them habits thought appropriate for the respectable working class, such as obedience, discipline, honesty, cleanliness and sobriety. To achieve this character reformation, administrators demanded an indeterminate policy of sentencing, allowing incarceration for periods of up to three years because, as one prison commissioner put it, 'six months is too short a period for any real impression to be made upon a rebellious character.'[11] It was widely believed that the most effective cure for irregular and immoral habits learned in the slums was to place the contaminated city child in a country setting, where direct contact with nature would lead to moral and physical regeneration. The consequent decision to locate many reformatories in rural environments was, of course, just one expression of the middle-class fear of the disruptive effects of urbanization that we have already examined, but it created the paradox that rebellious slum children were removed into institutional settings in the countryside in order to equip them to become respectable and law-abiding citizens in the city.[12]

What were the characteristic internal features of these institutions, and what was the extent and significance of working-class youths' resistance to them? The precise nature and development of reformatories between the 1890s and the 1930s were extremely complex, for institutions varied according to their administrative staff, their size, their financial resources and, most important, their specific purpose. Thus while truant schools administered a 'short, sharp shock', usually of four weeks' duration, to irregular school attenders, Borstal attempted a much longer-term character reformation of the hardened teenage delinquent. Also the internal organization of reformatories was not static or fixed. There was, for example, a gradual movement away from an exclusively punitive and coercive approach towards more subtle character-forming methods, which aimed not just at the conditioned response of obedience but rather at the internalization of the principles of discipline and duty. However, despite these variations, three features are discernible in most reformatory institutions during our period. First, they were characterized by the invasion of all spheres of life. The inmate enjoyed no rights, no privacy and no free time. Second, external control was exercised through the organization of the entire day into a series of formalized and closely supervised routines. The imposition of a uniform and compulsory sequence of tasks, such as washing, meals, school lessons, work and so on, was designed specifically to eliminate any independent thought or action among the inmates and to replace them with habits of conformity, obedience and submission to authority. Third, the regimented routine was enforced by recourse to harsh disciplinary methods, and any inmate who resisted regulations was liable to suffer brutal punishment. This form of institutional regime does, of course, bear some resemblance to the typical elementary school described in previous chapters; however, there was an enormous qualitative difference in the degree of control and manipulation to which schoolchildren and reformatory inmates were subjected. Not only was regimentation more rigid and punishments more frequent and severe in reformatories than in schools but, crucially, the psychological pressure that reformatories were able to exert upon the individual was far more relentless and unremitting in its impact than any sanction that the most authoritarian school could impose. For whereas the elementary schoolchild experienced authoritarian control in the classroom for only about a third of his waking life and the school's influence was modified by personal relationships and informal codes of conduct within the family, the neighbourhood and the independent street culture, the reformatory inmate was isolated from parental or peer-group support and was subjected to absolute control. The reformatory, then, was an institution of class control, in which all daily activities were part of an overall plan to liquidate the inmate's former personality and reshape it into a conformist mould. In this context resistance, even though it was severely punished, was essential if the inmate was to maintain a personal, as opposed to an institutional, identity.[13]

One important area of resistance to the regimented daily routine was related to the formal manner in which reformatory institutions provided for the inmates' physiological needs, such as eating, washing and sleeping. It was frequently claimed by apologists of reformatories that their inmates were more healthy and robust than normal children from poor backgrounds, because they were able to provide a more nutritious diet and to establish higher standards of hygiene, cleanliness and medical care than some working-class families could attain. However, although prior to incarceration many children were underfed and in poor health — often due to circumstances beyond their parents' control — basic family activities such as eating, washing and sleeping usually took place in an atmosphere of emotional warmth, spontaneity and solidarity, which compared favourably with the uniform, depersonalized and rigidly supervised organization characteristic of the reformatory. Anger and resentment at the bureaucratization of activities associated with family life occasionally inspired acts of resistance, such as those of Ivy Petherick's sister at Muller's Orphanage in the pre-World War I period.

It was like a prison, ingraining the routine into you — hygiene, soap and water and cleanliness, tidiness, all that sort of thing. I've never been able to get out of the habit. We had to be up every morning at six o'clock. We all had to file into the washroom, and there was the tin bowls filled with cold water and carbolic soap. We had to strip to the waist, every morning, summer and winter, and plunge into this cold water, and there was this medical lady would stand in the room to see we all did it. There was no talking. Very few broke the rules, but my sister did. She broke the rules, talking to one of the girls, and she had to stand in the passage with her hands on her head, and I think she had to stand there nearly all day. And sometimes if we did break a rule, we were put in silence for a fortnight. We weren't allowed to speak or no one was allowed to speak to us. I was terrified, you know, even if I heard the trains rumbling by (we were near Stapleton Road station). I thought the end of the world had come. That was the sort of effect it had on you. . . . Our meals we had to eat off long white tables, and it was corned beef, potatoes and cabbage every Monday, every Wednesday and every Friday, and that was it, the same thing. And we had porridge for breakfast, and before we could have our porridge, there was a pulpit in the dining-room and a man used to go up and read a portion of the Bible and say a prayer, and we were very hungry. We'd had nothing between five o'clock and the next morning. Now my sister was difficult. She refused to eat the porridge, so they lay her on a form and poured it down her throat, and she spat it at them. She was very wilful, my sister, and a good thing she was, but in my case I was intimidated. Well, she wouldn't eat it, but in the end she had to give in because she was hungry.[14]

Official reports increasingly argued that the depersonalized relationship between children and staff undermined the character-forming purpose of the reformatory, and the need to recreate a family atmosphere within institutions was often stressed. Thus from the 1890s onwards many local authorities attempted to develop smaller-scale family units for children in care, such as 'cottage homes', complete with 'housemothers'.[15] Similarly, in Borstal institutions housemasters were encouraged to act as substitute father-figures in inculcating conformist values through firm leadership, personal examples of fairness and honesty and concern for individual inmates.[16] However, despite the alluring label given to cottage homes, the forerunners of the 'community homes' of the post-World War II period, both oral and documentary evidence suggest that the attempt to break down barriers of resistance and to encourage the acceptance of institutional values by establishing bonds of trust between inmates and staff met with little success. This failure was due in part to overcrowding, to the high ratio of inmates to staff and to the proliferation of unqualified staff, who frequently resorted to authoritarian methods as the simplest method of maintaining control.[17] Most important, though, was the fundamental contradiction between the coercive purpose of the reformatory institution, one aim of which was to eliminate the informal and independent aspects of working-class family life, and the attempt to recreate affectionate relationships between children and adults. This contradiction is clearly illustrated by the memories of Ivy Petherick, whose sister, having experienced tolerant and non-authoritarian family life prior to incarceration, refused to submit to the harsh, bureaucratic regime of Muller's Orphanage. She resisted two key assumptions that infused the organization of all reformatories: first, that hard work was a duty to be undertaken for meagre rewards and, second, that the satisfaction of primary needs such as hunger was to be regulated according to the clock and not according to individual desires and preferences. If detected, such resistance usually met with both physical coercion and moral reprobation.

The teachers, they were on to a very good thing, because each teacher had allotted to her two or three girls to do the cleaning of her room and even her sewing and things like that. My sister was a good lace-knitter and she used to knit the most marvellous lace for one teacher there, Miss Lewis. . . . She used to do it for their tablecloths and things, yards and yards of lace, in her own time. So when she finished, oh, enough for a great big afternoon teacloth, she took it in to her and she gave her one sweet out of a box. And my sister thought, well, this isn't much; whether they sold it or have it for their own use, it was worth a lot more than that. So on the afternoon that she [Miss Lewis] was supposed to go out, she watched her go and thought, she won't be back 'til the evening, so she went in and opened the lid and took out four more sweets. She thought, well, I'll pay meself, and all of a sudden she heard footsteps and Miss Lewis had evidently forgotten something. My sister crawled under the bed and there she had to lie. 'Course, she would have 'ad it if they'd found out. She daren't move a limb and she seemed to be ages. And after about an hour she crawled out. She said, 'That was a sticky time for me,' she said, 'I'll never forget that, Ivy. I sweat drops.' . . . When you leave there, if you've a pretty good record, you have a box of clothes for service, a tin trunk and you have a Bible with your name written in. I was a good girl. I had my name put in the Bible. My sister didn't. She never had her name put in because one day when she was working in the kitchens she stole a crust of bread which was mouldy and ate it because she was hungry. And it was green and she was had up before the teachers for theft. That went down in their record book.[18]

The appropriation of food was one of the most common acts of resistance in reformatories. This crime was frequently perpetrated in a collective and clandestine manner by members of the dormitory subcultures formed by inmates in opposition to the institution and its regulations.[19] Evenings spent in the dormitory offered inmates some of their rare opportunities to establish friendships without staff interference and control, and they would often exploit brief moments of privacy to plan and engage in anti-institutional activities. In the following extract, for example, George Nott recalls one such activity, which came to be called the 'laugh-up' tradition, in which boys at the Ongar cottage homes in Essex would illicitly steal and consume food and fruit after 'lights out'.

Sometimes at night, when it got dark, we used to wander round, and if we felt particularly hungry, we used to what we called 'laugh up'. Then we used to go to the larder of two cottages away, open a window and see what we could get. . . . Well, there was something missing one day, and the bandmaster punished us. And he turned round and he said, 'Huh, now this is where the small boys laugh up their sleeves at the big boys.' So, of course, when we got out we say, 'We'll go and see what we can find.' And when we came back we said, 'Now, this is where the big boys laugh up their sleeves.' Laugh up. . . . We had a wonderful big grass oval in the centre of the school in between the boys and girls, and all round the edge of the oval were apple trees that used to bear fruit. And the consequence was that we used to fancy some of this fruit at times. So what used to happen at night time, we used to wait and watch the nightwatchman, wait till he'd gone a certain distance away, then we used to get out the window, onto the fire escape, down the fire escape, a couple of us, run to these trees. One used to shake the tree while the other one held out his night shirt to catch the apples. Take 'em back to the dormitory and eat them. Well, it was all right until one day there was about six of us taken with diarrhoea. And, of course, they rumbled what it was.[20]

Another common preoccupation of the dormitory subculture was the hatching of devious plots to meet members of the opposite sex, for most reformatory institutions insisted upon rigid sex segregation as a safeguard against the precocious sexual behaviour that, it was assumed, would result if the inmates' immoral instincts were allowed free expression.[21] Sexual misdemeanours, however innocuous, were often viewed as grave sins, to be punished by a bread-and-water diet, the dispersal of guilty dormitory members and the expulsion of ringleaders, as Edie Bailey, recalling one such incident at Newark Orphanage, Leicestershire, in the 1900s, remembers:

The big girls, in church, used to look at the choirboys. . . . And one evening the under-matron, Miss Wilcock, she was going out and the girls were at the front bedrooms . . . and they were letting these letters down, on string, to the choirboys. They were hiding round the corner. . . . Luckily, I got away with that. . . . I wasn't punished for that. But the big girls were punished. They had to come into the little girls' bedrooms and us, the little ones . . . went into the big room. . . . That was their punishment. And when we went to church, the big ones, girls, naturally would sit at the front. But after that, they were — had to sit at the back. And they used to have bread teas for a long, long while. They had bread teas for that. Yes, one girl was expelled.[22]

As sexual desire and love were usually denied any heterosexual expression, inmates were forced to look to their friends for sexual gratification. Thus among teenagers mutual masturbation, sodomy and exhibitionist displays became important features of the dormitory subculture, as is illustrated by the following heavily bowdlerized recollection of Borstal written by a former inmate in the 1940s.

I awake to the harsh clatter of the electric bell. Some idiot walks through the dormitory shouting, 'Come on, get out of it, you lazy bastards.' He goes over to one of the beds and strips the clothes off, revealing a boy completely nude. 'What, you on heat?' shouts the idiot. The boy on the bed laughs. A titter runs round the dormitory. The idiot picks up a slipper and swipes at the offending object. The boy on the bed, who is one of the 'leery' (which means rough, crude, rude, ignorant) boys of the house, begins to strut down the dormitory. This delights the rabble who encourage him with shouted remarks. The leery boy stoops, if it is possible to stoop from this position, to ridicule. He places one hand upon his hip and purses his lips, making a sucking noise. 'Ah, yer lovely thing,' he says in an affected manner.[23]

The most dramatic and secretive form of resistance within the dormitory subculture was the planning and execution of escape attempts. Absconding or 'scarpering', as it was commonly referred to among inmates, was a recurrent feature of institutional life, and there were few reformatories that did not experience several such attempts by individuals or groups each year. Many young people who were incarcerated were committed because of their irregular school and work records, as they had chosen truancy, absenteeism and involvement in the independent and semi-delinquent street culture rather than conforming to the monotonous daily routine of the respectable poor. To working-class rebels such as these, the long hours of tedious manual labour, the rote learning in schoolrooms, the enforced silence, the military discipline and the severe punishments, all of which were characteristic of reformatory institutions, were often an intolerable restraint. Thus boys like Sam Jenkins, who was committed to a training ship anchored in the River Thames at the turn of the century, would willingly risk drowning or a birching by jumping overboard in a bid to swim to freedom rather than submit to the harsh, regimented routine of the reformatory.

I was always one for running away from school. I didn't like school at all. I detested it. . . . When I run away from school and mother brought me back, he used to give me six with the cane. Because I kept hopping the wag, playing hookey . . . I was sent to the training ship. Took me there, they put me in uniform and read the riot act out to me and that was that. There was a man there, a schoolmaster, Mr Ferguson. He was spiteful, used to cut me hands off. . . . Always hungry. Hard biscuits, no bread, never had bread, the old seafaring biscuits, you know, hard ones. . . . When we had a bath, they were like horse troughs in this barrack room, and we all stripped naked and there was an officer sitting down in a chair and a man alongside of him with a big tub of soft soap and as he went by he slapped a dollop on the top of your nut. . . . Tell you my number, 3747, and that was me official number, same as a convict had a number, and my number on the ship's company was 196, and I was in 15 mess, and that was imprinted on my mind. . . . I learned to swim, oh yes, I learned it. I used to try and sneak away, to escape. I jumped over the side and further on there was what they call piers, like, jetty, and I got between there. The boat shot round the other side and caught me coming through. I got twelve strokes with the birch then.[24]

Few escape attempts were successful. Most absconders were quickly arrested and returned to face a public flogging before the assembled reformatory inmates, which was intended to act as a severe warning to children with similar inclinations. Absconders were hindered by their uniform, which was conspicuous and easily identified, by their lack of money and by their ignorance of local geography, for they were rarely allowed outside the reformatory grounds and were normally incarcerated long distances from their homes. And, as Ivy Petherick remembers, though unhappy children often devised daring and ingenious escape attempts — involving, for example, a secret letter to a parent or a rapid change of clothes to avoid detection — their freedom was cut short after only a few hours or days.

I remember there was a girl, and her mother had married again, and she used to write to her daughter. Once you go in there, you're there, and you can't get out. They don't train you for somebody to come and say, as soon as you're old enough to work, they want you home — that didn't happen. But if parents did remarry, they could demand their child to come out. Well, my sister was a daredevil, really. She wrote a letter for this girl. She took a chance — where she got the stamp from I don't know — but she wrote about this girl, how she was always crying and she was unhappy and she wanted to come home, and my sister went out and posted it. The postbox was just outside the double gates, and that was a terrible crime to go out of the grounds. We never went what we called out into the world; we never had any contact with the outside world at all. . . . We never went out from that building, only once a year, and we filed out in crocodile line past Stapleton Road station and across the fields. We had to walk and walk and walk to a huge building in this field. I expect it was some big country house. We had capes, green and black, and straw bonnets, and we were a spectacle really for everyone to look at. . . . I remember there was a room where they put all our clothes. When we come in they took all our nice clothes, and they kept them up in a room. Well, these girls must have found out about this room, and five of them went up there and they all got their clothes one morning, and they dressed up and ran away. But, 'course, there was a real outcry because the police eventually found them, and I shall never forget when those girls came back. They had a terrible time. They were stood out in front of all the school, the whole school, North and South, and they were severely caned, you know, but they only ran away because they were so unhappy.[25]

Public birchings were the most severe punishment that reformatory institutions were permitted to inflict upon inmates. There is much evidence to suggest that there was a significant decline in the frequency with which reformatories resorted to this psychologically damaging ritual during the period under study.[26] For most day-to-day misdemeanours officials preferred to use less drastic sanctions, such as the cane, solitary confinement, a restricted diet, deprivation of earnings or play, the postponement of letters and visits or down-grading. However, oral interviews indicate that absconding was an offence for which even the youngest children continued to be brutally punished. For example, Reg Chubb, recalling his incarceration at the Russell Coates Nautical School in Parkstone, Dorset, after World War I, remembers how he, together with three other boys, was required to hold down his seven-year-old brother while he was publicly birched for attempting to escape.

My brother had the birch just because he ran away. He wanted to get out of it so he ran away. He was round about seven. Anyway they caught him in a

London train, in the toilet. I remember holding 'im down on the table meself, an' the rest of the school was all brought in to see the public flogging as an example to the rest if they absconded — they'd know what they was going to get. . . . They birched him six times. Four of us children held him down, two at hands an' two at legs, and a person in authority to give him the birch.[27]

Punitive treatment was notoriously brutal on training ships controlled by retired naval officers, and the innumerable delinquent and neglected teenagers who were placed in boy service in the Royal Navy were commonly subjected to severe punishments by the naval authorities, which collaborated with reformatory institutions and the courts.[28] Eric Walsh, who took the option of enlisting for three years' boy service rather than going to jail for persistently loitering on the streets of Manchester at the turn of the century, quickly discovered that birchings were often administered for petty offences such as smoking and swearing. Paradoxically, however, his acts of rebellion resulted in a premature discharge, a consequence of the excessive number of floggings he received.

I used to be summonsed many a time you know. . . . I was going for some sugar for me mother, it was only half a pound of sugar, and I'm going up Rossall Street to the top and the lads are stood at the corner, you see. Well, when they sees them [the police] coming, they flew away. They run, and I'm just going to the top of the street and he gets hold of me, Haydock did, said I'd been loitering there with them. Well, me mother knew that I'd only just gone out of the house, but they wouldn't take any notice, took me down and fined me five shillings or three days. I said, 'I'm not going to pay any more fines,' I said. 'I'll stop this. I'd rather go to Strangeways.' . . . So I went in, he put me down for seven days, I was still only sixteen. . . . So the next time he [the police officer] caught me, he says, 'Now, look here, I know you're defying me, and I don't want to keep you doing it. It doesn't matter how much I summons you, you won't pay. You'd rather go to jail.' I said, 'I would, 'cos I'm in the right. I'm doing no wrong.' 'Well,' he says, 'I think you've got a lot of bad. You're among a lot of bad pals. Will you go in the navy, if I let you go, go and join the boys' service?' . . .
    Well, I was only there a fortnight, on HMS *Caledonia*, at South Queensferry, Scotland. I had to do three years' boys' service, you see. Well, I was only there about a fortnight when they caught me smoking. That was when I was sixteen. Broke me heart, that did. When they flogged me it disheartened me altogether. . . . The birch, it's the same as them long brushes [for] sweeping up. They've got nine big things sticking out of it. Strip me like, put a loin cloth round so they wouldn't catch me loins. Then they rang the bell on ship to let them see me getting flogged, you see.
    Well, anyway, I thought to myself, well, I'm going to get away from this. Punish us terrible there. Up aloft at four o'clock in the morning with

weather, you know, bare feet and had to swim half a mile with your clothes on in the sea. Well, I says, 'There's a starboard watch to go into the field this afternoon and when I get ashore,' I said, 'I'm going to get away some road.' Well, I got away, me and [a friend] got away, and I said, 'Where do you live?' He says, 'Glasgow.' 'We get there,' he says, 'mother'll see us all right.' Well, anyway, we gets there and as soon as his mother saw him she summoned the police. I flew and I got away, you see. But I told him that there's a pit there at Borness. I said, 'I'll try there for to get a job.' They didn't catch me; they catched him. They fetched him back and he told 'em where I'd gone and they come for me. Well, I got twenty-four cuts with the birch, sixty days' leave and pocket money stopped and my long vacation leave. Well, after they'd given me twenty-four cuts it knocked me out, had to put me in hospital and all. And this doctor heard about me being flogged. Took me about three or four days to get round. So he put me down for me discharge, you see. Unfit.[29]

The general concensus among reformatory staff that birching was a legitimate last resort to maintain control derived in part from a crude application of utilitarian and behaviourist principles to the organization of institutional life, which contained built-in rewards as incentives and punishments as sanctions in order to encourage conformity. More important was the widespread assumption that the inmates were physically as well as morally degenerate, and that the most appropriate corrective treatment for lazy and shifty youths was a harsh physical regime, involving early rising, cold showers, vigorous exercise, strenuous labour, military drill — and, if necessary, severe corporal punishment. Surprisingly, however, from the 1920s onwards Borstal institutions, which generally contained the toughest and most violent delinquents, were more restrained in their infliction of corporal punishment and birching than reformatories containing children who were guilty of only minor infringements of the law or who had committed no criminal offence whatsoever. This paradox was to a large extent a consequence of the missionary zeal of Alexander Paterson, who pioneered the reorganization of Borstal in the 1920s and 1930s, recruiting university graduates as officers and attempting to transplant some features of the public school into reformatory life.[30] The press, politicians and penal experts heaped lavish praise upon the new-style Borstal system, with its emphasis upon sport and inter-house competitions as a means of grafting middle-class traditions of 'muscular Christianity' on to a rebellious working-class youth culture. It was claimed by Dr Methuen, the Governor of Borstal, 'that a distinct tradition was growing up amongst the boys, and they looked forward to a time when the traditions of Borstal would be at least equal to those of Eton and Harrow. . . . The Borstal "Blue" feels just as much pride in his colours as if he had won a Varsity Blue by his sporting prowess.'[31] The success of Borstal's methods of character reformation and the benefits that it conferred on the inmates were grossly exaggerated — one magistrate, when sentencing a young offender, assured him that 'Borstal is a public school, with all the advantages you get there.'[32] However, there is no doubt that the dedication of the staff in some Borstals helped to forge closer relationships with the inmates, which reduced the necessity for the regular infliction of corporal punishment that was characteristic of other types of punitive institution.[33] The disciplinarian clerics who dominated the committees of reformatory and industrial schools had little compunction in recommending severe birchings in their institutions. For example, the Reverend Vine, warden of Farm Hill School, Surrey, stated in 1896: 'I do not think eighteen strokes of the birch rod is anything of a punishment for a great, big, strong, healthy fellow . . . of eighteen or nineteen years of age. . . . I should give three dozen and have done it.'[34] Government inspectors throughout the period often complained of the rigid authoritarianism and the excessive use of corporal punishment in many of these institutions. In fact, revelations concerning the death of several inmates under suspicious circumstances at Akbar (Heswall) Nautical Training School in 1911 stimulated a series of sensational exposés in the press; reformatories were accused of inflicting such brutal punishments for petty offences that children were attempting to commit suicide in order to escape sadistic torture.[35] Although the subsequent official inquiries denied these allegations, there is much evidence to suggest that irregular and brutal punishments were inflicted upon young people who resisted control, particularly on those who persistently absconded or who were re-convicted for criminal offences. To illustrate this point I wish to quote at length from the recollections of a former approved-school inmate, documented by a 'mass observation' survey in 1949.

I had been writing for about five minutes when I heard the teacher call a boy's name. The boy came out and received a bashing for some sums which he had done wrong in the morning. The teacher hit him on both sides of the face, and then punched him in the stomach and finally kicked him in the backside and sent him back to his seat. When he got to his seat he was still crying, and the teacher went to him and told him to pipe down and gave him another smack across the ear. After seeing this, I felt a bit rotten and homesick. . . . One Sunday morning we went for a walk in the country and one boy with us . . . messed his trousers, and when he got back the officer took his trousers off and rubbed them all over his face. The stuff went into his eyes, his mouth and his hair, so that you could not see his face from the brown mess. . . . I did not get on very well. One day the Governor came up to me and said, 'How would you like to go home tomorrow?' I said I should like that very much. . . .

I had only been home a day, however, when I received a letter saying that if I did not get a job within four days, an officer would come down and fetch me back for another year and seven months. On the next morning I got a job as errand boy for a greengrocer. I could not find a decent job, however, and started to go wrong again. I first started by stealing from my boss to make more of my wages which I earned. But I got the sack because someone told my boss that I had been to an approved school. I had a hard time getting work, and all the time I was unemployed I was getting worse and worse. I had to get a living somehow, and I could not get it by honest means, so I had to get it by other means, which is the same thing as saying by stealing. At last I was caught red-handed in a shop with a man of forty-two at 4 o'clock in the morning. I was tried and sent to Wormwood Scrubs Prison, and then was sent back to the approved school. When I arrived I received a sound bashing up from the head and from the officers, and in two days I was properly fed up, and within a week I ran away again. . . . I was sleeping under a hedge when a policeman came up and asked me my name, and I replied, 'Bill Sykes.' He asked me where I lived, and I said I had left home to look for work. He did not believe me and asked me to turn out my pockets, and he found a letter with the address of the school on it. . . . When I got back there the head gave me a hot time with his cane, which he kept in pickle, and my backside hurt me so much that I could hardly sit down. I also received the same the next day. I once more ran away. . . . [He was again arrested by the police after stealing a police officer's car.]

The next night I went into the Governor's office. First, he started by getting hold of me by the hair and giving me two black eyes. He then kicked me in the stomach and winded me. I ran to the fireplace and picked up a poker and threatened to hit him with it. Then two officers pounced on me and held me down whilst the head beat me something terrible. When I got to my feet it was only to be knocked down by a terrific blow on the mouth. He then laid me across a chair and gave me fourteen strokes with the cane on the back and backside. After this he took off his coat and belted me all round the office. I must have lost consciousness because I remember coming round crying, 'Father, father, stop, stop.' I was completely out of my head. When he had finished beating me he led me down to the showers, kicking me all the way. I had a cold shower, which brought me to my senses a bit. When I was putting on my shirt again I saw it was covered with blood. When I had dressed one of the officers went to fetch the best boxer in the school. When he arrived, we went into the gym and the boy put on boxing gloves and I was made to fit on a pair, and then the boy was told to tan me. But as he was one of my mates he refused, only to be told that if he did not do so, he would get a beating. So we started, but he never hit me and I could not hit him, as I was nearly all in. My face, when I woke in the morning, was a sight. I could hardly see, for my eyes were nearly closed up and my mouth was swollen about an inch out, and it was all cut and hurt me to eat. . . . One ear had been bleeding in the night, for there was blood all over the pillow. . . . I was put in a field to work next morning, and I was that all in, I fainted for the first time in my life. Well, things went on all right for a week, and at the end of two weeks my face had healed up and I escaped once again and got all the way down to my home in Sussex, about 270 miles from the school. I was again caught and handed over to the police. I was sent to Wormwood Scrubs Prison when I received three years' Borstal for a shop-breaking offence. And I can only tell you that I would rather do six years' Borstal than go through all that treatment again what I had at the approved school.[36]

We have examined the conflict between the repressive regime of the reformatory, which sought to shape the inmates in a conformist mould by exercising control over all aspects of their life, and the dormitory subculture, which sought to create a release from the regimented routine and to maintain the inmates' personal identity through acts of resistance and escape attempts. In order to qualify our definition of reformatories as institutions of *class* control, we must add a more specific class dimension to our analysis of their organization. The social purpose of reformatories is most clearly evidenced by their attempt to inculcate rigid discipline through compelling older children and youths to perform semi-skilled and unskilled labouring tasks for long hours each day. This concern with the ingraining of regular work habits featured prominently in the rules, regulations and reports of all reformatories. For example, a conference of reformatory school managers in 1893 was informed that at Plymouth truant school, an institution said to be representative of its type,

the discipline is strict, continuous and inexorable. They [the inmates] are there because they love play better than work; and therefore they are kept at work almost all the day long, from six in the morning until eight at night.[37]

A militaristic demonstration of shoe-shining at Upton House Industrial School, London, at the turn of the century. Like other reformatory institutions, Upton House sought to impose mechanical habits of work upon rebellious working-class children.

Many institutions insisted upon long periods of silence to ensure the internalization of mechanical work habits, uninterrupted by the moments of humorous distraction, horseplay and repartee that characterized the shop-floor culture, as we have seen. Thus a government Report of 1896 noted that in truant schools

silence is enforced as part of the punitive system. . . . On the first readmission the half-hour for play and talking is taken away for a fortnight, during which period therefore the boy has no play and no freedom to talk at any hour of the day. On the second readmission the complete deprivation of play and free talking lasts for a month . . . and on the third . . . the complete deprivation of play and free talking is enforced throughout the whole of the twenty weeks.[38]

It is indicative of the social purpose of reformatories that Alexander Paterson, one of the most liberal and progressive administrators in this field, accepted uncritically the capitalist nature and unequal organization of the work process. He wrote that the fundamental purpose of Borstal was to transform the delinquent boy's reluctant attitude to work, so that

by the end of his training . . . he will be able to keep any sort of job, however laborious and monotonous it may be. . . . Many were born to be hewers of wood and drawers of water. . . . For them labouring work, arduous and continuous, is the best preparation for the life that ensues. . . . It is the duty of every Borstal officer to preach the gospel of work, not because it is easy or healthy or interesting, but because it is the condition of an honest life.[39]

To make this situation more palatable to young working-class rebels, reformatories often emphasized elements of this subordinate position in which they might take some pride, such as hard work, honesty, patriotism and service to superiors.[40] As the Governor of Rochester Borstal put it to his inmates:

without being angels we can all be sportsmen. . . . It means someone who can be depended upon to play the game. . . . Whatever work or game you take up can be performed or played to the best of your ability. . . . It's no use asking a carthorse to win the Derby, but he can win a ploughing match with equal credit. So, realize your own limitations and don't set out to equal those whose lives lead to higher spheres than those of your own.[41]

The cropped hair, the bowed head, the stark uniform and the numbered desk all betray the fact that harsh discipline and obedience were foremost among the lessons that these boys were being taught at Borstal in the 1920s.

Although reformatories frequently claimed that they taught inmates a trade, in fact very few provided facilities for any form of apprenticeship — they merely manufactured a highly regimented reserve army of unskilled labour, equipped to perform the most lowly paid, menial tasks, which the majority of working-class youth was reluctant to undertake. The reformatory training in military discipline and obedience prepared boys for a life in the army, naval service on the lower decks, unskilled agricultural labouring or routine factory work.[42] Girls were usually trained to enter domestic service, an occupation that from the late nineteenth century onwards, was becoming increasingly unpopular among young working-class people, who resented the long hours, the low pay and the petty interference of employers with their moral conduct and leisure.[43] The arrangements for placing boys and girls in suitable jobs, which might involve a move to any part of Britain or the Empire, were often made by the institution responsible for their care, and inmates usually had little or no choice in this official process of disposal.[44] Thus the reformatories' organization of work corresponded closely with the demands of the labour market, and the tight control of work within these institutions offered little opportunity for resistance. Even those like eight-year-old Reg Chubb and his seven-year-old brother, who were fortunate enough to be boarded out in a family, often discovered that their substitute parents viewed them as a cheap labour supply, to be exploited ruthlessly whenever possible.

I got boarded out on a farm, an' my brother was boarded out with me in Herefordshire, an' he was a wicked father an' so she was. . . . Start at six o'clock. Before I went to school I had to be out in the fields, top-'n-tailing turnips for the old farmer to come in and pick 'em up with the horse and cart. . . . And we 'ad to be home by a certain time after school closed, which meant we 'ad to run all the way to get home by that time, an' if we weren't home, the old farmer used to take his belt off an' give us the buckle strap, not the strap but the buckle end. [My brother] 'ad to work indoors making the butter, turning the churn an' making the cream, cleaning the house and doing the baking an' all this and that, and I was out doing the fields an' the cows an' the horses. And these people had two sons, and this is the part that annoyed me, because they never done a stroke. . . . I can give you one incident which shows how callous these people were. My brother and I used to sleep together. Well, sometime or another there must've been a hole in the sheet, but you know what children are, wriggle through the night, an' we happened to tear the sheet, with our toes, I suppose, from end to end. And this was a Christmas Eve, and she made us sit down with a needle and cotton each, he start one end and I the other, and we finished sewing this sheet up to the middle. That was the Christmas Eve before we went to bed. . . . And we stayed there in fear for three years because when the people came round to inspect you, to look at you, these people used to say to us, 'Now, look, tell these people that you're treated alright or else.' And I said to my brother one day, 'Now, look, let's face it. Let's tell these people how we're being treated . . . let's speak up. Don't be frightened to tell 'er.' Because you was living on your nerves.[45]

It is worth examining the recollections of Reg Chubb in some detail, for, like many other institutional children, his experience of regimentation and exploitation did not produce the desired effect of subservience to authority, but instead reinforced a proud and rebellious identity. After narrowly escaping being sent to Australia — his brother was removed to New Zealand — the Stepney Causeway headquarters of Dr Barnardo's Home found him employment at Munsley Sanatorium in Norfolk, where he worked as a cleaner for pocket money of only one shilling a week. Here, as a teenager, he began to adopt an aggressive attitude towards his employers, fiercely demanding basic rights and physically attacking anyone whom he suspected of being patronizing towards him. Although his rebellious stance was ultimately defeated by the sanatorium authorities, his frequent acts of resistance helped him to maintain personal dignity and to transcend the humiliation of his subordinate position.

You used to get a lot of rotten food. Then, of course, one day we got together an' said, 'Now, look, we've 'ad enough of this 'ere rotten food. C'mon, let's take it down.' So we all marched down to the doctor's dining-room with our plates an' stuck it on the table and said, 'Now you eat it.' So, of course, it was a private-run concern an' they said, 'Right, now, everyone, a month's notice.' Well, we gradually dwindled, so they [the protesters] got their jobs back. And I said, 'No, I'm not going to swallow my pride. To hell with it, I'm going to go.' I was the only one left out of three hundred; I was standing me ground. I was big-headed, you know. Believe me, I was a swine. I used to fight every day of the week, you know. If someone looked at me the wrong way, I'd go over and belt him one. I was a wicked man. I had to be. I had to stand my grounds. I got the sack because I would not say I wanted to make an apology. I had a pair of boots supplied by 18 Stepney Causeway while I was there, an' I said, 'Right, I've got to go and catch the train to 18 Stepney Causeway.' And I had to pass the golf course on my way there, which belongs to the home, an' I threw my boots over the hedge. I was really in a temper. Anyway, I got me bike onto the guard's van (don't ask me what I paid with — I don't know), but I had no boots. I said, 'To hell with them.'[46]

Reg Chubb was subsequently removed to a hotel in Clevedon, Somerset, where he worked as a cleaner, again receiving only one shilling a week but compensating for this low wage by pilfering cigarettes.

At that time I liked a cigarette, and I had to clean the bar round an' all this sort of thing. Anyway, I couldn't buy them, an' I thought I was clever being a boy, see. I used to take a packet from the bottom instead of the top [of the pile], not thinking they'd fall down. This went on for quite a while an' nothin' was said, so, of course, I never smoked all I took. I used to take 'em up me bedroom an' stick 'em in me case, so I could have a cigarette when I wanted one. I used to take a packet every day, only tens.

Anyway, one afternoon I went to the pictures — I think it was tuppence to go in in those days, an' you 'ad to read the words an' the music was playin'. I was sittin' there and I could hear the word going around, 'The police are looking for so-and-so'. I said, 'It's me. Well, this is it.' I sat there for a bit longer an' I said, 'Well, you aren't going to get me,' and I went out. I thought, well, you might as well take the bull by the horns, Reg, and I went back to the hotel. I didn't wait for the police to take me back. And he [the manager] said, 'I want you.' 'Yes.' He said, 'Where did you get all those cigarettes from?' 'You know where I got them from, but the point is, who told you to go into my trunk? You're equally guilty as I am. You went to my case to find 'em. You had no right to go into my room, no more than I had the right to pinch 'em.' 'Ah, well,' he said, 'the police are looking for you.' I said, 'Yes, I know all about it. I've heard. But they aren't going to 'ave me,' I said, 'nobody is.' He said, 'No? Oh, well, you can stay here the night and then tomorrow you'll be shifted back to 18 Stepney Causeway.' I said, 'Yes, that's alright,' and I thought, yes, that's what you think, mate.

I went to bed an' I waited until everything was all quiet and peaceful, an' I thought everyone had gone to sleep, an' then I got up an' I wen' out. Now I left there, an' I thought the best thing I can do is try to make my own way to Plymouth to find me mother. Never seen me mother before, mind, an' I didn't even know what she looked like. I tramped the roads to Plymouth. I didn't 'ave a lift on a cart or anything. I didn't 'ave nothing. I lived on water in the gutter an' banana skins what I could pick up. I never went to a door to beg an' I never even asked for a cup of water. I think it took the best part of a week to get there though, sleeping rough in the hedge and the ditch, you know. . . .

[Reg eventually contacted his mother through an elder sister he remembered. His mother had remarried and had eighteen children, but agreed to let him stay.] As I say, she wasn't no bloody good. She used to drink. She never used to keep house. She used to go out an' flog herself, all this kind of bloody business. I didn't worry mind, but I had to 'ave somewhere. There was one particular time I was playin' football on the brick fields with me step-brother an' he didn't like me because I could dribble the ball away from him. It was as tense as that, you see. He came to me and, of course, I had a temper, you see, because it was me and me alone. I had to stick by meself because otherwise I was cowed, an' I said, 'I ain't going to be cowed.' Anyway, I gave him a good hiding. I belted him one, you see. 'Course, he goes back home an' starts crying to mother an' so she starts on me. 'Out!' Now, that was the time when I threatened my mother with an open razor blade, you know, the cut-throat, and I would've killed 'er. Straight up, I would've killed 'er. Oh, she went mad. She told me to get me things an' get out and this and that, and I said, 'You aren't going to put me out. You're supposed to be my mother, but you ain't never been a mother to me. But I ain't going to get out, not until I'm ready to go.' And I 'ad her against the wall an' I was going to slash 'er throat with this cut-throat. 'Course, me temper started to cool down. I went out, an' she told the police. The police was comin' for me. I said, 'Well, Reg, you got to get out now, boy.' I thought, they aren't going to get me.[47]

Reg Chubb's experiences highlight the enormous difficulties confronting teenagers with no money, no skills and no family support, who wished to sever their links with reformatory institutions, many of which were able to exercise direct or indirect control over former inmates' working lives. It was only through constant struggle and determination that he was able to withstand the psychologically damaging effects of social isolation and insecurity and to resist the immense pressure exerted upon reformatory youths to accept their lot humbly. However, although many reformatory inmates like Reg succeeded in their struggle to maintain an independent and rebellious working-class identity, the personality of many others was ruthlessly crushed by the institutional regime.

The question of the powerful constraints imposed by reformatories, which restricted independent thought and action among their inmates, brings us finally to an assessment of their effectiveness in modifying working-class youths' behaviour and of the significance of resistance to corrective treatment. It is extremely difficult to quantify with any exactitude the impact of reformatories in either eliminating or reinforcing rebellious behaviour, partly because official records tend to exaggerate grossly the efficiency of these institutions — for example, in the 1920s 'industrial' and reformatory schools claimed a non-reconviction rate of between 85 and 90 per cent.[48] However, despite these distortions, which were often a consequence of inaccurate returns and reports, it is likely that in the majority of cases reformatories were fairly successful in manufacturing a conformist and submissive identity. Although traditions of resistance and dormitory subcultures insulated inmates from control and manipulation to some extent, for many children this psychological support was insufficient, in the long term, to enable them to withstand the powerful pressure to conform. Interviewees whose friends were incarcerated in reformatories noted that as soon as an inmate's resistance crumbled, he or she was invariably reduced to an automaton by the institution. Frank Vowles, for example, became a lifelong opponent of corporal punishment after witnessing the virtual destruction of his friend's personality after serving three years in Borstal for a minor offence.

Corporal punishment such as the birch, I'm very much against it, because of an experience with an older boy than me. He'd stolen some fruit, I think, from a shop in Bedminster, and he was caught and taken to the police station and to the court, juvenile court, and he had to have so many lashes with the birch and he was sent to Portland [Borstal] near Weymouth. . . . He pinched an orange or an apple. . . . That's all. I mean, we hadn't sort of progressed far, we hadn't, not in the twenties, from the eighteenth century, when they were so cruel to people, where they hung a man for stealing a sheep. In the twenties we had almost that kind of situation, I mean for children. When he came back, which was three or four years later, this boy was lifeless, you know, he was a different being. Instead of being a boy full of nonsense and fun and daredevil, he was a cold person. I just can't explain what he appeared to be. He was dead; he was soulless; there was something gone. All my life when I hear people talking about they ought to bring back the birch, well, you've got to see somebody that's had the birch and realize that you can't do that to human beings.[49]

The dehumanizing effects of the reformatory were sometimes compounded by the experience of isolation and ostracism when a young person was released and resumed life in the working-class community. This process of stigmatization is clearly illustrated in the case of Bill Bees's friend, who was committed to a reformatory training ship after violently protesting against the teachers' victimization of Bill at the village school in Hanham, south Gloucestershire, in the 1930s. When the young man returned he was rejected by the community, partly because he had become uncommunicative and conformist but principally because of a deep-rooted fear among former friends and neighbours that association with an offender known to the police might lead to prosecution for their own illegal activities.

He was put away for so many years an' he came out of there a different young man altogether. Although he would be your best friend, he'd hardly speak to you. And people despised him after, they'd call him the 'Borstal boy'. He wouldn't discuss it. He wouldn't go out like he used to, stealing, going over people's gardens stealing apples at night times an' doing damage, because he knew that he'd go back there again. And I used to say to myself, 'Well, it's no use foolin' around with him, Bill, 'cos you'll be along with him, and quick.' I used to think of my parents, I used to think, you'd better not, Bill, 'cos you've got a lot to do at 'ome.[50]

The ostracism of convicted delinquents as a form of community protection against police interference was rare, however. More often, the hostility of working-class youths towards the police was inflamed by their traumatic encounters with friends discharged from reformatories, whose personalities were so scarred that they could not even speak of their harrowing experiences. This powerful antipathy was further aggravated by the knowledge, often shared by members of the street culture, that each individual risked being singled out at random for exemplary punitive treatment, as Arthur Burley, recalling his childhood in the Cornish village of Perranwell, remembers:

Back in those days when you see a policeman, my God, you go quiet right away, even the chaps in the village, grown up, seventeen to twenty-five, perhaps. They'd be down on the bridge and they're having some fun there, an' somebody say, 'Tremerick is coming' — that's the policeman. Well, all the chaps would go quiet. They all go quiet now, until he go out of sight, you know. The policeman in the village back in those days . . . you had to watch your step, because you always had in the back of your mind that you might be going to Borstal. We'd heard how the children were treated in these places an' if you done something wrong, well, that's where you go, see, to Borstal. . . . I don't even know where the place was. 'Twas up the country somewhere, an' they used to give corrective training. You had to do everything on the run, apparently. If you was told to do something, you didn't walk, you 'ad to run to it. And when you come back, you was different altogether, like. I knew two brothers went to Borstal, an' before they went they was full of life, used to play with us, full of life they was. . . . I think they went down to a mill, which I've done myself, an' other boys done it, went down to the mill and got into the great waterwheel. This waterwheel used to drive all the machinery in the mill. Then the man the mill belonged to, he contacted the police, an' he come down an' catched 'em in this waterwheel. That's what they was sent away for. They never hurt nothing, really, they didn't do no damage or anything, but you done things like that back in those days an' you was punished for it. . . . When they come back from Borstal they was quiet, like, an' you had a job to get 'em to speak. Yes, they was changed altogether from what they was when they went away. And we couldn't understand it, an' we could never get the brothers to talk about it. They wouldn't tell us anything. But I think they 'ad a hard time.[51]

Such a deep rift developed between working-class youth and the penal authorities that if delinquents were able to remain proud and defiant throughout their period of incarceration, they were often admired and celebrated as heroes by their friends when they returned home. This inversion of official values and objectives most commonly occurred after the victimization of youths for popular acts of resistance to tyrannical authority figures, as Ernie Till, recalling his schooldays in Bristol in the 1920s, remembers:

We used to 'ave student teachers come as a trial, see. It might only be a month. They come from the university an' they'd take over a class. Well, of course, they didn't know the kids at all. There was one ginger one — they always used to say ginger people is slightly mad; that was a rumour at that time — an' he used to use the cane wildly, across the back. The master in the end 'ad 'im up an' told 'im off. But he done it to this kid an' this kid was the same height as he, an' he just picked the cane up, broke it across 'is knee an' hit 'un on the jaw. He was took to court, his parents an' all, an' he was sent to reform school. I think it was a month he got. He come back a hero after. They all thought he was marvellous for punching he.[52]

Many penal experts became increasingly aware that harsh punitive treatment was often counter-productive in its effects, frequently leading to a loathing of the police, a contempt for the law and rapid reconviction for similar offences. Indeed, this resistance to intimidation of a hard core of working-class youth influenced the growing preference among penal authorities for persuasive methods of character reformation as opposed to coercive methods such as the birch.[53] For example, the 1938 Cadogan Report concluded:

there is a very real danger that a boy who has been birched may be regarded as a hero among companions of his own age. . . . His main desire will be to show that he has not been intimidated by the punishment; and we have had evidence that, only too often, he seeks to prove this by going off at once and committing a further offence.[54]

Any attempt to establish the precise proportion of youths who resisted punitive and corrective treatment must, of course, to a large extent be speculative. Resistance varied according to a number of important factors, principally the nature of the institution in which youths were incarcerated and their character, family background, age and sex. Young people with criminal records were generally more difficult to control and reform than orphans, the destitute and the poverty-stricken. Thus Borstal institutions, dealing exclusively with young delinquents, tended to record higher reconviction rates than other reformatories — for example, the number of youths reconvicted within a two-year period after release from Borstal increased from 25 per cent in 1923 to 46.3 per cent in 1940.[55] It was often admitted among the most incorrigible youths were those who had enjoyed the independence and freedom of a semi-delinquent, street-trading life, the experience of which led to a profound loathing of any form of control or regimentation.[56] Penal experts viewed this resistance as a consequence of the corrupting influence of the city environment. They frequently claimed that corrective treatment was most effective among younger inmates because their habits of indiscipline and delinquency were less deeply ingrained, and because children were less practised in the art of dishonesty and deception than older teenagers, whose character had been shaped by the independent street culture.

Another recurrent theme of official reports was that although there was only a small minority of delinquent girls, they were much more fiercely resistant to character reformation than delinquent boys.[57] Regular complaints were made that domestics trained in reformatories were sullen, disrespectful and likely to steal clothing and jewellery from their employers. For example, in 1896, Miss Poole, Secretary of the Metropolitan Association for Befriending Young Servants, warned that former industrial school girls were 'violent and rough. . . . We constantly have cases of dishonesty and if we get their previous history and find that they went in for dishonesty, it seems to me that they are very seldom really cured by being sent into the school.'[58] The intransigence of delinquent girls is an extremely complex phenomenon, which cannot be discussed fully here, but it is explicable partly in terms of a determination to defy moral convention and the law in order to engage in part-time or full-time prostitution — an occupation that offered attractive working-class girls more money, freedom and independence than almost any other form of employment available to them.[59]

We noted earlier the exaggerated success rates of reformatory institutions, many of which claimed that at least three-quarters of their former inmates subsequently entered respectable employment and were not reconvicted. The most fundamental flaw in these optimistic estimates was their failure to take account of the extent and significance of hidden crime and resistance. For it requires only an elementary knowledge of criminology to realize that most illegal activities remain undetected or unsolved, and it is likely that the bitter resentment aroused by reformatories motivated innumerable hidden acts of revenge against authority.[60] To illustrate this final point, it is instructive to return to the recollections of Reg Chubb. Although appearing to earn an honest living, he not only obtained his job as a wine waiter under false pretences, but he then proceeded to pilfer from the upper-class customers he despised by giving short change. After escaping from the police Reg applied for a job as a dish-washer in a hotel:

I came down, no luggage, just as I stood up, with one suit, ass out of the trousers, one pair of shoes. Oh, I did take me waiter's suit with me as well! When she saw me she said, 'You poorish looking morsel.' [He only weighed seven stone.] First thing I said to 'er was, 'Madam, I'm a waiter by trade and I got my uniform upstairs,' an' I said, 'I want the job an' I want a roof over my head, but I'm telling you this, as soon as I see a job for a waiter, I'm off.' 'That's alright', she said, 'I admire your pluck. There's nothing of you, but I admire your pluck.' After three weeks . . . I saw the head waiter an' he said, 'Can you do wine waiting?' and I said, 'Yes.' I lied, you know, because I couldn't do it but I wouldn't say. I had a pound float an' I went to the first table an' I said, 'Can I get you anything to drink, sir?' He asked for a whisky and one for his friend, so I said, 'Thank you,' an' he give me a five-pound note. So I got the drinks, told 'im how much it was. I said, 'I'll bring you your change later on, sir, because you gave me a fiver and they ain't got the change for it at the moment.' 'That's alright, later on in the evening.' Yes, I thought to meself, you've 'ad that, you ain't gonna' get no bloody change, mate. I thought to myself, I've been poor all my life, now I'm serving the rich I'm going to start meself now.
   It went on through the evening, an' I was giving change here, owing change there. This one with the fiver, I didn't give him his change at all. I'd get an odd tanner tip an' I wasn't doing too badly — actually, I was richer then than I'd ever been in me life, see. So I said, 'This is alright Reg. Carry on, you're doing alright.' And towards the end of the evening, this fellow came to me an' he said, 'Waiter, do you know, you never gave me my change.' I said, 'I beg your pardon, sir, I did give you your change. As a matter of fact, I can tell you exactly how I done it. You was very engrossed talking to the gentleman next to you. I dropped your change on the table and tapped you on the shoulder and said, "There's your change," and you didn't give me a tip.' 'Well,' he said, 'it seems as though you've got it off pat. I can't remember what I did with it.' 'Well, that's nothing to do with me, is it?' I said. But he didn't 'ave his bloody change, I kept it. [Laughter][61]

In conclusion, the reformatory must be seen as the ultimate weapon deployed by the middle class and the state to contain and control those elements within working-class youth culture that most threatened their continued domination. The repressive aims and organization of reformatories are an indication of the essentially coercive and manipulative nature of the broader provision of educational welfare and leisure for working-class youth during the period under study. They constituted the final punitive thrust of a more general ideological assault upon working-class youth culture that sought to reproduce and reinvigorate capitalist society by instilling habits of regularity and conformity and by inculcating attitudes of dependence on, and deference towards, middle-class adults. For young people who stubbornly resisted bourgeois institutions through sabotage at school and work, persistent truancy, violent conflicts with teachers, social crime and street-gang subcultures were, as we have seen, major targets for disciplinary and corrective treatment in the reformatory. But this opposition could not be completely suppressed, despite the constant resort to brutal authoritarian methods. The recollections of old people clearly reveal that this powerful undercurrent of resistance, which obstructed official aims even in institutions such as the reformatory, cannot be dismissed simply as an expression of the ignorance, immorality and immaturity that middle-class commentators have commonly attributed to working-class youth. Instead this resistance can best be understood as a discriminating response to the contradictions and inequality that were experienced in all spheres of life. Working-class people's memories of childhood and youth illuminate the fundamental importance of anger, resentment and hostility in motivating the antisocial, delinquent and un-disciplined behaviour of which they stand accused in the official records.

Notes and References

The letters B, E and M, which precede interview reference numbers, denote that a tape is held in the Bristol, Essex or Manchester oral history collections. Interviews for which no reference number is given were conducted by the author. For details, see 'A Brief Guide to Oral History Material', p. 269. It should be noted that pseudonyms have been used where requested by respondents and that some quotations have been edited to avoid unnecessary repetitions and digressions.

The titles of certain academic journals have been abbreviated. These are: *British Journal of Educational Studies* — BJES; *Economic Journal* — EJ; *History of Education* — HE; *History of Education Quarterly* — HEQ; *Journal of Contemporary History* — JCH; *Oral History Journal* — OHJ; *Past and Present* — PP; *Victorian Studies* — VS.

CHAPTER 1: *Deprivation and Depravity: A Review of the Theory*

1 Liberal educational historians maintain that the growth of state education was democratic and progressive, both in its intentions and in its effects. See G. Lowndes, *The Silent Social Revolution* (London, 1937); S. Curtis, *History of Education in Great Britain* (London, 1965); D. Wardle, *English Popular Education 1780-1970* (Cambridge, 1970). The orthodox interpretation of youth organizations parallels this celebration of schooling, viewing them as civilizing agencies providing healthy, character-forming, recreative and moral standards for deprived and brutalized working-class children. See, for example, W. McG. Eagar, *Making Men: The History of Boys' Clubs and Related Movements in Great Britain* (London, 1953). Similarly, the emergence of social work and welfare professions and the development of penal institutions aimed at reforming and rehabilitating 'problem' children have been portrayed by liberal historians as inspired by

evangelical zeal, humanitarian concern and the new middle-class collectivism, all of which culminated in the growth of a benign welfare state. There is a huge hagiographic literature in this tradition; for some of the most influential works, see A. F. Young and E. T. Ashton, *British Social Work in the Nineteenth Century* (London, 1967 edn.); M. P. Hall, *The Social Services of Modern England* (London, 1960 edn.), esp. pp. 171-274; I. Pinchbeck and M. Hewitt, *Children in English Society*, vol. 2, *From the Eighteenth Century to the Children Act 1948* (London, 1973).

2   See M. Katz, 'The Origins of Public Education: A Reassessment', in *HEQ*, vol. 16, no. 4 (1976), pp. 381-407; R. Johnson, 'Educational Policy and Social Control in Early Victorian England', in *PP*, no. 49 (1970). For a powerful statement of the theoretical importance of applying the concept of hegemony to the study of working-class youth culture, see S. Hall and T. Jefferson (eds.), *Resistance Through Rituals: Youth Subcultures in Post-War Britain* (London, 1976), pp. 9-74.

3   During the 1970s there was a steady accumulation of revisionist works that examined critically the origins and nature of schooling, youth movements, welfare and penal institutions provided for youth and the social definition of adolescence and youth. See, for example, J. Springhall, *Youth, Empire and Society* (London, 1977); G. Grace, *Teachers, Ideology and Control: A Study in Urban Education* (London, 1978); G. Pearson, *The Deviant Imagination* (London, 1975); P. Young, 'A Sociological Analysis of the Early History of Probation', in *British Journal of Law and Society*, vol. 3, no. 1 (1976), pp. 44-58; G. Mungham and G. Pearson (eds.), *Working Class Youth Culture* (London, 1976); J. Gillis, *Youth and History* (London, 1974).

4   For useful general analyses, see S. Giner, *Mass Society* (London, 1976); J. Agassi, 'The Worker and the Media', in *Archives européenes de sociologie*, vol. 2, no. 1 (1970), pp. 26-66; P. Golding, *The Mass Media* (London, 1974), pp. 4-7.

5   H. Dendy, 'The Children of Working London', in B. Bosanquet (ed.), *Aspects of the Social Problem* (London, 1895), p. 36.

6   R. Bray, *The Town Child* (London, 1907), pp. 50, 51.

7   T. R. Fyvel, *The Insecure Offenders: Rebellious Youth in the Welfare State* (London, 1969 edn.), p. 85.

8   See, for example, the Albermarle Report, *The Youth Service in England* (London, 1958); T. R. Fyvel, *The Unattached* (London, 1963); M. Morse, *The Unattached* (London, 1965).

9   See P. Dunae, 'Penny Dreadfuls: Late Nineteenth Century Boys' Literature and Crime', in *VS*, vol. 22, no. 1 (1979), pp. 133-50.

10   E. Salmon, 'What Boys Read', in *Fortnightly Review* vol. 39, no. 2 (February, 1886), pp. 258, 257.

11   C. F. G. Masterman, 'Where Ignorant Armies Clash by Night', in the *Commonwealth* (August 1901).

12   R. Hoggart, *The Uses of Literacy* (London, 1958), pp. 188, 249, 250.

13   For a graphic illustration of this type of simplistic approach, see D. Thompson (ed.), *Discrimination and Popular Culture* (London, 1964), esp. pp. 9-22.

14   G. Orwell, *Keep the Aspidistra Flying* (London, 1962), quoted in R. Collins, 'The Film', in D. Thompson (ed.), *Discrimination and Popular Culture*, rev. edn. (London, 1973), p. 215.

15   See D. Reeder, 'Predicaments of City Children: Late Victorian and Edwardian Perspectives on Education and Urban Society', in D. Reeder (ed.), *Urban Education in the Nineteenth Century* (London, 1977), pp. 75-94; J. Marchant, *James Paton, Educational and Social Pioneer* (London, 1909); M. Whitehouse, *Cleaning Up TV* (London, 1967).

16   C. Booker, *The Neophiliacs* (London, 1969), pp. 60, 61.

17   See, for example, O. Newman, *Defensible Space* (London, 1974); Fyvel, *The Insecure Offenders*, esp. pp. 9-26.

18   See, for example, R. Parks, E. Burgess and R. McKenzie, *The City* (Chicago, 1925); F. Thrasher, *The Gang* (Chicago, 1927); T. Morris, *The Criminal Area* (London, 1957).

19   The founding fathers of sociology, notably Tonnies, Weber and Durkheim, built into many of their theories the key assumption that the processes of industrialization and urbanization were leading to increasing isolation and atomization. Individuals were torn away from rural and village communities characterized by collective solidarity and strong kinship bonds and were transplanted into anonymous towns and cities dominated by formal, rational and competitive relationships. For the most incisive summary of this sociological concern with the breakdown of community solidarity, see R. A. Nisbet, *The Sociological Tradition* (London, 1971 edn.), esp. pp. 47-106. The parallel literary tradition, embracing such influential writers as Dickens, Gissing and D. H. Lawrence, in which the image of the organic country community is juxtaposed with that of the anonymous city crowd, is brilliantly analysed in Raymond Williams's *The Country and the City* (London, 1973), esp. pp. 142-81, 215-47, 289-306.

20   W. Morrison, *Juvenile Offenders* (London, 1896), p. 29.

21   B. Wilson, *Youth Culture and the Universities* (London, 1970), pp. 88-90.

22   H. Zehr, *Crime and the Development of Modern Society* (London, 1976), esp. pp. 57-87; F. Musgrove, *Youth and the Social Order* (London, 1964), pp. 125-49; F. Milson, *Youth in a Changing Society* (London, 1972), esp. pp. 19-48.

23   J. J. Tobias, *Crime and Industrial Society in the Nineteenth Century* (London, 1967), pp. 244-7, 255.

24   See Reeder, 'Predicaments of City Children'.

25   See M. Casson, *Youth Unemployment* (London, 1979), esp. pp. 9-29, 126-8.

26   See, for example, R. Bray, *Boy Labour and Apprenticeship* (London, 1911); R. H. Tawney, 'Economics of Boy Labour' in *EJ*, vol. 19, no. 4 (December 1909), pp. 517-37; K. Liepmann, *Apprenticeship: An Enquiry into its adequacy under Modern Conditions* (London, 1960), pp. 13-23.

27   See, for example, M. E. Sadler (ed.), *Continuation Schools in England and Elsewhere, their Place in the Educational System of an Industrial and Commercial State* (Manchester, 1907); Bray, *Boy Labour and Apprenticeship*, esp. pp. 176-240; A. Greenwood, 'Blind Alley Labour', in *EJ*, vol. 22, no. 2 (1912), pp. 309-14.

28   A useful bibliography of the vast literature published in the early part of the century on the boy labour problem appears in A. Freeman, *Boy Life and Labour* (London, 1914), pp. 233-48.

29   Bray, *Boy Labour and Apprenticeship*, p. 170.

30   For a discussion of the ambivalent and apprehensive middle-class response for urbanization, see, for example, S. Pierson, 'The Way Out', in H. Dyos and M. Wolff (eds.), *The Victorian City, Images and Realities*, vol. 1, (London, 1973), pp. 873-89.

31   For a general discussion, see G. Pearson, *The Deviant Imagination* (London, 1977 edn.), esp. pp. 160-76.

32   See, for example, C. Burt, *The Young Delinquent* (London, 1938 edn.), p. 302; *Sunday Chronicle*, 21 May 1916; Wilson, *Youth Culture and the Universities*, p. 92; D. Holbrook, 'Magazines', in Thompson, *Discrimination and Popular Culture* (1973 edn.), p. 205.

33   See S. Cohen, *Folk Devils and Moral Panics* (London, 1973).

34   ibid. For an analysis of similar 'mugging' moral panics in the 1970s, see S. Hall, C. Critcher, T. Jefferson and B. Roberts, *Policing the Crisis: Mugging, the State and Law and Order* (London, 1978).

35   The most virulent attacks on mass teenage culture have emerged from the Frankfurt School of Marxists; see, for example, T. W. Adorno, *Prisms* (London, 1967) and H. Marcuse, *One-Dimensional Man* (Boston, 1964).

36 C. Parker, 'Pop Song: The Manipulated Ritual', in P. Abbs (ed.), *The Black Rainbow* (London, 1975), p. 139.

37 For a useful summary of these arguments, see S. Hall and P. Whannel, *The Popular Arts* (London, 1964), esp. pp. 365-70.

38 P. Morgan, *Delinquent Fantasies* (London, 1978), pp. 11, 13.

39 For a comprehensive bibliography of the vast literature on 'popular' culture — the polite term for mass culture — see *Current Sociology* (Winter 1978), esp. pp. 71-154, compiled by George Lewis. And for a valuable discussion of the origins and development of the language of 'masses' and the way in which it has acted as an alternative to the language of 'class', thereby disguising and depoliticizing class relationships, see A. Briggs, 'The Language of "Mass" and "Masses" in Nineteenth Century England', in D. Martin and D. Rubinstein (eds.), *Ideology — the Labour Movement* (London, 1979), pp. 62-83.

40 For an extensive discussion and bibliography, see Hall and Jefferson, *Resistance Through Rituals*.

41 See, G. Murdock and R. McCron, 'Youth and Class — The Career of a Confusion', in Mungham and Pearson *Working Class Youth Culture*, pp. 10-26.

42 See, for example, Hall and Jefferson, *Resistance Through Rituals*.

43 For a short review of the many youth culture histories that have been produced in America in the past decade, see D. Reimers, 'On the History of Youth', in *HEQ*, vol. 18, no. 3 (1978), pp. 357-64.

44 See, for example, Musgrove, *Youth and the Social Order*; Gillis, *Youth and History*; P. Thompson, 'The War with Adults', in T. Vigne (ed.) *OHJ*, vol. 3, no. 2 (1975), pp. 29-38.

45 F. Galton, *Classification of Men according to their natural gifts* (London, 1892), quoted in S. Wiseman (ed.), *Intelligence and Ability* (London, 1967), p. 30.

46 See, for example, B. Gilbert, *The Evolution of National Insurance in Great Britain* (London, 1966); Reeder, 'Predicaments of City Children', esp. pp. 80-6.

47 G. Sims, *The Black Stain* (London, 1907), pp. 11, 12, 150.

48 Some of the more influential works include R. Bray, *The Town Child*; A. Paterson, *Across the Bridges* (London, 1911); C. Russell, *Manchester Boys: Studies of Manchester Lads at Work and Play* (Manchester, 1905); E. J. Urwick (ed.), *Studies of Boy Life in Our Cities* (London, 1904).

49 Freeman, *Boy Life and Labour*, p. 72.

50 Russell, *Manchester Boys*, p. 54.

51 For a valuable discussion of the influence of atavistic, biological and medical theories of criminality from the late nineteenth century onwards, see I. Taylor, P. Walton and J. Young, *The New Criminology: For a Social Theory of Deviance* (London, 1977 edn.), esp. pp. 31-66.

52 C. Burt, *The Young Delinquent* (London, 1931 edn.), pp. vii, viii.

53 See, for example, G. S. Hall, *Adolescence: Its Psychology and its Relations to Physiology, Anthropology, Sociology, Sex Crime, Religion and Education*, 2 vols. (New York, 1904). Leading psycho-historian Lloyd de Mause claims that 'the history of childhood is a nightmare from which we have only recently begun to reawaken.' Previous generations and cultures, he claims, grossly abused the fundamental physical and psychological needs of children and adolescents, thus frequently producing adults with damaged personalities. See Lloyd de Mause, 'The Evolution of Childhood', in L. de Mause (ed.), *The History of Childhood: The Evolution of Parent-Child Relationships as a Factor in History* (London, 1974), pp. 1-73. Given this type of perspective, behaviour that might legitimately be explained in terms of resistance is instead conceptualized as an expression of the psychic problems associated with middle-class adolescence in the post-war period. Thus, for example, Steven Smith views the riots, political activitism and fraternal solidarity of apprentices in seventeenth-century London to some extent as expressions of adolescent problems such as 'role experimentation' and 'identity confusion'. See S. Smith 'The London Apprentices as Seventeenth Century

Adolescents', in *PP*, no. 61 (1973), pp. 149-61.

54 See Gillis, *Youth and History;* Musgrove, *Youth and the Social Order,* pp. 13-17, 33-57.

55 See M. May, 'Innocence and Experience. The Evolution of the Concept of Juvenile Delinquency in the Mid-Nineteenth Century', in *VS*, vol. 18, no. 1 (1973) pp. 7-29; Gillis, *Youth and History*, pp. 61-6; Reeder, 'Predicaments of City Children', pp. 75-94.

56 Blacker's Presidential Address to the NUT, quoted in the *Schoolmaster*, 13 April 1901, p. 566.

57 Hall, *Adolescence*, vol. 2, p. 458.

58 For a graphic example of the pathological approach to juvenile delinquency, see W. Norwood East, *The Adolescent Criminal: A Medico-Sociological Study of 4,000 Male Adolescents* (London, 1942).

59 For a classic illustration of social class defined in terms of cultural deprivation, see B. Sugarman, 'The Subcultures of Social Classes', in M. Craft (ed.), *Family Class and Education* (London, 1970), pp. 244-9.

60 See, for example, A. H. Halsey, Jean Floud and C. P. Anderson (eds.), *Education, Economy and Society* (London, 1961); J. B. W. Douglas, *The Home and the School* (London, 1965); B. Bernstein, 'A Socio-Linguistic Approach to Social Learning', in J. Gould (ed.), *Survey of the Social Sciences* (London, 1965), pp. 144-68.

61 For a critical discussion of cultural deprivation theory and an extensive bibliography, see K. Giles and R. Woolfe, *Deprivation, Disadvantage and Compensation,* Open University Course E202, Schooling and Society, Units 25-6 (Milton Keynes, 1977), pp. 32-68.

62 L. McDonald, *Social Class and Delinquency* (London, 1969), pp. 26, 27.

63 R. Bray, 'The Boy and the Family', in Urwick, *Studies of Boy Life in Our Cities,* p. 60.

64 H. Trevor Roper, 'The Past and the Present − History and Sociology', in *PP*, no. 42 (1969), p. 12.

65 A summary of the theories of psychologists, political scientists and sociologists concerning working-class authoritarianism is contained in S. Lipset, *Political Man* (London, 1971), pp. 97-130.

66 For a discussion, see S. Yeo, 'On the Uses of Apathy', in *Archives européenes de sociologie*, vol. 15, no. 2 (1974), pp. 279-311.

67 Lipset, *Political Man,* p. 126.

68 Both quoted and discussed in Lipset, *Political Man,* pp. 103, 117, 118.

69 Pinchbeck and Hewitt, *Children in English Society,* vol. 2, pp. 347, 653.

70 For a valuable discussion and bibliography, see M. May, 'Violence in the Family: An Historical Perspective', in J. P. Martin (ed.), *Violence in the Family* (London, 1978), pp. 135-67.

71 J. Samuelson, *The Children of our Slums* (London, 1911), pp. 22, 23.

72 G. Stedman Jones, *Outcast London* (London, 1971), pp. 341, 343.

73 G. Lowndes, *The Silent Social Revolution* (London, 1955 edn.), pp. 235, 236, 239.

74 For accounts that emphasize the ignorant, violent and semi-criminal aspects of 'rough' working-class culture see, for example, K. Chesney, *The Victorian Underworld* (London, 1970); G. Best, *Mid-Victorian Britain* (St Albans, 1973), esp. pp. 150-2, 240-3, 293-7.

75 See for example, N. Keddie (ed.), *Tinker, Tailor . . . The Myth of Cultural Deprivation* (London, 1973); H. Rosen, *Language and Class* (Bristol, 1972).

76 For a useful introductory discussion and bibliography of phenomenological sociology and cultural relativism, see M. Sarup, *Marxism and Education* (London, 1978), esp. pp. 13-103.

77 P. Marsh, *Aggro − the Illusion of Violence* (London, 1978), pp. 11, 12.

78 See, for example, Marsh, *Aggro;* P. Marsh, E. Rosser and R. Harré, *The Rules of Disorder* (London, 1978).

79   See, for example, D. Lockwood, 'Sources of Variation in Working-Class Images of Society', in *Sociological Review* vol. 14, no. 3 (1966), esp. p. 249; G. Pearson, ' "Paki-Bashing" in a North East Lancashire Cotton Town: a Case Study and its History', in Mungham and Pearson, *Working Class Youth Culture*, pp. 48-81.

80   See P. Robinson, *Education and Poverty* (London, 1976), esp. pp. 30, 31.

81   For one of the most interesting recent attempts to combine an ethnographic and a Marxist approach to the study of working-class youth culture, see P. Willis, *Learning to Labour* (Farnborough, 1977) pp. 119-93.

82   R. Price, *An Imperial War and the British Working Class* (London, 1972), pp. 4, 242.

83   ibid., pp. 237, 241.

84   G. Stedman Jones, 'Working Class Culture and Working Class Politics in London 1870-1900: Notes on the Remaking of a Working Class', in *Journal of Social History* (Summer 1974), pp. 460-508.

85   ibid., p. 490.

86   See, for example, P. Cohen, 'Sub Cultural Conflict and Working Class Community', in *Cultural Studies*, no. 2 (Birmingham, 1972).

CHAPTER 2: *Subverting the School Syllabus*

1   Born 1904, Fishponds, Bristol. Bus conductress. Father, bricklayer.

2   The information for this discussion was drawn from log and punishment books relating to the period 1889-1939 held by the Bristol and Exeter Record Offices and from records held privately by a number of West Country schools.

3   For elaboration of this point, see P. McCann (ed.), *Popular Education and Socialisation in the Nineteenth Century* (London, 1977), editor's introduction, pp. x-xii. Character formation is a recurrent central concern of British educationalists; see M. Katz, 'From Bryce to Newsom: Assumptions of British Educational Reports 1895-1963', in *International Review of Education*, vol. 11, no. 3 (1965), pp. 287-302.

4   For a general discussion of the development of the liberal educational ideology, see R. Dale and G. Esland, Mass Schooling, Open University Course E202, Units 2-3 (Milton Keynes, 1977).

5   See M. Mathieson, *The Preachers of Culture* (London, 1975).

6   See, for example, R. J. W. Selleck, *The New Education: The English Background 1870-1914* (London, 1968), pp. 78-151.

7   For a general analysis, see D. W. Dean, 'Conservatism and the National Education System 1922-1940', in *JCH*, vol. 6, no. 2 (1971), pp. 150-65; B. Simon, *Education and the Labour Movement 1870-1920* (London, 1965), pp. 176-246; B. Simon, *The Politics of Educational Reform 1920-1940* (London, 1974), esp. pp. 65-77, 217-24, 296-322.

8   For analyses of the development of a missionary ideology within the teaching profession, see G. Grace, *Teachers, Ideology and Control* (London, 1978), pp. 9-50; Mathiesen, *The Preachers of Culture*.

9   For a valuable study, which argues that despite the steady decline in popular support for the Churches in the twentieth century, the influence of religion in schools was in fact maintained and in some ways increased up to the 1940s, see C. Cannon, 'The Influence of Religion on Educational Policy 1902-1944', in *BJES*, vol. 12, no. 2 (1964), pp. 143-60.

10   For evidence of this bureaucratization of religion into a depersonalized routine, see E. Holmes, *What Is and What Might Be: A Study of Education in General and Elementary Education in Particular* (London, 1917 edn.), pp. 87-101.

11   Interview no. B.015, p. 2. Born, 1901, Easton, Bristol. Labourer, store keeper, collier. Father, seaman.

12   For details, see note 1.

13   Interview no. B.065, p. 13. Born 1922, St George, Bristol. Blacksmith striker, ladder maker, toy maker, builder and saw-mill worker. Father, docker and merchant seaman.

14   Interview no. E.151, pp. 11, 12. Born 1889, Bolton. Labourer, cardboard factory worker and shop assistant. Father, railway plate-layer.

15   Interview no. B.047, pp. 6, 15. Born 1906, Barton Hill, Bristol. Errand boy, bus conductor, warehouseman and truck driver. Father, candle maker.

16   Interview no. B.061, pp. 32, 33. Born 1910, Bedminster, Bristol. Machinist in tobacco factory. Father, general labourer.

17   Interview no. B.001, pp. 2, 8, 9, 22-7. Born 1896, St Phillip's Bristol. Domestic servant, then brewery worker. Father, labourer.

18   See, for example, K. S. Inglis, *Churches And the Working Classes in Victorian England* (London, 1963), esp. pp. 1-20, 48-57, 322-36.

19   Interview no. E.22, p. 24. Born 1904, Great Bentley, Essex. Farmworker, bricklayer, shepherd, roadman, then thatcher. Father, shepherd.

20   There was a tendency among large sections of the Church during the Victorian and Edwardian periods to view military discipline as a form of moral strength, to idealize death in war as a supreme sacrifice for God and the state and to encourage recruitment into the armed forces. For a discussion, see A. Summers, 'Militarism in Britain before the Great War', in *HWJ*, no. 2 (1976), pp. 104-23; O. Anderson, 'The Growth of Christian Militarism in Mid-Victorian Britain', in *English Historical Review* vol. 86, no. 1 (1971), pp. 46-72.

21   Interview no. B.039, p. 5. Born, 1896, Bristol. Clerk, then packing-case maker. Father, boot and shoe maker.

22   See, for example, H. McLeod, *Class and Religion in the Late Victorian City* (London, 1974), pp. 72-80, 96-100; W. M. Walker, 'Irish Immigrants in Scotland: The Priests, Politics and Parochial Life', in *Historical Journal* vol. 15, no. 4 (1972), pp. 649-67.

23   Interview no. B.063, pp. 7, 27, 28. Born 1905, St Paul's, Bristol. Clerk. Father, cabinet maker.

24   For a valuable discussion, see S. Yeo, *Religion and Voluntary Organisations in Crisis* (London, 1976), esp. pp. 117-84, 291-331.

25   For an extensive bibliography and discussion, see S. Yeo, 'On the Uses of Apathy', in *Archives européennes de sociologie* vol. 15, no. 2 (1974), pp. 279-311.

26   ibid.

27   The clearest evidence of this dissassociation is provided by patterns of Sunday school attendance. By 1900 the Churches had achieved a level of five million regular Sunday school scholars, but only a small proportion of these progressed to become adult members of Churches, and the vast majority left as soon as they achieved wage-earning status and were no longer compelled to attend by parents. See R. Currie, A. Gilbert and L. Horsley, *Church and Churchgoers: Patterns of Church Growth in the British Isles since 1700* (Oxford, 1977), pp. 86-9, 114, 115, 167-92.

28   See Simon, *Education and the Labour Movement*, pp. 165-75; B. Gilbert, *The Evolution of National Insurance in Great Britain: The Origins of the Welfare State* (London, 1966), pp. 102-58.

29   See V. Chancellor, *History for their Masters: Opinion in the English History Textbook 1800-1914* (Bath, 1970), esp. pp. 137, 139-42; J. Springhall, 'Lord Meath, Youth and Empire', in *JCH*, vol. 5, no. 14 (1970), pp. 97-111.

30   See, C. Dyhouse, 'Social Darwinistic Ideas and the Development of Women's Education in England, 1880-1920', in *HE*, vol. 1, no. 1 (1976), pp. 41-58; A. Davin, 'Imperialism and Motherhood', in *HWJ*, no. 5 (1978), pp. 9-65.

31   For a general discussion of the public school origins of this ethos, see N. Vance,

'The Ideal of Manliness', and G. Best, 'Militarism and the Victorian Public School', both in B. Simon and I. Bradley (eds.), *The Victorian Public School* (London, 1975), pp. 115-28, 129-46.

32 See P. McIntosh, *Physical Education in England Since 1800* (London, 1952), pp. 133-94.

33 Interview no. B.021, p. 12. Born 1904, Hotwells, Bristol. Domestic service, cook. Father, docker.

34 Interview no. B.007, p. 7. Born 1898, Bedminster, Bristol. Paper boy on trains, packer and case maker in saw mill. Father, soldier and worker in iron foundry.

35 For work on imperialism in juvenile literature and its impact on working-class youth, see P. Dunae, 'British Juvenile Literature in the Age of Empire 1880-1914', unpublished Ph.D. thesis (Manchester, 1975); L. James, 'Tom Brown's Imperialist Sons', in *VS*, vol. 18, no. 1 (1973), pp. 89-99.

36 Interview no. B.005, pp. 7, 8. Born 1902, St Phillip's, Bristol. Labourer. Father, engineer.

37 Mass volunteering during World War I must partially be explained in terms of the presence of militaristic and patriotic feelings among working-class youth. See, for example, Summers, 'Militarism in Britain before the Great War'.

38 Interview no. B.061, p. 11 (for details, see note 16).

39 Interview no. B.014, pp. 2, 6, 7. Born 1895, Bristol. Tram and bus conductor. Father, labourer.

40 See Springhall, 'Lord Meath', pp. 109, 110, and 'Boy Scouts, Class and Militarism', in *International Review of Social History*, vol. 16, no. 1 (1971), pp. 140-55.

41 Born, Bristol, 1905. Errand boy, engineer, draughtsman. Father, engineer.

42 See B. Simon, 'Classification and Streaming: A Study of Grouping in English Schools 1860-1960', in B. Simon, *Intelligence, Psychology and Education, A Marxist Critique* (London, 1971), pp. 200-36.

43 For details, see note 21.

44 Interview no. B.144. Born 1906, Perranwell, near Truro, Cornwall. Dock labourer, then lorry driver. Father, quarry worker.

45 See, for example, 'Suggestions for the Consideration of Teachers and Others Concerned in the work of Public Elementary Schools' (London, 1905), in *The Companion to the Red Code* (London, 1908), pp. 6, 7, 138, 140.

46 For a valuable introduction to the work of Marxist theorists and historians who argue that the state schooling system has served to reproduce class structures and relationships in a capitalist society, see R. Dale and G. Esland, Schooling and Capitalism, Open University Schooling and Society Series, Course E202, Block 1 (Milton Keynes, 1977).

47 Elementary schoolteachers were often recruited from the 'respectable' working class. Their rigid imposition of school rules can be explained to some extent in terms of their contempt for the appearance and attitudes of 'rough' working-class pupils and parents whose lifestyle represented everything that ambitious teachers sought to escape from and eliminate. For a general discussion of the status anxieties of the emerging schoolteaching profession, see A. Tropp, *The Schoolteachers: The Growth of the Teaching Profession in England and Wales from 1800 to the present day* (Westport, Connecticut, 1977), pp. 26-43, 147-50.

48 See P. Gordon and D. Lawton, *Curriculum Change in the Nineteenth and Twentieth Centuries* (London, 1978).

49 For discussion, see G. Chanan, 'Culture and Equality in Education', in *Educational Research*, vol. 18, no. 12 (1976), pp. 108-16; Katz, 'From Bryce to Newsom', pp. 287-302.

50 Interview no. B.011, pp. 7, 9. Born 1897, Hotwells, Bristol. Factory operative. Father, docker.

51 See, for example, J. Hurt, *Elementary Schooling and the Working Class 1860-1914* (London, 1979), pp. 102, 133; P. Horn, *Education in Rural England 1800-1914* (London, 1978), pp. 120, 121, 141.

52 Interview no. B.132. Born 1911, Exeter. Laundress. Father, labourer.
53 Attendance regulations are discussed in detail in chapter 3.
54 For an account of the domestic chores and part-time jobs undertaken by working-class schoolchildren, see E. Roberts, 'Learning and Living: Socialization outside School', *OHJ*, vol. 3, no. 2 (1975), pp. 14-28.
55 Interview no. B.019, p. 10. Born 1886, Kingsdown, Bristol. Domestic servant. Father, carpenter and joiner.
56 W. Healy and M. Healy, *Pathological Lying, Accusation and Swindling*, Criminal Science Monograph no. 1 (1915), contains a summary of research into the pathological origins of children's lies.
57 Interview no. B.051, p. 19. Born 1913, Ynysabwl, Wales; moved to Bristol, 1914. Errand boy, junior warehouseman and fishmonger. Father, professional soldier and bank messenger.
58 See, for example, Dyhouse, 'Social Darwinistic Ideas and the Development of Women's Education'.
59 Interview no. B.015, p. 4 (for details, see note 11).
60 For a general discussion, see R. Williams, *The Long Revolution* (London, 1971), pp. 145-75; Simon, *The Politics of Educational Reform*, pp. 270-83.
61 For the most comprehensive bibliography of this movement, see H. Silver, 'Education and the Labour Movement: A Critical Review of the Literature', in *HE*, vol. 2, no. 2 (1973), pp. 173-202. However, oral and documentary evidence suggests that many working-class parents and pupils viewed compulsory state education as a harsh imposition, to be avoided whenever possible. For discussion, see chapter 3.
62 See, for example, G. Bernbaum, *Social Change and the Schools, 1918-1944* (London, 1967), esp. pp. 12, 13, 20, 21, 52-72.
63 See Simon, *The Politics of Educational Reform;* R. Barker, *Education and Politics 1900-1951, a Study of the Labour Party* (Oxford, 1972).
64 *Report of the Departmental Committee on the Teaching of English in Schools* (Newbolt Report) (London, 1921), pp. 59, 64, 65, 66.
65 Interview no. B.038. Born, 1909, Hanhan, south Gloucestershire. Coal screener. Father, quarryman and miner.
66 For details, see note 1.
67 Interview no. B.016, p. 9. Born 1906, Ashton, Bristol. Blacksmith. Father, engineer.
68 Interview no. B.015, p. 11 (for details see note 11).
69 Interview no. B.133. Born 1912, Exeter. Domestic servant. Father, Post Office engineer.
70 Born 1921, Burslem, Stoke on Trent. Clerk, later insurance broker. Father, miner.
71 For details, see, for example, R. Bray, *Boy Labour and Apprenticeship* (London, 1911), pp. 151-5; Simon, *Education and the Labour Movement*, pp. 133-41, 278-91.
72 See K. Lindsay, *Social Progress and Educational Waste* (London, 1926), pp. 145-61.
73 Interview no. B.058, pp. 3, 6. Born 1911, Cardiff; moved to Bristol as a child. Builder, hairdresser, plumber, worker for motor accessory firm, soldier. Father, jobbing builder.
74 See A. Little and J. Westergaard, 'Trends of Class Differentials in Educational Opportunity in England and Wales', in *British Journal of Sociology*, vol. 15, no. 4 (1964), pp. 301-15.
75 For a useful summary of the findings of a number of investigations, see Bernbaum, *Social Change and the Schools*, esp. pp. 92-7.
76 See Lindsay, *Social Progress and Educational Waste*, esp. pp. 1-48.
77 The withdrawal of scholarship children from grammar schools after they had just begun or when they were half-way through their courses was a recurrent problem, and many did not remain long enough to take their School Certificate

examination. See O. Banks, *Parity and Prestige in English Secondary Education* (London, 1955), pp. 61-71.

78 For details, see note 68.

79 Interview no. B.043, pp. 2, 3, 12, 24, 34, 35. Born 1914, Preston, near Yeovil, Somerset. Fitter. Father, engineer and musician.

80 For details, see note 69.

CHAPTER 3: *Challenges to Classroom Coercion*

1   Interview no. B.014. Husband born 1895, Bristol. Tram and bus conductor. Father, labourer. Wife born 1898, Bristol. Machinist, tailoring trade. Father, general labourer.

2   For a more detailed definition and discussion of the 'hidden curriculum', see I. Illich, *Deschooling Society* (London, 1973).

3   This is a rough estimate based principally on the calculations of two historians, D. Withrington, 'Attitudes to Truancy: Anxieties over Withdrawal from School, Historical Comment', in *Research Intelligence*, vol. 1, no. 2 (1975), p. 20 and A. Ellis, 'Influences on School Attendance in Victorian England', *British Journal of Educational Studies*, vol. 21, no. 3 (1973), p. 315.

4   Interview no. B.051, p. 27. Born 1913, Ynysbwl, Wales; moved to Bristol in 1914. Errand boy, fishmonger. Father, professional soldier and bank messenger.

5   For a general discussion, see 'The Working Class and Leisure: Class Expression and/or Social Control: Conference Report', in *Society for the Study of Labour History Bulletin*, no. 32 (1976), pp. 5-18.

6   See, for example, T. W. Kline, 'Truancy as Related to the Migratory Instinct', in *Pedagogic Seminary*, vol. 5, no. 3 (1898), pp. 381-420; W. Healy, *The Individual Delinquent* (London, 1915).

7   See, for example, H. Marten, 'Inhumanity in Schools', in *Humane Review*, vol. 1, no. 1 (1900), pp. 22, 23; C. Burt, *The Young Delinquent* (London, 1938 edn.), pp. 457-9, 498-501; A. Ellis, 'Influences on School Attendance in Victorian England', in *BJES*, vol. 21, no. 3 (1973), pp. 313-26.

8   Interview no. B.002, pp. 2, 7, 10, 11. Born 1899, St Phillip's, Bristol. Factory operative, domestic. Father, naval engineer, then miner.

9   For an account of the gradual improvement in the standards of nutrition among schoolchildren and the development of a school health service during the period under study, see S. Leff and V. Leff, *The School Health Service* (London, 1959), esp. pp. 11-90.

10 The most detailed analysis of poverty as the major determinant of non-attendance is D. Rubinstein's *School Attendance in London 1870-1904, A Social History* (Hull, 1969), esp. pp. 56-109.

11 Interview no. B.005, pp. 11, 12. Born 1902, St Phillip's, Bristol. Labourer. Father, engineer.

12 See D. Ellis, 'Influences on School Attendance in Victorian England'; Withrington, 'Attitudes to Truancy'; D. Rubinstein, 'Socialization and the London School Board 1870-1904: Aims, Methods and Public Opinion', in P. McCann (ed.), *Popular Education and Socialization in the Nineteenth Century* (London, 1977), pp. 231-58; J. Hurt, *Elementary Schooling and the Working Class 1860-1914* (London, 1979), pp. 188-213.

13 Hurt, *Elementary Schooling and the Working Class*, pp. 188-213; P. Horn, *Education in Rural England* (London, 1978), pp. 138-140, 266, 267.

14 See, for example, the socialist and trade union movement's campaign for state intervention to abolish the half-time system, whereby until 1918 older children were able to work in local industries on a half-time basis before attaining the school-leaving age. This campaign is documented in E. Frow and R. Frow, *A*

Survey of the Half-Time System in Education (Manchester, 1970).

15   See E. P. Thompson, 'Time, Work Discipline and Industrial Capitalism', in *PP*, no. 38 (1967), pp. 56-97. The poverty and harsh working conditions produced by industrialization reinforced the kinship bonds of working-class families, for solidarity was essential to survival, and children in many industries worked alongside, and under the guidance of, parents and relatives. See M. Anderson, *Family Structure in Nineteenth Century Lancashire* (Cambridge, 1972); J. Gillis, *Youth and History* (London, 1974), esp. pp. 56-61.

16   During the period 1888 to 1916, truancy was the second most common offence, and in peak years there were as many as 100,000 prosecutions of working-class parents. See Hurt, *Elementary Schooling and the Working Class*, p. 203. One of the richest sources of evidence for the essentially coercive and punitive role played by the state in enforcing attendance regulations is Ernest Pomeroy's collection of press reports relating to the prosecution of working-class parents during the years 1908 and 1909; see *The Education Tyranny* (London, 1910).

17   For a valuable overview, see J. Clarke, *The Three R's: Repression, Rescue and Rehabilitation. Ideologies of Control for Working Class Youth*, CCCS stencilled paper (Birmingham, 1975).

18   Born 1898, St Jude's, Bristol. Wheelwright. Father, publican.

19   Punishment books and official reports both suggest a gradual decline in corporal punishment; see P. W. Musgrave, 'Corporal Punishment in Some English Elementary Schools, 1900-1939', in *Research in Education* no. 17 (1977), pp. 1-11.

20   For evidence of the sadistic practices of teachers, see P. Thompson, *The Edwardians* (London, 1975), p. 67.

21   The clearest evidence of the survival strategies used is contained in the autobiographies of former elementary schoolteachers. See, for example, K. Runciman, *Schools and Scholars* (London, 1887); G. Christian, *English Education from Within* (London, 1922); P. Ballard, *Things I Cannot Forget* (London, 1937); F. Spencer, *An Inspector's Statement* (London, 1938). Physical strength and brute force were important assets in the battle for control, and women teachers seem to have been most vulnerable to the violent opposition and disruptive activities of pupils. For a vivid description of this, see Flora Thompson, *Lark Rise to Candleford* (Oxford, 1963), pp. 198-200; see also G. Grace, *Teachers, Ideology and Control. A Study in Urban Education* (London, 1978), pp. 31-50; S. Humphries, 'Hurrah for England: Schooling and the Working Class in Bristol 1870-1914', in *Southern History*, vol. 1 (1979), pp. 171-208. For a discussion of teachers as exponents of 'recipe knowledge', see G. Esland, Pedagogy and the Teacher's Presentation of Self, Open University Course E282, Units 5-8, *The Social Organisation of Teaching and Learning* (Milton Keynes, 1975), pp. 30-2.

22   See the analysis of teaching manuals in R. J. W. Selleck, *The New Education: The English Background 1870-1914* (London, 1968), pp. 61-3; J. Hurt, 'Drill, Discipline and the Elementary School Ethos', in McCann, *Popular Education and Socialization in the Nineteenth Century*, esp. pp. 180-3.

23   See R. J. W. Selleck, *English Primary Education and the Progressives 1914-1939* (London, 1972), pp. 120-8.

24   Despite a gradual reduction in the size of classes from the 1890s onwards, in 1927 the Board of Education reported that there were still over 20,000 classes containing upwards of fifty pupils. See G. Bernbaum, *Social Change and the Schools 1918-1944* (London, 1967), p. 49.

25   For an account of the conflict in London between the teachers' union, which defended the right of assistants to inflict canings, and angry parents, Radical Working Men's Associations and the ILP-influenced Society for the Reform of School Discipline, which demanded tight controls on the use of corporal punishment, see M. Highfield and A. Pinsent, *A Survey of Rewards and Punishments in School* (London, 1951), pp. 41-57; B. Simon, *Education and the Labour Movement* (London, 1965), pp. 146, 147. For evidence of teachers'

refusals to abide by prohibitive regulations on caning in Bristol, see Humphries, 'Hurrah for England', pp. 191-6; and for evidence of the protests of assistant teachers in other cities (for example, Birmingham, Leamington and Manchester), see *School Board Chronicle*, 6 May 1893, p. 518; 20 May 1893, pp. 561, 690.

26   As late as 1949 a survey of 136 local education authorities showed that thirty-seven still failed to have any rules concerning the infliction of corporal punishment. Many issued regulations during the inter-war period, often as a result of parental protests over unjust canings. The regulations that were issued usually held the headteachers responsible for all corporal punishment in the school, allowed them to devolve the right to punish to certificated teachers, recommended that women teachers should administer punishments to girls and required school managers to inspect punishment books regularly. See Musgrave, 'Corporal Punishment in Some English Elementary Schools', p. 3. Regulations that restricted or denied the right of assistants to inflict summary corporal punishment on disobedient children were fiercely opposed by teachers' unions; see, for example, *Education*, 4 October 1929, p. 306, and 18 February 1938, pp. 201, 202. The teachers' press was unsympathetic to attempts to raise the issue of corporal punishment in schools as a subject for debate and legislation in Parliament; see, for example, *Education*, 28 March 1930, pp. 360, 361, 424. Indeed, the teaching profession was so successful in arousing public support for the idea that corporal punishment was necessary for the maintenance of discipline and had no adverse effects on the young victims that even the Cadogan Report of 1938, which made the radical recommendation that birching should be abolished as a form of punishment for criminals, endorsed uncritically the practice of caning in schools. See *Report of the Departmental Committee on Corporal Punishment* (Cadogan Report), Cmnd 5684 (London, 1938).

27   *Hansard*, LXXXVII c. 1375, 11 May 1900; *ibid.*, XCIV c. 593, 20 May 1901, quoted in Hurt, *Elementary Schooling and the Working Class*, p. 226.

28   Interview no. B.002, p. 3 (for details see note 8).

29   Interview no. B.080. Born 1905, Bath. Paper boy, then gardener. Father, gardener.

30   Recollections of the infliction of these punishments recur with some consistency in both the Bristol and the Essex collections of interviews. See P. Thompson, 'The War with Adults', in T. Vigne (ed.), *Oral History*, vol. 3, no. 2 (1975), pp. 32, 33. Reports of irregular punishments, which occasionally resulted in permanent physical damage such as deafness, were not uncommon in the contemporary press. See for example, R. Henderson, 'Irregular Punishments in Elementary Schools', *Humane Review*, vol. 10, no. 3 (1909), pp. 175-80.

31   For details and discussion, see I. Gibson, *The English Vice: Beating Sex and Shame in Victorian England and After* (London, 1978), esp. pp. 233-319; D. P. Leinster-Mackay, 'Regina v. *Hopley*: Some Historical Reflections on Corporal Punishment', in *Journal of Educational Administration and History*, vol. 9, no. 1 (1977), pp. 1-5.

32   Interview no. E.155, pp. 61, 62. Born, 1900, South Shields. Various kinds of work in coal mines, then bus driver. Father, foreman boilermaker.

33   Born 1919, Bedminster, Bristol. Factory operative. Father, labourer.

34   This was by no means uncommon, for, as Burt put it, 'the boy from the poor home seldom takes his caning in the same sportsmanlike spirit as the boy from the public school. He is more likely to nurse a secret feeling of resentment, resolving to demonstrate his high indifference, when the first chance offers for a backhanded reprisal' (*The Young Delinquent*, p. 123).

35   Born 1900, St Jude's, Bristol. Boot and shoe factory operative, lorry driver. Father, boot and shoe factory operative.

36   The fiercest resistance was often accompanied by biting, kicking and punching. See A. Lowndes, *The Silent Social Revolution* (London, 1969 edition), pp. 11-14; Horn, *Education in Rural England*, pp. 144, 145.

37 Born 1900, Hanham, south Gloucestershire. Carpenter. Father, carpenter.
38 There is a massive accumulation of sociological and historical research that stresses the conformity and deference of women as compared with men. This orthodoxy has recently been challenged by feminist writers, who argue convincingly that the resistance of women to all forms of oppression has been grossly underestimated and undervalued. See, for example, S. Rowbotham, *Hidden From History* (London, 1974); R. Cloward and F. Piven, 'Hidden Protest: The Channelling of Female Innovation and Resistance', in *Signs, Journal of Women in Society*, vol. 4., no. 4 (1979), pp. 651-69.
39 See Humphries, 'Hurrah for England', pp. 193-5.
40 The most comprehensive study of school punishment books to date revealed that only 9.1 per cent of all recorded disobedience relates to girls; see Musgrave, 'Corporal Punishment in some English Elementary Schools', p. 9.
41 Interview no. B.003, p. 3. Born 1885, Bedminster, Bristol. Apprentice in printing trade, shop assistant, operative in paint and brush factory, labourer. Father, labourer.
42 Born 1899, Warmley, south Gloucestershire. Operative in slipper factory. Father, boilermaker.
43 Girls tended to view corporal punishment as much more abhorrent and degrading than boys. See, for example, K. D. Hopkins, 'Punishment in Schools', in *British Journal of Educational Psychology*, vol. 9, no. 1 (1939), pp. 18-27.
44 Interview no. B.002, p. 4 (for details, see note 8).
45 Working-class parents who refused to use corporal punishment themselves and who disagreed on principle with the caning of their children were often ridiculed by magistrates, education committees and teachers, who viewed this gentle approach as evidence of a failure of parental duty. It was often commented that it was folly for a working-class parent to object to punishments that were taken in good spirit by public school boys and their parents. See H. Salt, 'The Ethics of Corporal Punishment', in *Humane Review* vol. 7, no. 1 (1906), pp. 18, 19. Indeed, the objections of poor parents and their children to corporal punishment were rather amusing to the educational press and its readers; see, for example, *School Board Chronicle*, 19 August 1893, p. 169.
46 Interview no. B.001, p. 5. Born 1896, St Phillip's, Bristol. Domestic servant, then brewery worker. Father, labourer.
47 See Humphries, 'Hurrah for England', pp. 195, 196.
48 Interview no. E.389, p. 75. Born 1891, Portobello Road, London. Sorter clerk. Father, jobbing gardener.
49 Interview no. B.004, p. 5. Born 1897, Bedminster, Bristol. Various factory occupations. Father, shop assistant.
50 Interview no. B.029. Born 1901, Lawrence Hill, Bristol. Operative in box factory. Father, warehouseman.
51 Interview no. B.038. Born 1909, Hanham, south Gloucestershire. Coal screener. Father, quarryman and miner.
52 It is difficult to estimate the precise extent of this type of vandalism, but contemporary accounts suggest that it was common in the first decades of board schools. As one writer, describing certain parts of London, put it, 'building a Board School was like planting a fortress in an enemy's country. The building was the symbol of tyranny and oppression, and often the school keeper had difficulty in protecting it from malicious damage.' H. Philpott, *London at School: The Story of the London School Board 1870-1904* (London, 1904), p. 40. And during the inter-war period educational journals occasionally noted widespread vandalism in schools in some areas — see, for example, the report of vandalism in Rhondda schools in *The Schoolmaster*, 10 December 1926, p. 886.
53 See for example, P. Thompson, *The Edwardians* (London, 1975), pp. 66-8, and 'The War with Adults', esp. pp. 32, 33.
54 Interview no. B.005, pp. 2, 3 (for details see note 11).

55 In a series of cases since the mid-nineteenth century magistrates have rigorously
    defended the school's right to inflict almost any amount of corporal punish-
    ment, providing that it does not result in permanent physical injury, on the
    grounds that parents delegate full disciplinary powers to teachers by choosing to
    send their child to school — despite the.fact that they are compelled to do so by
    law. See P. Newell (ed.), *A Last Resort? Corporal Punishment in Schools* (London,
    1972), pp. 43-60; G. Barrell, *Teachers and the Law* (London, 1966), pp. 180-9.
    Even when parents summonsed teachers for assault on delicate infants their
    protests received little or no sympathy, as is illustrated by the following
    characteristic comment of a London magistrate passing judgement on the case of
    a six-year-old who had been caned by his teacher for dishonesty: 'I consider the
    telling of lies to be a grave moral offence and nothing could be better for the boy.
    The schoolmistress has done her best in doing what the mother ought to do. The
    summons is therefore dismissed.' *School Board Chronicle*, 18 May 1895, p. 549.
    In parts of London parental interference in the classroom and assaults on
    unpopular teachers were so common that the school board was forced to offer
    bonus payments to attract teachers to accept posts in such areas. See Highfield
    and Pinsent, *A Survey of Rewards and Punishments*, pp. 47, 48. For cases of
    assault on schoolteachers in other areas see Horn, *Education in Rural England*,
    pp. 143, 144; Hurt, *Elementary Schooling and the Working Class*, pp. 163, 164;
    Humphries, 'Hurrah for England', pp. 195, 196.
56 Interview no. B.144. Born 1906, Perranwell, near Truro, Cornwall, Dock labourer,
    then lorry driver. Father, quarry worker.
57 Interview no. B.023, p. 5. Born 1912, Ashton Gate, Bristol. Errand boy, butcher's
    assistant, then joined the army. Father, docker.
58 Born 1904, Fishponds, Bristol. Bus conductress. Father, bricklayer.
59 For a detailed examination of the rift that developed between the working-
    class community and provided state schools in Bristol, see Humphries, 'Hurrah
    for England', pp. 171-208. In some instances, teachers who brutally punished
    children had to be provided with police protection from angry mothers and
    fathers; see Hurt, *Elementary Schooling and the Working Class*, pp. 163, 164.
60 Mrs Melhuish, quoted in Federation of Worker Writers and Community Publishers
    (eds), *Writing* (London, 1978), p. 27.
61 See *Newcastle Commission* (P.P. 1861), 2794-i, XX (Part 1), pp. 78-83.
62 See *The Times*, 30 January 1875, p. 7; Humphries, 'Hurrah for England',
    p. 196.
63 For this analysis I am indebted to Phillip Gardner's research into working-class
    private schools, which he is undertaking for a doctoral thesis at the University of
    Sussex.

CHAPTER 4: *School Strikes: Pupils and Parents Protest*

1 Letter to author. Born 1910, Manchester. Master barber and antique dealer.
   Father, hand cloth dyer and antique dealer.
2 D. Marson, *Children's Strikes in 1911* (Oxford, 1973).
3 P. Horn, 'The Herefordshire School Strike of 1914', in History of Education
   Society, *Studies in the Local History of Education* (Leicester, 1977), pp. 46-52.
4 B. Edwards, *The Burston School Strike* (London, 1974).
5 This information was obtained from my own interviews and correspondence
   with many old people throughout Britain who remembered school strikes.
6 Interview no. E.134, p. 61. Quoted in P. Thompson, 'The War with Adults', in
   T. Vigne (ed.), *Oral History*, vol. 3, no. 2 (1975), p. 33.

7   Interview no. M.272. Born 1912, Broughton, Manchester. Decorator. Father, decorator and glazier.
8   See *Scotsman*, 9 October 1889, p. 7.
9   *Llanelly Mercury*, 7 September 1911.
10 The information for the diffusion of school strikes in 1889 is based upon my own research into local press reports in all the major towns and cities throughout Britain. Information concerning the extent of the 1911 strikes is based primarily upon Marson's *Children's Strikes in 1911* but is supplemented with references to other strikes that I have myself discovered in newspapers and school logbooks.
11 *Educational News*, September 1911, p. 968.
12 It is significant that the nationwide waves of school strikes in October 1889 and September 1911 occurred in months and years in which industrial conflict was particularly intense, and my research has revealed a close correspondence between the strike action of parents and of pupils in particular localities.
13 Born, Eastville, Bristol, 1900. Lamplighter. Father, canal boatman.
14 *Educational News*, 5 October 1889, pp. 685, 686; 12 October p. 702; 19 October pp. 719, 720.
15 Letter to author. Born 1899, Hull. Signalman, North-Eastern Railway. Father, permanent way sawyer, North-Eastern Railway.
16 See, for example, Marson, *Children's Strikes in 1911*, pp. 3-29.
17 *School Board Chronicle*, 19 October 1889, p. 361.
18 ibid.
19 Letter to author. Born Hull, 1900. Confectionery van salesman. Father, inspector for shipping firm, then egg and butter merchant.
20 *Pall Mall Gazette*, 10 October 1889, p. 7.
21 *Dundee Advertiser*, 11 October 1889, p. 5.
22 Quoted in *School Board Chronicle*, 19 October 1889, p. 361.
23 ibid., p. 349.
24 See, for example, *Truth*, 10 October 1889, pp. 640, 641, and 17 October 1889, p. 684; *Scotsman*, 9 October 1889, p. 7; *Dundee Courier and Argus*, 2 October 1889; *Liverpool Daily Post and Mercury*, 14 September 1911; *Birmingham Daily Mail*, 14 September 1911; *The Times*, 13 September 1911, p. 4, and 14 September 1911, p. 6.
25 See Marson, *Children's Strikes in 1911*, pp. 17-19; interviews reveal that attendance officers visited neighbourhoods on strike, warning mothers of the legal consequences should their children fail to return to school immediately.
26 For details see note 19.
27 Interview no. E.453, pp. 84, 85. Born 1899, Cardiff. Merchant seaman, labourer, later foreman. Father, merchant seaman.
28 See D. Marson, *Children's Strikes in 1911*, pp. 1-23, and other press reports of the 1889 strikes cited in the footnotes.
29 Letter to author. Born 1898, Oswaldtwistle, Lancashire, Army. Father, dairy farmer.
30 See, for example, *Educational News*, 5 October 1889, p. 687; 12 October 1889, p. 702; 26 October 1889, pp. 738, 739; *Scotsman*, 9 October 1889, p. 7; *Truth*, 10 October 1889, p. 640, 641, and 17 October 1889, p. 684.
31 For a general historical analysis of attempts to eliminate rowdy and disruptive working-class leisure traditions and to replace them with rational and respectable recreation, see P. Bailey, *Leisure and Class in Victorian England: Rational Recreation and the Contest for Control 1830-1885* (London, 1978).
32 *Education*, 27 September 1912, p. 189; see also *Bradford Daily Telegraph*, 9 September 1912, 23 September 1912, 24 September 1912, 29 September 1913. For examples of the arguments used to suppress Feast Tide holidays for the children in Idle, see *Bradford Elementary Education Sub Committee Meeting Minutes* (Bradford Records Office), 11 February 1904, pp. 234, 235; 14 February 1911, p. 187; 11 February 1913, p. 165.

33   See *Bedworth Observer*, 8 April 1914, p. 5, and 15 April 1914, p. 5; *Education* 6 March 1914, p. 141, and 24 April 1914, p. 265.

34   See, *Northampton Daily Chronicle*, 27 October 1920; *Northampton Daily Echo*, 27 October 1920; *Northampton Herald*, 29 October 1920, p. 8; *Northampton Independent* 30 October 1920, p. 9.

35   See, for example, *Northern Daily Mail*, 9 and 15 September 1911; *Birmingham Daily Mail*, 13 September 1911.

36   Born 1900, St Jude's, Bristol. Operative in boot and shoe factory, army service, then lorry driver. Father, operative in boot and shoe factory.

37   See, B. Simon, *Education and the Labour Movement* (London, 1965), pp. 133-7, 278-286.

38   *Sunderland Daily Echo*, 19 November 1917, p. 4, and 21 November 1917, p. 5.

39   ibid., 21 November 1917, p. 5.

40   Durham County Chronicle, 23 November 1917, pp. 2, 3.

41   This account is based on Horn, 'The Herefordshire School Strike of 1914'.

42   For the background to the dismissal of married teachers in Keighley, Yorkshire, see *Keighley News*, 28 February 1922, p. 8; 8 April 1922, p. 9; 3 June 1922, p. 7; 15 July 1922, p. 13.

43   I am indebted to Ian Dewhirst, Reference Librarian, Keighley Library, for this information, which was obtained from the Eastwood school log book and from the recollections of his mother, a former pupil at the school.

44   See *Keighley News*, 15 and 29 July 1922; 2 September 1922.

45   Interview by Ian Dewhirst. Born Keighley, Yorkshire, 1912. Shorthand typist, then housewife. Father, book-keeper at joinery works.

46   See *Keighley News*, 2 September 1922, p. 7; 9 September 1922, p. 7.

47   See *South Wales Argus*, 6 March 1924. For a similar strike in Haslington, near Crewe, see *Education*, 22 August 1913, p. 113.

48   Born 1904, Fishponds, Bristol. Bus conductress. Father, bricklayer.

49   Interview no. B.159. Born 1904, Bideford, North Devon. Shop assistant, bus conductor. Father, tailor.

50   Board of Education, *The Education of the Adolescent, Report of the Consultative Committee* (Hadow Report) (London, 1927)

51   See *Education*, 16 December 1938, p. 655.

52   Quoted in *Education*, 2 December 1938, p. 591.

53   The Rathven school strike aroused immense local controversy, and the grievances of the parents, together with their resistance to coercion by the education authorities, are both given extensive coverage in the columns of the *Banffshire Advertiser;* see, in 1913, 28 September, 4 October, 11 October, 18 October, 9 November, 6 December, 13 December, 20 December, 27 December; in 1914, 4 January, 8 January, 15 January, 22 January, 29 January, 5 February, 19 February, 26 February, 5 March, 12 March.

54   One of the most elaborately organized protests by an urban working-class community was the East Ham strike of 1929. The parents' campaign was reported in detail in the local press; see, for example, *Echo, Mail and Chronicle* (East London), 12 July 1929, p. 5; 19 July, p. 5; 26 July, p. 5; 2 August, p. 6; 30 August, p. 5; 6 September, p. 2; and *East Ham Echo*, 6 September 1929, p. 1; 13 September, p. 1; 20 September, pp. 1, 5; 27 September, pp. 1, 5.

55   *Eastern Daily Press*, 18 April 1928, p. 10.

56   *The Schoolmaster and Woman Teacher's Chronicle* 19 September 1929, p. 431.

57   Information concerning these strikes was obtained from the following sources. For Rathven, see note 53. For Pont Yates, see *Glasgow Daily Herald*, 13 February 1914, p. 9. For Gilfach Goch, see *The Times*, 15 December 1919, p. 11. For Waterfoot, see *Education*, 23 April 1926, p. 452. For Eaton, see note 55. For Winsford, see *Teacher's World*, 4 September 1929, p. 1086. For Llansamlet, see *Teacher's World*, 11 September 1929, p. 1168; *South Wales Daily Post*, 2 September

1929, p. 1; 3 September, p. 3. For Newmains, see notes 63-5. For Patcham, see *Brighton Evening Argus*, 7 January 1929, p. 6; 8 January, p. 5; 9 January, p. 5; 11 January, p. 3; 15 January, p. 7. For Audley, see *Evening Sentinel* (Stoke-on-Trent), 1 September 1938, pp. 1, 5; 2 September, p. 7; 7 September, p. 5; 9 September, p. 9; 20 September, p. 5; 1 October, p. 5; 7 October, p. 9; 11 October, p. 4; 12 October, p. 5; 18 October, p. 7; 22 October, p. 5; 26 October, p. 7; 1 November, p. 7; 3 November, p. 1; 14 November, p. 7; 17 November, p. 3; 21 November, p. 5; 26 November, p. 1; 28 November, p. 1; 6 December, pp. 1, 12.

58 Information for these strikes was obtained from the following sources. For Harringay, see *The Times*, 7 April 1914, p. 10; *Hornsey Journal*, 3 April 1914, p. 4, and 10 April, p. 4. For Edinburgh, see *Glasgow Herald*, 3 September 1925, p. 3; 4 September, p. 5; 5 September, p. 5; 8 September, p. 5; 21 September, p. 9; 6 October, p. 6. For East Ham, see note 54. For Downham, see *Bromley Mercury*, 17 September 1926, p. 6; 1 October, p. 7; 29 October, p. 9; 5 November, p. 3; 12 November, p. 10; 10 December, p. 11; 17 December, p. 9; 21 January 1927, p. 4. For Watford, see *West Hertfordshire Post and Watford Newsletter*, 5 September 1929, p. 9; 12 September, p. 9; 7 October, p. 7; 14 October, p. 9; 17 October, p. 12. For Bradford, see *Bradford Telegraph and Argus*, 30 August 1929, p. 9; 31 August, p. 4. For Rowley Regis, see *Dudley Herald*, 26 October 1929, p. 11; 2 November, p. 7; 9 November, p. 15; 30 November, p. 5. For Dumfries, see *Dumfries and Galloway Standard and Advertiser*, 31 August 1929, p. 5; 4 September, p. 4; 7 September, p. 6; 11 September, p. 5, 14 September, p. 7; 21 September, p. 15; 25 September, p. 7; 2 October, p. 11; 23 October, p. 7; 2 November, p. 15; 6 November, p. 5; 27 November, pp. 7, 8; 4 December, p. 10; 18 December, pp. 8, 11; 21 December, p. 12; 29 January 1930, p. 6; 8 February, pp. 5, 9; 15 February, pp. 7, 9; 22 February, p. 12; 22 March, p. 4; 26 March, p. 10. For Leicester, see *Leicester Mercury*, 8 September 1930, p. 11; 9 September, p. 9; 10 September, p. 11; 12 September, p. 14; 13 September, p. 14; 15 September, p. 12; 16 September, p. 10; 17 September, p. 16; 23 September, p. 6; 24 September, p. 4; *Education*, 12 September 1930, p. 236. For Port Talbot, see *Port Talbot Guardian*, 7 April 1933, p. 1; 13 April, p. 1; 28 April, p. 8; 5 May, p. 5; 2 June, p. 5. For Bedford, see *Bedford Record*, 6 April 1937, p. 11; 13 April, pp. 1, 10; 20 April, p. 11; 18 May, p. 2; 25 May, p. 2; 1 June, p. 2; 8 June, p. 8. For Chatham, see *The Times*, 22 April 1938, p. 7; *Kent Messenger and Observer*, 23 April 1938, p. 1, and 30 April, p. 3; *Rochester, Chatham and Gillingham Journal*, 27 April 1938, p. 3.

59 *Everybody's Weekly*, quoted in *East Ham Echo*, 13 September 1929, p. 2.
60 See *Glasgow Herald*, 5 April 1929, p. 7.
61 *Glasgow Herald*, 26 September 1929, p. 8; 30 September, p. 12; 14 October, p. 10.
62 Mr May, quoted in *Glasgow Daily Herald*, 31 December 1929, p. 10.
63 *Glasgow Herald*, 25 September 1929, p. 15; 27 September, p. 10; 28 September, p. 10; 29 September, p. 6; 1 October, p. 2; 2 October, p. 14; *Hamilton Herald and Lanarkshire Weekly News*, 3 October 1929, p. 6; *Glasgow Herald*, 18 March 1930, p. 7.
64 *Glasgow Herald*, 16 November 1929, p. 7; 14 December, p. 12; 17 December, p. 3; 14 May 1930, p. 8; 5 July, p. 10; 31 July, p. 5.
65 *Glasgow Herald*, 27 April 1929, p. 9; 21 August, p. 9; 18 January 1930, p. 7.
66 See Edwards, *The Burston School Strike*, pp. 13-44.
67 Emily Wilby, 'Our School Strike', quoted in Edwards, *The Burston School Strike*, pp. 116-18.
68 Violet Porter, quoted in Edwards, *The Burston School Strike*, p. 179.
69 Edwards, *The Burston School Strike*, pp. 9-12, 112-69.

CHAPTER 5: *Larking About: Pranks and Parody*

1 Born 1900, Exeter Devon. Bus conductor. Father, labourer.
2 Interview no. E.166, p. 25. Born 1886, Lerwick, Shetland. Butcher's boy, then shoemaker. Father, seaman.
3 For elaboration, see D. Douglas, *Pit Life in County Durham* (Oxford, 1972); A. Green, 'Only Kidding: Joking among Coalminers', unpublished paper presented to the British Sociological Association Conference 1978; R. Martin, *The Triumph of Wit, a Study of Victorian Comic Theory* (London, 1974).
4 Interview no. B.007, p. 21. Born 1903, Montpelier, Bristol. Journeyman compositor. Father, blacksmith.
5 See 'The Working Class and Leisure: Class Expression and/or Social Control', Conference Report, in *Society for the Study of Labour History Bulletin*, no. 32 (1976), pp. 5-18; P. Thompson, *The Edwardians* (London, 1975), pp. 197-205.
6 Born 1898, St George, Bristol. Factory operative. Father, bakery boiler stoker.
7 Interview no. B.001, p. 6. Born 1896, St Phillip's Bristol. Domestic servant, then brewery worker. Father, labourer.
8 Interview no. B.148. Born 1913, Babbacombe, Torquay. Agricultural labourer, various casual jobs, then plasterer. Father, agricultural labourer.
9 Interview no. 001, pp. 1, 6 (for details, see note 7).
10 Interview no. E157, p. 18. Born 1906, Shetland. Fisherman and merchant seaman. Father, carpenter and fisherman.
11 Born 1900, Norwich. Domestic servant. Father, labourer.
12 See D. Gifford, *The Evolution of the British Comic* (London, 1974), pp. 357, 358.
13 Born 1904, Kingswood, Bristol. Bus conductress. Father, bricklayer.
14 Interview no. B.144. Born 1906, Perranwell, near Truro, Cornwall. Docker, bus and lorry driver. Father, quarry worker.
15 Interview no. B.044, pp. 6, 7. Born 1914, Preston village near Yeovil, Somerset. Apprentice fitter and turner, motor mechanic. Father, musician.
16 Born 1889, Manaccan, Cornwall. Quarry labourer. Father, gardener.
17 I. Opie and P. Opie, *The Lore and Language of Schoolchildren* (London, 1959), pp. 3-5.
18 Interview no. B.047, p. 7. Born 1906, Barton Hill, Bristol. Errand boy, bus conductor, truck driver. Father, candle maker.
19 Interview no. B.011, p. 19. Born 1897, Hotwells, Bristol. Cigarette factory operative. Father, docker.
20 Born 1905, Bristol. Errand boy, engineer, draughtsman. Father, engineer.
21 Interview no. B.148 (for details, see note 8).
22 For details, see note 6.
23 Born 1922, Fishponds, Bristol. Clerk, salesman. Father, engineer.
24 See L. Lewis Shiman, 'The Band of Hope Movement: Respectable Recreation for Working-Class Children', in *VS*, vol. 18, no. 1 (1973), esp. pp. 69-74; J. Marchant, *James Paton: Educational and Social Pioneer* (London, 1909), p. 214.
25 Over 15 million children have passed through the ranks of the Boy Scouts, Boys' Brigades and Girl Guides since their inception in the late nineteenth and early twentieth centuries. See J. Springhall, *Youth, Empire and Society* (London, 1977), p. 13.
26 See, J. Brophy and E. Partridge, *The Long Trail: What the British Soldier Sang and Said 1914-1918* (London, 1965), esp. pp. 11-18.
27 See, for example, R. Price, *An Imperial War and the British Working Class* (London, 1972), esp. pp. 1-11, 233-42; and G. Stedman Jones, *Outcast London, a Study in the relationship between classes in Victorian Society* (London, 1976), pp. 77, 78.

28 This anxiety is most clearly expressed in the literature of the social purity movement; see, for example, Marchant, *James Paton*, esp. pp. 197-267. For the best discussion and bibliography of this literature, see E. J. Bristow, *Vice and Vigilance: Purity Movements in Britain since 1700* (Dublin, 1977).

29 See Bristow, *Vice and Vigilance*, esp. pp. 94-228; D. Reeder, 'Predicaments of City Children: Late Victorian and Edwardian Perspectives on Education and Urban Society', in D. Reeder (ed.), *Urban Education in the Nineteenth Century* (London, 1977), pp. 84-7, 93, 94; and J. Gillis, *Youth and History: Tradition and Change in European Age Relations 1770-Present* (London, 1974), pp. 156-9.

30 See, for example, R. Price, 'Society, Status and Jingoism: The Social Roots of Lower Middle Class Patriotism 1870-1900', in G. Crossick (ed.), *The Lower Middle Class in Britain* (London, 1977), esp. pp. 92, 93, 95, 102.

31 Interview no. B.080. Born 1905, Bath. Paper boy, then gardener. Father, gardener.

32 H. Dendy, 'The Children of Working London', in B. Bosanquet (ed.), *Aspects of the Social Problem* (London, 1895), p. 31.

33 For details, see note 13.

34 Interview no. B.133. Born 1912, Exeter, Devon. Domestic service. Father, Post Office engineer.

35 See, for example, L. Davidoff, *The Best Circles* (London, 1973), esp. pp. 49-54; for a general discussion, P. Cominos, 'Late Victorian Sexual Respectability', in *International Review of Social History*, vol. 8 (1963), pp. 18-48, and vol. 9 (1963), pp. 216-50.

36 E. Partridge, *Dictionary of Catch Phrases* (London, 1977), p. 47.

37 C. E. B. Russell, *Manchester Lads at Work and Play* (Manchester, 1905), p. 116.

38 W. Besant, 'From Thirteen to Seventeen', in *Contemporary Review* (March 1886), pp. 417-19.

39 The evidence of school log books, punishment books and oral interviews, for example, indicates that girls who wore rings, bracelets or, occasionally, coloured ribbons in their hair were likely to find them confiscated by the school authorities, especially during the late Victorian and Edwardian periods.

40 Interview no. B.056, pp. 4, 11-13. Born 1912, Bristol. Domestic service, shop assistant then waitress. Father, army.

41 See, for example, E. Matthias, 'The Young Factory Girl', in J. J. Findlay (ed.), *The Young Wage Earner* (London, 1918), pp. 87-96; L. Montagu, 'The Girl in the Background', in E. J. Urwick (ed.), *Studies of Boy Life in Our Cities* (London, 1904), pp. 233-54.

42 For a description and discussion of the conditions experienced in domestic service, see P. Horn, *The Rise and Fall of the Victorian Servant* (Dublin, 1975). The best account of the conditions of shop girls appears in W. Whitaker, *Victorian and Edwardian Shopworkers: The Struggle to Obtain Better Conditions and a Half Day Holiday* (Newton Abbot, 1973). And for general accounts of factory and sweated labour by women, see, for example, S. Meacham, *A Life Apart: The English Working Class 1890-1914* (London, 1977), pp. 95-115; J. Burnett, *Useful Toil* (London, 1974), esp. pp. 48-54.

43 J. Shelley, 'From Home Life to Industrial Life', in Findlay, *The Young Wage Earner*, p. 254.

44 Extract from the unpublished autobiography of Iris Hutchings (née Bradford). Born 1921, Bedminster, Bristol. Tobacco factory worker and shop assistant. Father, unemployed for long periods, became postman.

45 For details, see note 13.

46 For details, see note 3. The most vivid record of working-class humour during the period under study is contained in autobiographies and fictional accounts; see, for example, P. J. Keating, *The Working Classes in Victorian Fiction* (London, 1971), esp. pp. 78, 189-91, 202-3, 211-18.

47 Interview no. E.12, p. 41. Born 1903, Halstead, Essex. Ironmoulder. Father, ironmoulder.

48 Interview no. E.14, pp. 54, 55. Born 1899, Halstead, Essex. Various kinds of work in silk mills. Father, labourer, silk mills.
49 Interview, Alf Drury, engineer and regular soldier, quoted in R. A. Leeson, *Strike: A Live History 1887-1971* (London, 1973), p. 65.
50 See Meacham, *A Life Apart*, pp. 182-4.
51 For details, see note 6.
52 Interview no. B.152. Born 1903, St Denis, near Truro, Cornwall. Dressmaker. Father, clayworker.
53 Interview no. B.002, p. 12. Born 1899, St. Phillip's, Bristol. Factory worker. Father, engineer, then miner.
54 Interview no. B.077. Born 1903, Bristol. Factory operative. Father, cook on steam ships.
55 See, for example, E. P. Thompson, 'Time, Work Discipline and Industrial Capitalism', in *PP*, no. 38 (1967), pp. 56-97.
56 For summaries of the findings of investigations into absenteeism during the period under study, see P. Stearns, *Lives of Labour: Work in a Maturing Industrial Society* (London, 1975), pp. 241, 242; P. Froggatt, 'Short-Term Absence From Industry: A Statistical and Historical Study', unpublished D. Phil. Thesis (Belfast, 1967), esp. vol. 1, pp. 132-56.
57 For details, see note 44.
58 One of the few historical studies is G. Brown, *Sabotage: A Study in Industrial Conflict* (Nottingham, 1977).
59 Bob Stewart, quoted in R. A. Leeson, *Strike: A Live History*, (London, 1973), p. 22.
60 For description and discussion of these 'blind alley' jobs, see, for example, R. Bray, *Boy Labour and Apprenticeship* (London, 1911); Spencer J. Gibb, *The Problem of Boy Work* (Oxford, 1906).
61 Born 1914, Horfield, Bristol. Various casual jobs in retail and distributive trades. Father, docker.
62 Interview no. B.029. Born 1901, Lawrence Hill, Bristol. Factory machinist. Father, warehouseman.
63 See J. Gillis, 'The Evolution of Juvenile Delinquency 1890-1914', in *PP*, no. 67 (1975), pp. 96-126; J. Gillis, *Youth and History*, pp. 175-83.
64 See Opie and Opie, *The Lore and Language of Schoolchildren*, pp. 368-71.
65 Interview no. E.321, p. 43. Born 1899, Sneiton. Shop assistant. Father, pavier.
66 Interview no. E.296, p. 53. Born 1892, Tottenham, London. Wood machinist. Father, cabinet maker.
67 Interview no. E.90, p. 6. Born 1885, Pendleton, Manchester. Engineer, steam roller driver, chimney sweep. Father, armature winder.

CHAPTER 6: *Social Crime and Family Survival*

1 C. Burt, *The Young Delinquent* (London, 1938 edn.), pp. 248-52.
2 A valuable critical analysis of this tradition is contained in I. Taylor, P. Walton and J. Young (eds.), *The New Criminology: For a Social Theory of Deviance* (London, 1973).
3 For a useful discussion of the importance of the concept of social crime see J. G. Rule, 'Social Crime in the Rural South in the Eighteenth and early Nineteenth Centuries', in *Southern History*, vol. 1 (1979), pp. 135-53.
4 Unfortunately, criminal statistics on both a local and a national level rarely subdivided the annual number of convictions for simple and minor larceny into more specific categories, indicating the exact nature of the property that young people pilfered. See, for example, the discussion in A. M. Carr-Saunders, H. Mannheim and E. C. Rhodes, *Young Offenders — An Enquiry into Juvenile Delinquency* (Cambridge, 1942), pp. 112-18. My assertion that food and fuel were

the two principal items stolen is based on an extensive examination of the literature on juvenile delinquency.

5   Burt, *The Young Delinquent*, p. 22.

6   See, for example, Burt, *The Young Delinquent*, pp. 62-127; J. H. Bagot, *Juvenile Delinquency — A Comparative Study of the Position in Liverpool and in England and Wales* (London, 1941).

7   For the best summary of social and criminological research findings on this problem of the 'peak age' of juvenile delinquency in the pre-1940 period, see Carr-Saunders, Mannheim and Rhodes, *Young Offenders — An Enquiry into Juvenile Delinquency*, pp. 50-3, 120-6, 160-6.

8   See, for example, H. Ellis, *A Study of British Genius* (London, 1904); K. Pearson, *On the Handicapping of the First Born* (London, 1914): C. Goring, *The English Convict* (London, 1913), pp. 277-300.

9   G. S. Hall, *Adolescence: Its Psychology and its Relations to Physiology, Anthropology, Sociology, Sex Crime, Religion and Education* (New York, 1904), vol. 1, p. 325.

10 H. Jones, 'Group Sentiment and Delinquency', in *Mental Health*, vol. 8, no. 2 (1948), p. 41.

11 W. Norwood East, *The Adolescent Criminal, A Medico-Sociological Study of 4000 Male Adolescents* (London, 1942).

12 Burt, *The Young Delinquent*, p. 495.

13 For a summary of the theories and evidence of these pathological interpretations of delinquency, see B. Wootton, *Social Science and Social Pathology* (London, 1958), esp. pp. 21-156.

14 Bagot, *Juvenile Delinquency*, pp. 61, 62.

15 See, for example, B. Seebohm Rowntree, *Poverty: A Study of Town Life* (London, 1901) esp. pp. 152-72.

16 Interview no. B.059, p. 11-13, 25-7, 36. Born 1921, Baptist Mills, Bristol. Butcher's boy, then seaman. Father, bricklayer.

17 Quoted in H. Mannheim, *Social Aspects of Crime Between the Wars* (London, 1940), p. 300.

18 See S. Humphries, 'Bourgeois Deprivation Theory and the Resistance of Working-Class Youth to Control', unpublished paper given at University of Sussex History Research Seminar, summer 1979.

19 A valuable summary of criminological investigations, which revealed a close interrelationship between unemployment, strikes and juvenile delinquency, is contained in Mannheim's *Social Aspects of Crime Between the Wars*, esp. pp. 123-59.

20 Mannheim, *Social Aspects of Crime Between the Wars*, p. 299.

21 Interview no. B.038. Born 1909, Hanham, south Gloucestershire. Coal screener. Father, quarryman and miner.

22 See D. Hay, P. Linebaugh, J. Rule, E. P. Thompson and C. Winslow, *Albion's Fatal Tree: Crime and Society in Eighteenth Century England* (London, 1975); E. P. Thompson, *Whigs and Hunters: The Origins of the Black Act* (London, 1975).

23 Interview no. E.307, pp. 97, 98. Born 1891, Glasgow. Furnace man. Father, furnace man.

24 Interview no. E.380, pp. 20, 21. Born 1890, Tongwynlais, South Wales. Tinworker, fitter. Father, tinworker.

25 Burt, *The Young Delinquent*, p. 160.

26 Born 1899, Almondsbury, south Gloucestershire. Domestic. Father, farm labourer.

27 Interview no. E.42, pp. 14, 37, 74. Born 1893, Northleigh, Oxfordshire. Farm worker, builder's labourer, odd-job man and roadman for Oxford Corporation. Father, odd-job man.

28 See J. Rule, 'Wrecking and Coastal Plunder', in Hay *et al., Albion's Fatal Tree*, pp. 167-88.

29 Interview no. B.147. Born 1905, Newquay, Cornwall. Errand boy, undertaker's assistant, stonemason, fisherman. Father, stonemason.
30 Interview no. E.108, pp. 18, 19. Born 1904, Liverpool. Clerk, hospital porter. Father, packer.
31 Interview no. B.016, pp. 4, 5. Born 1906, Ashton Gate, Bristol. Blacksmith. Father, engineer.
32 For a useful discussion of this literature, see D. Reeder, 'Predicaments of City Children, Late Victorian and Edwardian Perspectives on Education and Urban Society', in D. Reeder (ed.), *Urban Education in the Nineteenth Century* (London, 1977), pp. 75, 94.
33 Interview no. E.377, pp. 14, 15. Born 1897, Edinburgh. Riveter's catch boy and dock labourer. Father, labourer.
34 Interview no. B.125. Born 1914, Horfield, Bristol. Various casual jobs in retail and distributive trades. Father, docker.
35 Born 1919, Bedminster, Bristol. Factory operative. Father, labourer.
36 A useful bibliography of the vast number of reports published during the 1900s relating to street trading and the government legislation of the period that sought to regulate the activities of young street traders appears in A. Freeman, *Boy Life and Labour* (London, 1914), pp. 233-48.
37 See Mannheim, *Social Aspects of Crime Between the Wars*, pp. 235-49.
38 *Report on the Employment of Schoolchildren* (London, 1901). Minutes of evidence, no. 4786.
39 Interview no. E.302, pp. 7, 8. Born 1900, Canning Town, London. Errand boy, labouring jobs, crane driver. Father, gas works labourer.
40 See, for example, J. Ditton, 'Perks, Pilferage and the Fiddle: The Historical Structure of Invisible Wages', in *Theory and Society*, vol. 4, no. 1 (1977), pp. 39-71; R. Gilding, *The Journeyman Coopers of East London* (Oxford, 1971).
41 Interview no. E.302, pp. 10, 12 (for details, see note 39).
42 Interview no. B.148. Born 1913, Babbacombe, Torquay. Various casual jobs, then plasterer. Father, agricultural labourer.
43 Interview no. E.369, pp. 6, 7. Born 1894, Stepney, London. Shoemaker. Father, carman.
44 Born 1898, Bath. Domestic servant, then valet in chocolate factory. Father, lorry driver and musician.
45 Interview no. E.287, p. 58. Born 1891, Balla. Domestic servant, herring girl. Father, fisherman.

CHAPTER 7: *Street Gangs: Revolt, Rivalry and Racism*

1 *London Echo*, 7 February 1898.
2 See, for example, Howard Association, *Juvenile Offenders, A Report based on the enquiry instituted by the committee of the Howard Association* (London, 1898), in which the general consensus among the police, magistrates and local authorities throughout Britain was that there should be a campaign for the 'vigorous and uncompromising suppression of the cruel and violent class of young ruffians or "scuttlers" who have increased in English cities' (p. 10).
3 Frequently, these law-and-order campaigns were localized, like the crusade against muggings and hooliganism in Cardiff launched by Justice Lawrence and enthusiastically supported by the local press in 1908. For a critical account of this campaign, which resulted in an increase in the use of the birch as a punishment for offenders, see W. J. Roberts, 'The Flogging Outbreak in Cardiff', in *Humane Review*, vol. 9, no. 1 (1908-9), pp. 65-75.

4   For a general account of the influence of the Boer War on social legislation
     relating to working-class children, see B. Gilbert, *The Evolution of National
     Insurance in Great Britain* (London, 1966), esp. pp. 59-61, 102-58. For evidence of
     attempts to comprehend and control juvenile delinquency during and immediately
     after World War I, see, for example, C. Leeson, *The Child and the War* (London,
     1917), and the Board of Education Juvenile Organizations Committee, *Report on
     Juvenile Delinquency* (London, 1920).
5   For example, the number of birchings ordered by courts in England and Wales
     increased from 2415 in 1914 to 5210 in 1917. See *Report of the Departmental
     Committee on Corporal Punishment* (Cadogan Report), Cmnd 5684 (London,
     1938), p. 19. And for evidence of the widespread demand during the Boer War for
     legislation to give magistrates broad discretionary powers to order the birchings
     of young offenders, see the Howard Report and the debate on the Youthful
     Offenders Bill, popularly referred to as the 'Whipping Bill' — *Hansard's
     Parliamentary Debates*, vol. 83, 14 May 1900 to 28 May 1900, pp. 808-55.
6   For one account of the class bias in press reports of the violence of young people,
     see S. F. Hatton, *London's Bad Boys* (London, 1931), pp. 14-28.
7   Grace Paithorpe, *Studies in the Psychology of Delinquency* (London, 1933), p. 88.
8   *Sunday Chronicle*, 21 May 1916.
9   Charles Booth, *Life and Labour of the People in London*, 3rd Series, vol. 2
     (London, 1902), pp. 112, 115.
10   C. Rook, *The Hooligan Nights* (Oxford, 1979 edn.), p. 16. Since I wrote the main
     body of the text a valuable book, *East End Underworld: Chapters in the Life of
     Arthur Harding* (London, 1981) has been produced by Raphael Samuel, based on
     interviews with a man brought up in the 'Jago', the most notorious criminal slums
     of late Victorian London. It contains a remarkable reconstruction of a boy's
     passage through delinquent gangs and the criminal underworld leading to Borstal
     and prison. The book lends support to many of my arguments on street gangs and
     resistance in this and the final chapter.
11   Rook, *The Hooligan Nights*, pp. 15, 16.
12   See, for example, N. Lucas, *Britain's Gangland* (London, 1973), esp. pp. 1-27.
13   Born 1922, Birmingham. Petty criminal, then cat burglar — 'recidivist'. Father,
     ball furnace man.
14   Interview no. M.124. Born 1910, Chorlton-on-Medlock. Butcher. Father, tailor.
15   Interview no. B.067. Born 1909, Bristol. Various occupations; became a tramp
     in his twenties. Father, factory foreman.
16   ibid.
17   Delinquent gangs proliferated in localities notorious for their poverty, deprivation
     or criminality. For example, in London most teenage delinquent gangs were
     concentrated in the Hoxton, Finsbury, Shoreditch and Bermondsey districts; in
     Manchester, the Ancoats area; in Bristol, the St Jude's and St Phillip's districts; in
     Birmingham, the St Lawrence's and St Martin's neighbourhoods; in Glasgow, the
     Gorbals, Calton and Bridgeton areas. The violent activities of gangs in these
     districts were often given detailed coverage in the local press and the Mitchell
     Library, Glasgow, holds a valuable collection of local press cuttings relating to
     hooliganism between the 1900s and the 1930s. For details of the enormous
     increase in juvenile delinquency, especially in inner-city areas, during World War
     I, see Leeson, *The Child and the War: Notes on Juvenile Delinquency*.
18   *London County Council Publications*, vol. 3 (Part 2) (London, 1930), pp. 76ff.
19   For descriptions and discussion of poverty and unemployment during the period
     under study, see, for example, B. S. Rowntree and B. Lasher, *Unemployment: A
     Social Study* (London, 1911); B. Gilbert, *The Evolution of National Insurance in
     Great Britain: The Origins of the Welfare State* (London, 1966), esp. pp. 59-158,
     233-88; A. Howkins and J. Saville, 'The Nineteen Thirties: A Revisionist History',
     in *Socialist Register* (London, 1979), pp. 89-100.
20   Interview no. B.047, pp. 19, 20. Born 1906, Barton Hill, Bristol. Errand boy, bus

conductor, truck driver. Father, candle maker.

21 Interview no. E.22, p. 63. Born 1904, Great Bentley, Essex. Farmworker, bricklayer, shepherd, roadman, then thatcher. Father, shepherd.

22 Interview no. E.155, p. 94. Born 1900, South Shields. Various kinds of work in coal mines, then bus driver. Father, boilermaker.

23 Interview no. B.147. Born 1905, Newquay, Cornwall. Errand boy, undertaker's assistant, stonemason, fisherman. Father, stonemason.

24 Interview no. B.011, p. 27, 28. Born 1897, Hotwells, Bristol. Cigarette factory operative. Father, docker.

25 Interview no. E.25, p. 47. Born 1896, Stoke on Trent. Errand boy, labourer in potteries and gas works. Father, stonemason.

26 Interview no. E.417, p. 26. Born 1899, Stepney, London. Messenger boy, sampler — Port of London Authority docks, ship's clerk. Father, crane driver.

27 See C. Burt, *The Young Delinquent* (London, 1938 edn), pp. 181, 351-4, 363; H. Mannheim, *Social Aspects of Crime Between the Wars* (London, 1940), pp. 284-7.

28 Interview no. B.067 (for details, see note 15).

29 *The Times*, 10 July 1914, p. 4.

30 See, for example, A. M. Carr-Saunders, H. Mannheim and E. C. Rhodes, *Young Offenders — An Enquiry into Juvenile Delinquency* (Cambridge, 1942), pp. 100-4; and, for the most comprehensive summary of the evidence of Prison Commissioners and social investigators that indicated a causal link between unemployment and juvenile crime, see Mannheim, *Social Aspects of Crime Between the Wars*, pp. 123-59.

31 For a characteristic moral condemnation of the young offender's belief that he or she had a fundamental right to a few simple pleasures in life, see S. Moseley, *The Truth About Borstal* (London, 1926), p. 23.

32 Born 1898, St Jude's, Bristol. Wheelwright. Father, publican.

33 For a useful summary and bibliography of social investigations into youth unemployment during the period under study, see M. Casson, *Youth Unemployment* (London, 1979), pp. 9-18, 126-8.

34 *The Times*, 22 July 1897, p. 13; 1 March 1898, p. 14, 19 August 1914, p. 9; 20 February 1917, p. 5; 7 January 1918, p. 3.

35 Interview no. E.55, pp. 15, 16. Born, 1882, Salford, Manchester. Leather craftsman. Father, iron fetler.

36 For an account of 'scuttling' in Manchester, see C. Russell, *Manchester Boys — Sketches of Manchester Lads at Work and Play* (Manchester, 1905), pp. 51-5.

37 See, for example, Burt, *The Young Delinquent*, pp. 467, 468.

38 *People's Journal* (Glasgow), November 18, 1916.

39 Interview no. M.189. Born 1897, Broughton, Manchester. Post Office worker, then salesman. Father, tailor.

40 For details, see note 32.

41 Interview no. E.167, p. 55. Born 1893, Jarrow on Tyne, Durham. Engineer. Father, ironmonger.

42 Interview no. M.189 (for details, see note 39).

43 Letter to author. Born 1910, Manchester. Master barber and antique dealer. Father, hand cloth dyer and antique dealer.

44 I am indebted to Bill Williams of Manchester Studies, Manchester Polytechnic, for kindly providing me with valuable information and interview material relating to the Napoo gang.

45 For details, see note 14.

46 Interview no. M.110. Born 1901, Waterproofer and seaman. Father, tailor.

47 See *The Times*, 8 April 1897, pp. 4, 16; 22 July 1897, p. 13; 9 August 1897, pp. 8, 9; 1 March 1898, p. 14; 18 May 1898, p. 4; 9 January 1899, p. 4; 19 August 1899, p. 2; 20 September 1899, p. 11; 6 June 1914, p. 4; 19 August 1914, p. 9; 20 February 1917, p. 5; 7 January 1918, p. 3; also John Mack, 'The Scarred Page', in

Scotland, vol. 10, no. 3 (1957), pp. 11-14.

48 Born 1900, St Jude's, Bristol. Operative in boot and shoe factory, army service, then lorry driver. Father, operative in boot and shoe factory.

49 See, for example, the series of articles on gang hooliganism by 'A Special Investigator' in *Glasgow Evening Citizen*, 4 August 1930, p. 7; 6 August, p. 8; 7 August, p. 8; 8 August, p. 8.

50 See C. Russell, *Lads' Clubs, their History, Organisation and Management* (London, 1932), esp. pp. 1-23, 250-67.

51 Russell, *Manchester Boys*, pp. 52, 53, and *Lads' Clubs*, p. 8.

52 See *Manchester City News*, 21 May 1892, p. 5.

53 See, for example, G. Stedman Jones, *Outcast London, a Study of the Relationship between Classes in Victorian Society* (London, 1976); M. Banton, *The Coloured Quarter* (London, 1955); A. Richmond, *Colour Prejudice in Britain* (London, 1954), and *The Colour Problem* (London, 1955).

54 See, for example, R. May and R. Cohen, 'The Interaction between Race and Colonialism: A Case Study of the Liverpool Race Riots of 1919', in *Race and Class*, vol. 16, no. 2 (1974), pp. 111-26; G. Alderman, 'The Anti-Jewish Riots of August 1911 in South Wales', in *Welsh History Review*, vol. 6 (1972), pp. 190-200.

55 Interview no. E.296 p. 77, 78. Born 1892, Tottenham, London. Factory boy, wood machinist. Father, cabinet maker.

56 Interview no. E.453, p. 21, 38, 51. Born 1899, Cardiff. Merchant seaman, labourer, then foreman at British Oxygen. Father, merchant seaman.

57 See, B. Williams, *The Making of Manchester Jewry, 1740-1875* (Manchester, 1976).

58 Interview no. M.5. Born 1907, Strangeways, Manchester. Waterproofer. Father, immigrant bespoke tailor.

59 Interview no. M.131. Born 1914, Broughton, Manchester. Baker and later engineering worker.

60 See, for example, C. Bermont, *Point of Arrival, a Study of London's East End* (London, 1975); P. Foot, *Immigration and Race in British Politics* (London, 1965), esp. pp. 85-110.

61 See, for example, C. Holmes, *Anti-Semitism in British Society 1876-1939* (London, 1979), esp. pp. 13-34, 128-38, 188-92, 227, 228.

62 *The Times*, 12 March 1897, p. 14.

63 For a more detailed theoretical and empirical statement of this position, see G. Pearson, ' "Paki Bashing" in a North East Lancashire Cotton Town: A Case Study and its History', in G. Mungham and G. Pearson (eds.), *Working Class Youth Culture* (London, 1976), pp. 48-81; and A. Phizacklea and R. Miles, 'Working-Class Racist Beliefs in the Inner City', in R. Miles and A. Phizacklea (eds.), *Racism and Political Action in Britain* (London, 1979), pp. 28-49.

64 Interview no. E.331, p. 59, 60. Born 1895, Stepney, London. Cigar maker. Father, railway messenger.

65 See, for example, E. P. Thompson, 'The Moral Economy of the Crowd in Eighteenth Century England', in *PP*, no. 50 (1971), pp. 76-136; G. Brown, *Sabotage, a Study in Industrial Conflict* (Nottingham, 1977).

66 For details of the harassment of Jews and the destruction of their property by gangs of working-class youths in Leeds, see *Yorkshire Evening Post*, 2 June 1917, p. 5; 4 June, p. 5; 5 June, p. 5; 6 June, p. 3; 7 June, p. 3. The important role played by 'hooligans' in the Liverpool race disturbances of 1919 is described in *Liverpool Courier*, 11 June 1919. And for an account of the involvement of working-class youths in the South Wales race riots of 1911 and 1919, see Alderman, 'The Anti-Jewish Riots of August 1911 in South Wales', pp. 192-4, and N. Evans, 'The South Wales Race Riots of 1919', in *Llafur: Journal of the Society for the Study of Welsh Labour History*, vol. 3, no. 1 (1980), esp. pp. 14-16, 24.

67 Interview no. M.110. Born 1901, Waterproofer and seaman. Father, tailor.

68 Interview no. M.242. Born 1902, Strangeways, Manchester. Waterproofer. Father,

Austrian immigrant, general dealer and synagogue *shamash*.

69 Interview no. M.214. Born 1902, Strangeways, Manchester. Raincoat machiner. Father, tailor's presser.

70 See I. Taylor, 'Soccer Consciousness and Soccer Hooliganism', in S. Cohen (ed.), *Images and Deviance* (London, 1971), pp. 134-65.

71 J. Gillis, 'The Evolution of Juvenile Delinquency 1890-1914', in *PP*, no. 67 (1975), pp. 96-126; J. Gillis, *Youth and History* (London, 1974), pp. 175-83; P. Thompson, *The Edwardians* (London, 1975), pp. 67, 68.

72 Interview no. E.417, p. 26 (for details, see note 26).

73 Interview no. B.008, p. 8. Born 1898, Bedminster, Bristol. Paper boy on trains, then packer and case maker in saw mill. Father, iron foundry worker.

74 Interview no. B.009, pp. 4, 5. Born 1899, Easton, Bristol. Machine driller, general labourer. Father, docker.

75 See, for example, *Evening Times* (Glasgow), 19 January 1920, 'Stories of the Glasgow gangs'.

76 For details, see note 68.

77 See, for example, R. Storch, 'The Plague of Blue Locusts: Police Reform and Popular Resistance in Northern England 1840-57,' in *International Review of Social History*, vol. 20, no. 1 (1975), pp. 61-90; R. Storch, 'The Policeman as Domestic Missionary: Urban Discipline and Popular Culture in Northern England', in *Journal of Social History*, vol. 9, no. 4 (1976), pp. 481-510.

78 Interview no. B.146. Born 1900, Charleston, St Austell, Cornwall. Milliner. Father, policeman.

79 See H. Hill, *Freedom to Roam: The Struggle For Access to Britain's Moors and Mountains* (Ashbourne, Derbyshire, 1980).

80 ibid., esp. pp. 50-83.

81 Interview no. M.59. Born 1909, Strangeways, Manchester. Tailor. Father, Russian-Jewish immigrant tailor.

CHAPTER 8: *Reformatories: Resistance to Repression*

1 Interview no. B.121. Born 1901, Barnstaple, Devon. Domestic servant. Father, picture frame maker, plasterer, then landlord.

2 See, for example, M. May, 'Innocence and Experience: The Evolution of the Concept of Juvenile Delinquency in the Mid-Nineteenth century', in *VS*, vol. 18, no. 1 (1973), pp. 7-29.

3 A. Thompson, *Social Evils: Their Causes and Their Cures* (London, 1852), quoted in W. B. Sanders (ed.), *Juvenile Offenders For a Thousand Years* (Chapel Hill, 1970), p. 183.

4 See J. Carlebach, *Caring for Children in Trouble* (London, 1970), pp. 4-80; A. Platt, *The Child Savers* (Chicago, 1969), pp. 46-74.

5 A. Paterson, 'Borstal Lads', *The Times*, 4 August 1925, quoted in R. Hood, *Borstal Re-Assessed* (London, 1965), pp. 106, 107.

6 For a general discussion, see A. Morris, *Juvenile Justice?* (London, 1978), esp. pp. 1-31.

7 See, for example, D. Bochel, *Probation and After Care: Its Development in England and Wales* (Edinburgh, 1976); S. Barman, *The English Borstal System: A Study of the Treatment of Young Offenders* (London, 1934), pp. 81-110.

8 For a general overview, see J. Clarke, *The Three R's, Repression, Rescue and Rehabilitation: Ideologies of Control for Working Class Youth*, CCCS stencilled paper (Birmingham, 1975).

9 *Report of the Departmental Committee on the Treatment of Young Offenders* Cmnd 2831 (London, 1927), p. 71.

10 *Report of the Departmental Comittee on Reformatory and Industrial Schools* Cmnd 8204 (London, 1896), p. 15.

11 Prison Commissioners' Report 1902-03, p. 85, quoted in Hood, *Borstal Re-Assessed*, p. 15.

12 See G. Pearson, *The Deviant Imagination: Psychiatry, Social Work and Social Change* (London, 1977 edn.), pp. 177-201.

13 Reformatories can properly be described as total institutions, for they combined all the classic features of authoritarian and bureaucratic control that Goffman defined as characteristic of this type of organization; see E. Goffman, *Asylums* (London, 1968). My analysis of reformatories is based upon an extensive study of official reports and investigations, principally the Annual Reports of Inspectors of Reformatory and Industrial Schools from 1889 onwards; *Report of the Departmental Committee on Reformatory and Industrial Schools* (1896); *Children Under the Poor Law* (T. J. Macnamara Report), Cmnd 3899 (London, 1908); *Report of the Departmental Committee on Reformatory and Industrial Schools,* Cmnd 8939 (London, 1913); *Report of the Departmental Committee on the Treatment of Young Offenders* (1927); *Report of the Care of Children Committee,* Cmnd 6922 (London, 1946). The most detailed accounts of the dehumanizing effects of these institutions are N. Middleton, *When Family Failed* (London, 1971); I. G. Briggs, *Reformatory Reform* (London, 1924).

14 For details, see note 1.

15 See Middleton, *When Family Failed*, pp. 92-7.

16 Hood, *Borstal Re-Assessed*, pp. 101, 110, 123, 124.

17 See, for example, Middleton, *When Family Failed*, pp. 92-7, 185-7, 321-2.

18 For details, see note 1.

19 The hidden subcultures of reformatories are recreated in most authentic detail in the autobiographies of former inmates. Two of the most outstanding of these are M. Benney, *Low Company* (London, 1936), and L. Edward, *Borstal Lives* (London, 1939).

20 Interview no. E.199, pp. 23-5. Born 1897, Brentwood, London. Army bandsman, then music hall and danceband musician. Father, walking-stick maker.

21 The child-saving and reformatory movement was closely associated with the enormously influential crusade for sexual purity in the late nineteenth and early twentieth centuries. See E. J. Bristow, *Vice and Vigilance: Purity Movement in Britain since 1700* (Dublin, 1977), esp. pp. 94-153.

22 Interview no. E.315, pp. 28, 29. Born 1901, Blackfriars, London. Domestic servant. Father, cab driver.

23 Quoted in H. Wilmott, *Mass Observation Report on Juvenile Delinquency* (London, 1941), p. 121.

24 Interview no. E.58, p. 28-34. Born 1889, London. Merchant Navy. Father's occupation unknown — died when respondent was a child.

25 For details, see note 1.

26 For a general account, see *Report of the Departmental Committee on Corporal Punishment* (Cadogan Report) Cmnd 5684 (London, 1938).

27 Interview no. B.135. Born, Plymouth, 1909. Cleaner, then waiter. Father, seaman.

28 See, for example, Middleton, *When Family Failed*, pp. 112-15, 251-3.

29 Interview no. E.90, pp. 17, 18. Born 1885, Pendleton, Manchester. Engineer, steam roller driver, chimney sweep. Father, armature winder.

30 Hood, *Borstal Re-Assessed*, pp. 32-57, 93-132.

31 Dr Methuen, quoted in ibid., p. 54.

32 Mr Mead, Marlborough Street magistrate, reported in *The Times*, October 1927, quoted in ibid., p. 37.

33 See, for example, S. Moseley, *The Truth About Borstal* (London, 1926); Briggs, *Reformatory Reform*, esp. pp. 131-81; Willmott, *Mass Observation Report on Juvenile Delinquency*, pp. 90-127.

34 *Report on Reformatory and Industrial Schools* (1896), p. 173.

35   For the subsequent government investigations, see *Report of Inquiry by C. F. G. Masterman, M.P., into charges made concerning the management of Heswell Nautical School*, Cmnd 5561 (London, 1911); *Report of the Departmental Committee on Reformatory and Industrial Schools* (1913).

36   Quoted in Wilmott, *Mass Observation Report on Juvenile Delinquency*, pp. 94-7. The survey stated: 'strange and improbable as such accounts may seem, this one is not unique in our files.'

37   *Report on Industrial and Reformatory Schools* (1896), p. 122.

38   ibid., p. 123.

39   A. Paterson, *The Principles* (London, 1932), quoted in L. Fox, *The English Prison and Borstal Systems* (London, 1952), p. 373.

40   See Hood, *Borstal Re-Assessed*, pp. 93-132.

41   Colonel Rich in *Borstolian*, vol. 1 (1923) quoted in Hood, *Borstal Re-Assessed*, p. 111.

42   See Middleton, *When Family Failed*, pp. 111-32, 247-69; Carlebach, *Caring for Children in Trouble*, pp. 68-70, 89.

43   For the increasing unpopularity of domestic service among working-class girls, see P. Horn, *The Rise and Fall of the Victorian Servant* (Dublin, 1975), esp. pp. 151-83.

44   See Middleton, *When Family Failed*, pp. 260-2; I. Pinchbeck and M. Hewitt, *Children in English Society*, vol. 2, *From the Eighteenth Century to the Children Act 1948* (London, 1973), pp. 546-81.

45   For details, see note 2.

46   ibid.

47   ibid.

48   Carlebach, *Caring for Children in Trouble*, p. 89.

49   Interview no. B.051, pp. 23, 24. Born Ynysabwl, Wales, 1913; moved to Bristol aged 1. Errand boy, junior warehouseman, then fishmonger. Father, professional soldier and bank messenger.

50   Interview no. B.038. Born 1909, Hanham, south Gloucestershire. Coal screener. Father, quarryman and miner.

51   Interview no. B.144. Born 1906, Perranwell, near Truro, Cornwall. Dock labourer, then lorry driver. Father, quarry worker.

52   Interview no. B.065, p. 18. Born 1922, Bristol. Blacksmith striker, ladder maker, toy maker, oil cake maker, builder, then sawmill worker. Father, docker and merchant seaman.

53   Apart from the war years, there was a steady decline in the number of birchings ordered by courts in England and Wales between 1900 and 1936. In 1900 there were 3385 birchings; in 1910, 1702; in 1916, 4864; in 1920, 1380; in 1926, 365; and in 1936, 166. By the late 1930s birching was used by courts in less than 2 per cent of the total number of cases in which there was power to apply it; birching remained much more common in Scotland, however. Cadogan Report, pp. 20-8.

54   ibid., p. 39.

55   Hood, *Borstal Re-Assessed*, pp. 206-11.

56   Youth workers frequently complained of the incorrigible nature of young street traders who, as Charles Russell put it, 'having from their earliest years enjoyed a freedom unknown to other children, are utterly opposed to any kind of restraint'. See Russell, *Lads' Clubs, their History, Organization and Management*, pp. 18, 19. For a useful summary of the child-saving literature that detected a close connection between street trading and imagined delinquency, see H. Mannheim, *Social Aspects of Crime Between the Wars* (London, 1940), pp. 235-49.

57   See for example, the 1927 *Report on the Treatment of Young Offenders*, p. 50.

58   Miss Poole, quoted in the 1896 *Report on Reformatory and Industrial Schools*, p. 80.

59   A fairly high proportion of delinquent girls were incarcerated for sexual misdemeanours, and the most serious of these offences, prostitution, can in some

circumstances be seen as a discriminating form of resistance to the restricted choice of lowly paid jobs that confronted working-class girls. See, for example, J. Walkowitz and D. Walkowitz, ' "We Are Not Beasts of the Field." Prostitution and the Poor in Plymouth and Southampton under the Contagious Diseases Acts', in M. Hartman and L. Banner (eds.), *Clio's Consciousness Raised* (London, 1973), pp. 192-225.

60 See, for example, S. Box, *Deviance, Reality and Society* (London, 1971), pp. 58-97; J. Ditton, *Part Time Crime, an Ethnography of Fiddling and Pilferage* (London, 1977).

61 Interview no. B.135 (for details, see note 27).

A Brief Guide to
Oral History Material

The interviews upon which this book is based were drawn from three oral history archives held by the University of Essex, Manchester Polytechnic and the Avon County Reference Library.

The Essex collection of tapes and transcripts was pioneered by Paul Thompson and Thea Vigne, and the book draws on a number of the 444 interviews that comprise the Family Life and Work Experience before 1918 Project. For a description of the formation and organization of this archive, see Paul Thompson, *The Voice of the Past* (Oxford, 1978).

The Manchester collection, which comprises over a thousand tapes of interviews with people in the Manchester area, was formed by Bill Williams and the Manchester Studies Unit of Manchester Polytechnic. For a full account of their work, see Audrey Linkman and Bill Williams, 'Recovering the People's Past. The Archive Rescue Programme of Manchester Studies', in *History Workshop Journal*, no. 8 (1979), pp. 111-26.

The Bristol archive, from which much of the interview material for the book was obtained, was created by several graduates who worked on the Bristol People's Oral History Project, a one-year special programme for the unemployed that I organized as an extension of my own research while a postgraduate student during 1979 and 1980. The project involved collecting the spoken and written recollections of childhood and youth of approximately two hundred working-class people in Bristol and the West Country born between 1890 and 1925. The archive we have formed comprises master tapes to be stored for posterity, cassette tapes for people to listen to in the library, teaching packs of tapes that are being distributed to local secondary schools, transcripts and written recollections. I have written a detailed account of the financing, the organization and the achievements of this project in the *Oral History Journal,* vol. 9, no. 1 (1981). In addition, I completed a further thirty-five interviews with elderly working-class Bristolians, from which I quote in the text but which do not at the moment form part of the Bristol collection of tapes and transcripts.

A total of approximately two hundred museums, libraries, public record offices and historical societies now hold tapes and transcripts relating to many aspects of social and political history. This material is indexed in the *Directory of British Oral History Collections* published in 1981 by the Oral History Society. Those who wish to find out more about oral history are strongly advised to read Paul Thompson's *The Voice of The Past* (cited above), which contains a valuable discussion on the reliability of oral evidence, as well as much practical advice on interviewing, project work and tape storage and a comprehensive bibliography on all aspects of oral history.

If you are interested in oral history and collecting the memories of older people you can join the Oral History Society which holds regular meetings, provides advice on how to interview and publishes a twice yearly magazine. Write to: Rob Perks, Curator of Oral History, National Sound Archive, 29 Exhibition Road, London SW7 2AS.

Further Reading

Since the first edition of *Hooligans or Rebels* there has been a proliferation of books exploring various aspects of childhood and youth in the first half of the century. There have also been a number of interesting studies of working-class culture during the late nineteenth and early twentieth century. What follows is an updated but very selective list of recent books containing material relevant to the social history of working class childhood and youth in Britain.

V. Bailey, *Delinquency and Citizenship: Reclaiming the Young Offender 1914–1948* (Oxford University Press, 1987)

J. Benson, *The Working Class in Britain 1850–1939* (London, 1989)

J. Bourke, *Working Class Cultures in Britain 1890–1960* (Routledge, 1994)

J. Burnett, *Destiny Obscure: Autobiographies of Childhood, Education and Family from the 1820s to the 1920s* (Penguin, 1984)

C. Chinn, *They Worked All Their Lives: Women of the Urban Poor in England 1880–1939* (Manchester, 1988)

A. Davies, *Leisure, Gender and Poverty: Working Class Culture in Salford and Manchester 1900–1939* (Open University Press, 1992)

E. Dunning et al, *The Roots of Football Hooliganism* (Routledge, 1988)

C. Dyhouse, *Girls Growing Up in Late Victorian and Edwardian England* (Routledge, 1981)

J. Field, *Learning Through Labour: Training, Education and the State 1890–1939* (University of Leeds, 1991)

P. Fryer, *Staying Power: The History of Black People in Britain* (Pluto Press, 1984)

P. Gardner, *The Lost Elementary Schools of Victorian England* (Croom Helm, 1984)

C. Hardyment, *Dream Babies: Child Care from Locke to Spock* (Jonathan Cape, 1983)

H. Hendrick, *Images of Youth: Age, Class and the Male Youth Problem 1880–1920* (Oxford University Press, 1990)

S. Humphries, *A Secret World of Sex: Forbidden Fruit, The British Experience 1900–1950* (Sidgwick and Jackson, 1989)

S. Humphries and P. Gordon, *Out of Sight: The Experience of Disability 1900–1950* (Northcote House, 1992)

S. Humphries and P. Gordon, *A Labour of Love: The Experience of Parenthood in Britain 1900–1950* (Sidgwick and Jackson, 1993)

S. Humphries and P. Gordon, *Forbidden Britain: Our Secret Past 1900–1950* (BBC Books, 1994)

S. Humphries, Joanna Mack and Rob Perks, *A Century of Childhood* (Sidgwick and Jackson, 1988)

G. S. Jones, *Languages of Class: Studies in English Working Class History 1832–1982* (Cambridge University Press, 1983)

M. Kohn, *Dope Girls: Birth of the British Drug Underground* (Lawrence and Wishart, 1992)

J. Lewis, *The Politics of Motherhood: Child and Maternal Welfare in England 1900–1939* (London, 1981)

J. Lewis, *Labour and Love: Women's Experience of Home and Family 1850–1940* (Oxford, 1986)

J. Mangan and J. Walvin, *Manliness and Morality: Middle-Class Masculinity in Britain and America, 1800–1940* (Manchester University Press, 1987)

F. Mort, *Dangerous Sexualities: Medico-Moral Politics in England Since 1830* (Routledge, 1987)

B. Murray, *The Old Firm: Sectarianism, Sport and Society in Scotland* (J. Donald, Edinburgh, 1984)

P. Panayi (ed.), *Racial Violence in Britain 1840–1950* (Leicester University Press, 1993)

G. Pearson, *Hooligan: A History of Respectable Fears* (Macmillan, 1983)

L. Pollock, *Forgotten Children: Parent–Child Relations from 1500–1900* (CUP, 1983)

E. Roberts, *A Woman's Place: An Oral History of Working Class Women 1890–1940* (Blackwell Publishers, 1984)

L. Rose, *Rogues and Vagabonds, The Vagrant Underworld in Britain 1815–1985* (Routledge, 1988)

M. Rosenthal, *The Character Factory: Baden-Powell and the Origins of the Boy Scout Movement* (Collins, 1986)

R. Samuel (ed.), *Patriotism: The Making and Unmaking of British National Identity*, 3 vols (London, 1989)

J. Springhall, *Coming of Age: Adolescence in Great Britain 1860–1960* (Gill and Macmillan, 1986)

P. Thompson, *The Voice of the Past* (OUP, 1992)

T. Thompson, *Edwardian Childhoods* (Routledge, 1981)

D. Waddington, *Contemporary Issues in Public Disorder: A Comparative and Historical Approach* (Routledge, 1992)

J. Walvin, *A Child's World* (Penguin, 1982)

C. Ward, *The Child in the Country* (Robert Hale, 1988)

J. Weeks, *Sex, Politics and Society: The Regulation of Sexuality Since 1800* (Longman, 1981)

J. White, *The Worst Street in London: Campbell Bunk, Islington Between the Wars* (Routledge, 1986)

E. and S. Yeo, *Popular Culture and Class Conflict 1590–1914: Explorations in the History of Labour and Leisure* (Brighton, 1981).

Index